Acclaim for Rick Moody's

THE BLACK VEIL

"A gripping memoir . . . intriguing and unforgettable. . . . A searing work of family history."   — Dylan Foley, *Cleveland Plain Dealer*

"A journey that is less bloodletting than blood sport, with Moody playing hunter and prey. . . . His writing, wit, and knowledge remain wonderfully intact."   — Thomas Cruwen, *Los Angeles Times Book Review*

"*The Black Veil* is shot through with indelible insights, humor, and the tenderness and sympathy that any fan of Moody has come to expect. . . . A muscular, eggheady exploration of self, patrimony, and the myths and stories that shape and define families, the stories that make us who we are. . . . Some of the most gripping and sensitively drawn passages in *The Black Veil* detail Moody's own story of survival."   — Deborah Hornblow, *Hartford Courant*

"Of course Moody writes wonderfully well. . . . *The Black Veil* concludes with a positively brilliant howling."   — John Leonard, *New York Times Book Review*

"Riveting. . . . This is the story of obsession, of coming of age in the grip of an unshakable, if obscure, sense of dread. . . . Rick Moody is an architect and a builder, a maker of compound-complex sentences that digress and subordinate, and at their best demonstrate as persuasively as any diagram the implicit complexity not just of thought, but of the invariably clotted-up inner life."   — Sven Birkerts, *Esquire*

"Moody's descriptions are lyrical, elegiac, and effortlessly compelling. . . . He is an extremely talented writer."   — Andrew Solomon, *Bookforum*

"*The Black Veil* is eloquent in its depiction of the stark isolation of an alcoholic and the miracle of one young person's recovery. And, as is consistently the case in Moody's increasingly impressive canon, it is beautifully written."   — Don Harrell, *Trenton Times*

"The dark far outweighs the light in this book, possibly because the dark is more engrossing. . . . Of course, no one is funnier than the person who is totally miserable, and Moody is often fall-down funny. Even the climax of his story is tinged with humor."
                    — David Kirby, *San Diego Union-Tribune*

"When he's on his game, Moody's prose gets at the tactile quintessence of lived life with an accuracy that can leave readers woozy."
                    — David Kipen, *San Francisco Chronicle*

"Like the works of W. G. Sebald, *The Black Veil* is difficult to categorize. It breaks the traditional mold of a memoir and creates its own category: part literary criticism, part intellectual autobiography, part family history, part testimony of depression. . . . In surging sentences that verge, like his personality I suspect, between spiraling out of control and maintaining an austere analytic precision, Moody adds to the discussion on why we still invent stories, and why narratives are sustained."
                    — David Lau, *Yale Review of Books*

"This is an enormously risky book, and its considerable innovations and accomplishments mark it as Rick Moody's most ambitious work yet, and also as one of the finest memoirs in recent years. Its timeless exploration of issues that are essential to what it means to be an American makes it likely that *The Black Veil* will take its place among classic American memoirs."   — Jeffery Smith, *Washington Post*

THE BLACK VEIL

THE

BLACK VEIL

A MEMOIR

For Susan

VT 2010

BY RICK MOODY

BACK BAY BOOKS

LITTLE, BROWN AND COMPANY

BOSTON NEW YORK LONDON

Originally published in hardcover by Little, Brown and Company, May 2002

First Back Bay paperback edition, May 2003

ISBN 0-316-57899-1 (HC) / 0-316-73901-4 (PB)
Library of Congress Control Number 2002090674

10 9 8 7 6 5 4 3 2 1

Q-FF

Designed by Jonathan D. Lippincott

Printed in the United States of America

For Dwight Francis Moody
and
Dylan Flynn Moody

CONTENTS

Preface   3

Children, with bright faces, tript merrily beside their parents,
or mimicked a graver gait . . .   11

The old people of the village came stooping along the
street . . .   26

The topic, it might be supposed, was obvious enough . . .   42

Customers came in, as the forenoon advanced, but rather
slowly . . .   54

Stooping somewhat and looking on the ground, as is customary
with abstracted men . . .   68

The deep pause of flagging spirits, that always follows mirth and
wine . . .   76

In his case, however, the symbol had a different import . . .   89

It takes off its face like a mask, and shows the grinning bare
skeleton underneath . . .   104

Mr. Hooper, face to face with his congregation, except for the black
veil . . .   120

If I had ever once been happy, methinks I could contentedly be shot
to-day . . .   137

If it be a sign of mourning, I, perhaps, like most other mortals,
have sorrows dark enough . . .   151

What is this world good for now that we can never be jolly
anymore . . .   176

I have suffered woefully from low spirits for some time
    past . . .   192
Every work, by an artist of celebrity, is hidden behind a
    veil . . .   211
Had her eyes provoked, or assented to this deed? She had not
    known it. But, alas!   220
A veil may sometimes be needful, but never a masque . . .   236
There being a heavy rain yesterday, a nest of swallows was washed
    down the chimney . . .   250
Hither coasters &c. and fishing smacks run in, when a storm is
    anticipated . . .   271
So far as I am a man of really individual traits, I veil my
    face . . .   293

"The Minister's Black Veil," by Nathaniel Hawthorne   305
Selected Bibliography   319
Acknowledgments   325

A Reading Group Guide   329

THE BLACK VEIL

So there's the matter of our crimes. The remembrance of our misdoings is grievous to us; the burden of them is intolerable. Lies, whispered, of friends' indiscretions; instances of envy — when we hate the people we love; peccadilloes; filched office supplies; inflated expense accounts; violent obsessions of all kinds; reckless speeding; a fender bender whose scene we left; the belt from Macy's we slipped into our own belt loops (they're the easiest thing to take); a copy of Montaigne, nineteenth-century edition, never returned to the library; a kiss stolen from someone else's lover; a night out of state upon a tanned mattress when the energy of adultery seemed so persuasive that we concealed from ourselves all memory of our spouses; gifts never sent; allegiances never acknowledged; inexplicable cruelties to people with bad luck; inexplicable cruelties to friends; the waiter we upbraided that time; we cheated at cards; we cheated at tennis; we cheated at backgammon or at chess or at some board game of our childhood; we tripped that guy in the backfield and then waltzed in for the goal; we took things for granted, took privileges for rights; we demanded things in no way due us. And then with some of us there are worse crimes, crimes unspeakable, though we might write of them, like robbery, battery, or rape. We fell into coercion or abuse or full-scale embezzlement or even murder, the murder of innocents, perhaps; we committed crimes of rage so that afterward we couldn't sleep, couldn't forget, couldn't think straight, and whispered to ourselves, revisiting these instances of our transgression. There's the matter of our crimes.

Down underneath New York City, in a network of tunnels and caverns, rat populated, perspiring, rumbling, lonely, I was troubled, as I have often been troubled, by these alarums of conscience. Who knows why? I was bothered, as you may be bothered yourself, by what I had gotten wrong or by some feeling that I might have done better, or I was bothered by the conviction that I might have done without some luxury, might have put aside some vanity or selfishness. What I liked about this particular cavern of archetypes, the New York City subway system, in the intoxication of conscience, was *the farthest end of the platform.* I liked to stand in unpopulated spots. To get there, at my particular station, the passage was at one juncture quite narrow, around a stairwell, around a pair of I beams (weekly repainted and that day deepest blue) dank with condensation. It was a setting dangerous in ways both actual and allegorical. Nonetheless, I was purposed upon the end of the platform because I liked to ride in *the last car,* the car most crowded with people who lived on the trains, with men and women doing their nine to five sprawled out lengthways, their faces turned from their compatriots toward the hard shell of benches. *If you are remorseful by nature, you believe that a great evil will befall you whichever way you turn.* If you are remorseful by nature, around every street corner is the speeding crack- or booze-intoxicated driver who will veer up on the sidewalk for blocks, flattening pedestrians, including yourself. Your death will be lingering and painful. Thus I often imagined in this particular dangerous setting that I would be pushed from the platform into the path of an oncoming train. I imagined the aftermath, the dismemberment, the morphine drip, a head injury that rendered me speechless or paralyzed. Headlines in the *Post.* In consideration of my fate — in the landscape of NYC nightmares, where the riders sometimes tongue-lashed one another — I was passing around the I beam I've described, through the narrowest spit of platform, when I came up short in front of an impasse. A fellow New Yorker. Lost in a dance of circumnavigation — should I go left, should I go right — I paid little attention to my dance partner until this New Yorker *began to hide,* like a sprite, like a pixie, behind the I beam that separated us. To allow my own unimpeded passage to the end of the platform? To push me to my death? Maybe. I intended to catch a look at him, if he were a he, as I passed around the sturdy navy blue I beam. I intended a bland smile of appreciation. I intended to acknowledge our mutual awkwardness by catching his eye, by catching the spot where his life's experience was etched for appreciation. The spot where his harried but polite New York visage might await me, or maybe his furrowed brow, his impatience and irritation, maybe his contempt.

But there was no face for me to see.

He was faceless. This guy. Instead of a face there was a large hooded garment, a sort of ski jacket, probably, an anorak, a cloak, just about, a costume from *The Seventh Seal,* and accordingly this hood hung down over his face, not just over his forehead, so that no face was apparent there at all, none whatever, no chin, no patch of unshaven neck, no stubble, no face at all but just *the hood,* in a kind of dusty, grimy taupe, swinging this way and that, a loose integument, so as to permit whatever infrared eyes my fellow New Yorker had beneath his garment to do little but steal a glimpse of the immediate ground before him, if that. The ski jacket was enormous, a body suit; it hung down about the knees, over gray, fouled chinos. He wore gloves. Work shoes. He had some kind of battery acid cologne. So here he was, Death, that personage of the Middle Ages. The guy from the Dürer engravings. He kept the I beam between us and then swiveled up the platform, like a pinball caroming off bumpers, startling locals up and down the platform, a gaggle of parochial-school kids, lawyers jabbering (fresh from the courthouse), the elderly, teens who shouldn't have been scared of anything, least of all another *subway freak.*

On American mass transit, I have, as all New Yorkers have, seen every variation on sorrow. Watched the guys in the two-seaters with their faces in their hands, wound into postures of despair, was even one of these guys myself, riding the express to midtown the morning of my sister's death, hunched over during rush hour, red and raw, mutely sobbing, with no fellow rider to ask, *Are you okay?* Subways are the high-volume freight carriers of despair. In time — through the triumph of deinstitutionalization — you learn on the trains a lot about disorders of the soul, you *live* with schizophrenics,

manic-depressives, drug addicts, homeless people, religious pilgrims, panhandlers, and thus, upon the platform, the sudden appearance that day of a man who entirely concealed his face from his
community should not have been entirely astonishing. But it was. I
did a jig with Death, he went left, I went left, and I gazed at him (*on
this dreary road, darkened by all the gloomiest trees of the forest*), and could
not move, was paralyzed until he fled. Was he badly disfigured? Did
he haunt the far end of the platform like an untouchable, secreting
himself to spare me the horror of his appearance? Was he driven by
hallucinatory voices? Was he evading pursuers, was he on the lam,
having ratted out some crime syndicate? And what's in a face, anyhow, except the uncomplicated story of a man? What's in a face that
makes it the nail on which we hang our ideas about people?

A train thundered into the station and I got on. In spite of the
certainty that I had long since seen all the worst that New York City
had to offer, I felt heavy with the dark reverberations of some spirit
world. Through subway windows covered with scratched names,
I watched that ghost make his way up the platform and I felt safer
for being shut away from him. His gait was reckless. Yet somehow
he was able to see beneath the hem of his cowl. He threw himself
impulsively about the platform. Parochial-school kids scattered out
of his path. My train lingered with the door open. Would he slip
ultimately onto the car? Would he sit with me? Could I talk to him?
Would he answer? What catalog of woes would he enumerate? And
what would his voice be like? Was it my own voice, a mockery of my
voice, flush with bad news about my failures? Don't be ridiculous.
Death had no intention of riding my train. *Death was not that method-
ical.* The doors rattled shut, and as they did, as we pulled away, this
familiar momentarily passed out of my waking thoughts.

Still, I began to imagine, in some other register of consciousness,
that unlike the permanent vagrant population of my neighborhood — the Vietnam vet by Borough Hall, the guy with the crutch
in front of St. Anne's Church — this apparition really was the pro-
jection of my troubled conscience, the personification called forth by
a certain average, guilty, middle-class taxpayer. He was *my* homeless
person, my particular deinstitutionalized person, my symbol, my

poltergeist. By which I mean that the ghost of the subway station, by his one appearance, ushered forth in me things that long preceded him or his appearance on the platform; the ghost of my subway station was a ghost from my childhood, and perhaps a ghost from *before* my childhood, so strong was his symbolic heft; like all enduring images, he was spectacularly uncanny, he was *something which should remain hidden but which has come to light,* he was part of the lore of *family,* of the very constitutional fabric of family.

What did he tell me? Was he just a mother's son, a guy named Horace, maybe, or Linwood, or Parker, a guy from New England, uncomfortable in the city, didn't care for it, stuck here now, living in tunnels, out of touch with what family remained, if any? Was he part of one of history's diasporas? Had they *all died* in the fire in which he was scarred, in which he was disfigured? We have our prejudices about who our homeless are, about their origins and their logic, but are these prejudices really valid? *Wasn't he related to all of us?* or so I began to argue, in certain insomniac settings. Wasn't he related to the mariners of the thirteen colonies or to the immigrants of the eighteenth and nineteenth centuries, this particular American, related *to me,* to my interlopers on the continent, authors of Manifest Destiny, sufferers of conscience, my settlers with their inventory of persecutions worried out like bad fevers through the troubled sleep of the centuries? Horace Cabot or Horace Adams or Horace Mather, or some such name, in his ragged cloak, sleeping badly, giving up on the consolations of family, village, and nation.

He began to appear to me regularly. Which period coincides with the beginning of these pages, the middle nineties. The Hooded Man on the R train. At Borough Hall, and later standing peacefully, arms folded, at the Canal Street Station or at City Hall. The Hooded Man, sentry, at Fifty-seventh. In the morning, in the evening, late at night, face covered. Emblematic. Occasionally placid, occasionally restless. I began to ask people. Had they ever seen this guy? Was anyone as preoccupied with him as I was? It turned out that *everyone* had seen him. He was a fixture in my New York City. On the way to rehearsal dinners and fancy society balls, book parties, press screenings, we had all seen him, dressed in our rental tuxedoes, wearing excellent perfumes, or maybe just in *business casual,* in sportswear, we had all found ourselves in the orbit of this celestial body. He'd made a celebrity of himself by zipping his hood, hiding his face. Or maybe that is simply my interpretation.

The disease of an evil conscience is beyond the practice of all the physicians of all the countries in the world, says W. E. Gladstone, or, according to an American thinker about inherited remorse: *The world should recline its vast head on the first convenient pillow, and take an age-long nap. It has gone distracted, through a morbid activity, and, while preternaturally wide-awake, is nevertheless tormented by visions.*

Readers in search of a tidy, well-organized life in these pages, a life of kisses bestowed or of novels written, may be surprised. My book and my life are written in *fits,* more like epilepsy than like a narrative; or: the process of this work is obsessive and like all obsessions is protean, beginning with the burden of conscience, moving through the narrative evocations of that sensation, shame, remorse, guilt, regret, into the story of a particular search for the original image of *the veil* in my life, the veil in the life of my family, the original image of *facelessness,* all this in an account of a five-day driving trip to Maine to locate the origin of the veil among Moodys, this five-day search woven like a braid into an account of my own difficulties, which are not entirely unlike the difficulties of the *hooded ghost on the R train.* Alas, this account never settles for the orderly where the disorderly and explosive can substitute, because obsession is not orderly, it is protean, like consciousness, it is one thing on a day sunny and cool with offshore breezes, quite another in winter, as in this preface, where there is description and then analysis, where there are disembodied quotations (some from Hawthorne, some from others) that float like ghosts of literature past. Encountering obsession is like encountering a whole person; obsession has its blind spots, it is occasionally inexplicable, it is worrisome, it is amazing and sometimes charming, it is both deceitful and forthright, it features *recurrent and persistent thoughts, impulses, or images that are experienced, at some time during the disturbance, as intrusive and inappropriate and that cause marked anxiety or distress;* you deal with obsession the way you deal with an unusual neighbor, uncertain about your right

to demand his complete story all at once, satisfied with the way
details are parceled out here and there, because that's how a life goes,
helter-skelter, like crows rising from a tree where a hawk has just
settled, famished. If birds will describe the obsession, I will break
away to describe the birds I have seen; if baseball will describe the
obsession, I will break away to speak of foul-outs and pop-ups of
my life; because *I am myself the matter of this book, you would be unreasonable to expend your leisure on so frivolous a subject,* as Montaigne advises.
Get to know my book the way you would get to know me: in the
fullness of time, hesitantly, irritably, impatiently, uncertainly, pityingly, generously.

CHILDREN, WITH BRIGHT FACES,
TRIPT MERRILY BESIDE THEIR PARENTS,
OR MIMICKED A GRAVER GAIT . . .

Fathers make fetishes of their cars. Mustang convertibles, sport-utility vehicles, Jaguars, Corvettes (fathers receding into their middle years), Audis, Saabs, the restored Nash Rambler, the MG, the Ferrari, Lexus, Lotus, Lincoln Town Car; there are souped-up motorcycles and fathers are out in the driveway, on their backs, fumbling for wrenches.

I'm concerned here with patrimony, with all the characteristics attendant thereupon, with self and the vain reiteration of self implicit in fathers and sons, with national pride, national psychology, national tradition, with inheritance, with all the eccentricities that run in families, so you will have no choice but to get to know my dad (to the almost complete exclusion of my mom, unfortunately), as you will also have to wrestle with certain long-standing rules of dads. My particular dad, Hiram Frederick Moody Jr., didn't appear in my life until I was nine. He was in residence before that, sure, throughout the early years, but in a way more capricious than fatherly. He made his way around the premises. He had thinning dark hair and glasses (worn with embarrassment since early childhood). He was slim. His most frequent expression was one of furrowed skepticism. He dressed casually but never sloppily. My dad wore Top-Siders and cable-knit sweaters and tweed jackets with patches on the elbows. And tortoiseshell glasses. He was, compared to me, very large. He was a behemoth. My childhood interest in dinosaurs, in the *T. rex* or the *pterodactyl*, was really a metaphorical interest in dads. He dispensed incontrovertible orders. We executed these orders. But my father was also a cipher to me, a mystery, an enigma — at least until my parents were divorced in 1970. This was all in Connecticut, in the suburbs. In Darien, mainly. Sun-dappled lawns, sprinklers, station wagons. My parents had to go as far as Mexico to secure their divorce. My mom had to go. That I hadn't been aware of any difficulties between them says more about what awareness is to a child than it says about their difficulties. My parents didn't talk to each other very often; they would pass through the kitchen or the front hall or on the way to the bar in the den and acknowledge each other in a miserly way. They didn't yell or bicker. They mostly agreed in public. But they managed to avoid being in a room at the same time, and we (my brother and sister and I) were rarely with the two of them in the family constellation, that I remember, except occasionally on our sailboat. I have the pictures of their wedding to attest to the fact that they were married at the same location and moment, but that is the only evidence. Dad turned up late, most nights, after my bedtime. Or, if earlier, he secluded himself in front of the network news, in a recliner, with a cocktail (*vodka martini very dry with twist*) and dry-roasted peanuts. Occasionally, I fitted myself into a small crevice beside him on the vinyl recliner, my head upon his shoulder, and watched the news with him, not understanding a word — Vietnamese body counts, riots at the convention — not talking to my dad, as my dad didn't talk to me. I absorbed the warmth of his sweaters and enjoyed the irrefutability of the head of household. When he took us out on weekends to play games, to engage in athletic contests, to school us in competition, he seemed distracted. Especially when baseball was involved. Baseball was too slow. Baseball was a game of the past, a nineteenth-century game, an Indian game. A game from the old America. *The pitcher is the only important player,* he observed. Why was anyone interested in it? My father watched football on the television in the den; he watched the New York Giants and grumbled at their performances, at Frank Gifford. We tried to excel at football as a result, even my sister, because we wanted to rouse him from distraction. Out on the lawn. In the space between crab apple trees and dogwoods. The neighbors came by and played too. Somebody's feelings were always hurt. *The rules had not been effectively stated! Someone was cheating!* I often tried to declaim facts about football in order to impress my dad, like that the Los Angeles Rams were very good, but my heart was not in it. I wasn't even in possession of genuine facts.

Fathers use acronyms. Fathers refold maps; fathers like to appear as though they have infallible knowledge of direct routes between any two points. Fathers are purveyors of ethics.

My brother is hard of hearing on one side because of chicken pox contracted as an infant. Because of his deafness, he never much trafficked in single words. There was no *dada* or *mama* or *doggy* or *kitty* period in his language development. When he learned to speak at all — in sentences — it was late, and he had a lot to say. Before language, he had a sentient glow but was unnaturally silent. Of course, silence is an incredibly powerful conversational gambit. He understood everything but reserved judgment. One day he was sequestered in the nursery, in his crib, and I was visiting him there while he passed time coloring, scribbling webs of color onto a pad in the tones of the old Crayola box. As I watched and offered commentary, he impulsively selected a certain yellow crayon and began to draw *on the wall of his room.* An eggshell wall, or perhaps a very pale linen–hued wall. Flat finish. Soon Dwight had made some compelling galaxies there. On the wall. The Crab Nebula. The Milky Way. Here were some really large-scale wall murals of a color-field sort. Like Motherwells or Rothkos. I watched this. It was fascinating because I knew intuitively that these designs did not belong on the wall of his room, and yet when no retribution was forthcoming (Mom was down the hall), I began to think that maybe I was wrong, maybe there were no parental regulations on the subject of coloring on the wall. Maybe everything was permitted. Maybe pandemonium was allowed. *Why hadn't we ever thought of this before? The wall offered many inviting planes onto which to fashion our creations!* It's a family trait to court trouble with authority, to incline toward trouble as though trouble were the sweetest grog. We were just coming into our inheritance.

My brother, however, having made a yellow scribble almost a crib length in diameter on the wall of his nursery, having filled in this scribble with swooping arcs of yellow sun-worshipping icons, petroglyphs, became bored with the exercise. He went back to his pad or went back to playing with his mostly decayed blanket, his *transitional object,* which accompanied all his peregrinations. I was not bored, however. I was just getting interested. I climbed up into the crib, stepped around my brother's diapered body, chose a purple crayon (the opposite of yellow), and made a small palm-sized quadrilateral smudge on the wall. The two drawings, it seemed to me, went well together. They were complementary.

Then my mother happened on the action. She darkened the threshold at the very moment when I, with crayon poised, was beginning to decorate my brother's decoration. *This linen-colored paint job just was not right. It needed a little zing. A little something.* Dwight was busy with some incredibly adorable three-year-old business that had nothing to do with defacing the house. Smiling his unforgettable smile, his snake charmer's smile. I was drawing on his wall. To my mother, fresh from another responsibility, it must have appeared as though I had myself made enormous yellow orbits on the wall and had now, in purple, begun to set off this yellow with some of my ideas about color harmony. There was a long, dramatic silence in which the enormity of the tableau sunk in. My mother slowly, incrementally, took note. Perhaps she fell tiredly against the door frame. But soon she seemed to regain her verve. In order to shout. She was not a person who *expressed her rage easily* (she was small and soft-spoken), but in this instance she made an indelible impact with words that had often been used before but until now only preemptively: *Wait till your father gets home.*

My parents were not committed to corporal punishment, to its theory or practice, to forms and styles of beatings, the belt, the open palm, etc. The threat was rare in our house, reserved only for really dreadful childhood crimes: maltreatment of our animal friends, theft, burglary, bodily harm of neighborhood children. In my brother's nursery, with my action paintings behind me, I suddenly knew, however, that I had placed myself on the list for such treatment. I was going to be spanked. My first thought was: *How do I pin this on Dwight?* It should have been easy. After all: my brother couldn't speak. I could say he had done anything. *He's hiding behind his disability! He stole your savings passbook! He strangled the dog! He made me do it! He did it all and I seized the crayon from him, anxious to spare the room the terrible yellow and purple scribbles! I was trying to supervise!* My brother's silence, however, had a sweetness that could have won over any jury. Look at that smile. Look at that blond mop. Look at those blue eyes.

And my mother believed him.

I spent the afternoon skulking around outdoors, playing alone with sticks and scraps of trash. (I was the middle child, I was left-handed, a brunet among blonds, I was covered with freckles, I was *a mutant, a criminal, a foundling, a monstrosity. I was going to perish.*) And then my father came home from the bank. He had barely loosed his tie, as I reconstruct it, before my mother, hands on hips, alerted him to the new interior decorating in my brother's nursery. Next, they stood in the doorway illumined by a dim ceiling light, silently inspecting the damage. Our circular artwork. *This is how much it will cost to repaint or this is the weekend that will be lost to do it ourselves.* My mother came to find me. I was guiltily attempting to hide in the family room, behind a Shaker chair. *Your father wants to talk with you.* My sister and brother avoided the whole contretemps. They knew what was up, and they were staying clear. *Serious trouble was communicable.* It might travel from one of us to another.

I refused to move. I screamed as my mother dragged me out into the hall. I grabbed on to furniture. The fullness of mortal terror emerged from me. I blamed Dwight. I blamed Meredith, my sister, who had been at school and had nothing to do with any of it. I blamed anyone who was at hand. I was misunderstood. I was unloved. I was a special case. I pleaded for my life, for mercy, for kindness. The whole neighborhood would know of my torture. Finally, my parents sequestered me in their bedroom. Pale gray walls. My father's suit pants were folded over the back of a chair designed to maintain their press. The closet in the bedroom was open, and inside cellophaned delicates shimmered. I remember the simplicity of Dad's hairbrush on the countertop. Tortoiseshell. Classic, masculine, functional. Was it plastic? Were plastics advanced enough for hairbrushes by the mid-sixties? The weapon had stiff brown bristles. Never before had it occurred to me to wonder which side of a hairbrush was used for a beating, bristle side or smooth surface, but now I knew. Bristles would have been *too* cruel. Or so I hoped. My father asked for no information on my wall-decoration project. This defendant was not encouraged to address the judiciary. In fact, my father didn't want to talk to me at all. He went through the business of *taking down my trousers* in silence. My skinny backside was exposed. And in some ways this was the worst part of the punishment, the Victorian spanking: the nakedness of it, the humiliation, the loss of self-determination. The spanking itself, one stroke only, was over instantly. Crimson indignity welled up in me alongside the sharp sting. I hopped around, gathering the complete text of my howl. I was left to hitch up my trousers myself.

My brother got off without a scratch.

Fathers may offer standard-issue praise, such as Attaboy! Stick with it! *or* Way to go! *Fathers are able to dispense paternal wisdom even in a semiconscious or unconscious state. Fathers dispense advice that they spurned themselves.*

He hated noise. The noise of kids, the footsteps of kids, herds of kids, mainly because he had gotten out of school, married immediately, spawned his first child ten months after marrying, two more by the time he was twenty-six. He had no idea how he was going to pay. How to get us through college, how to manage difficult teenage rebellions, how to play baseball with us (when he hated baseball), how to talk to children when they were clearly a separate species. The noise of kids made my father wild because he was not *actually* watching the New York Giants on television or the news or whatever he feigned watching. He was brooding about how he was going to pay. And plots must have abounded at the office. And there was the unhealthy quiet of his marriage. And there was the uncomfortable political ferment of the times. Up on the second floor of our house in Darien, the house where we lived while my parents were married, I would be throwing a pile of shoes, one by one, at my brother, trying to hit him in the head and *knock him unconscious,* and my brother would be crouched and screaming behind a desk, aiming a poison-tipped plastic spear at my face, when suddenly we would hear the sound of my father's voice in the stairwell, *What the hell is going on up there?* And we would fall into our shameful silence, an anxious silence so familiar as to have preceded our very births. Sometimes, intoxicated by the need to inflict bodily harm on each other, we ignored the initial warnings until we heard footsteps in the hall. Then at the door. And then the door would open.

Fathers speak in code. Fathers speak of equity or short positions or of the zero coupon or of the long bond; fathers speak of the need for a balanced portfolio; fathers shake their fists at the enduring misery of the bear market; fathers try to explain rate fluctuation, money supply, policy at the Fed. Fathers will have certain stirring anthems that they need to replay on the stereo again and again, such as anthems from Broadway shows or occasional hard-luck country ballads.

We were gathered around the fireplace, the kids, in Darien, one autumn evening when my mother explained that she and Dad couldn't get along anymore. His recliner, next to where we stood, was empty. To one side of the fireplace, the irons, the bellows. Wood smoke wreathed us. My mom was wearing plaid. I wasn't surprised by the direction of her remarks, though I had never seen any acrimony. There was a predictability about the whole discussion. A leaden disquiet to the scene. My brother was the only one who spoke up initially. By then he was a chatterbox. *Don't get divorced! Don't get divorced!* How did he know the word, since we were the first in the neighborhood to achieve that milestone? And though he stuttered much of the time, there was no stutter now. His plea was articulate and sad. My mother looked helpless. I tried to conceal myself behind my sister throughout the discussion, and this became my strategy later: *Don't draw attention.*

Mom journeyed south of the border and secured the paperwork, brought back certain gifts. I received a pair of ornamental spurs (they are somewhat rusted but still intact). My sister received a Native American hand drum that split along its length after a couple of New England summers. My brother's gift is lost to time. While my mom was in Mexico, Dad was in San Francisco, *on business,* or that was what we were told. Actually, he was banished. He brought me back a bar of Ghirardelli chocolate, a gigantic, monolithic chocolate bar weighing in at a couple of pounds. Therefore, we were rich in material distractors from the trouble of separation, but we were not distracted in full. When my parents' travels were over, so was their marriage. We anesthetized ourselves for days at a time. With television. While my parents drank. My mother slept on the couch for the next few weeks. They governed us in turns. Then we moved out. My mom and the three of us moved out, and there were the months of wrangling over visitation, child support payments. The bickering of lawyers. I had stomachaches. Just the words *macaroni and cheese* could produce a stomachache in me. *All-beef franks.* I could vomit over the idea of all-beef franks. I was the kid with the constant stomachaches, the kid who swilled Maalox and chomped Gelusil. And since my father was recovering from an ulcer himself, he not only identified with my woes but offered remedies and made dietary recommendations. Cream of Wheat and white toast. Mashed potatoes and chicken soup. It was an early *bonding experience.*

The arduous visitation schedule began, and we were in my father's company two Sundays and one long weekend a month and alternate holidays and August. We drove back and forth across Fairfield County on thruways. I knew every hill on the Merritt Parkway. I knew how many overpasses there were between Stamford and Darien. Lovely stone overpasses from the school of George L. Dunkelberger. On the first or second of these weekend visits, my father, at a tollbooth on the interstate, explained to us that he *couldn't understand why my mother was doing what she was doing,* and in the middle of offering this opinion, my father found that he could not go on. He covered his face with his hands. The car was stopped. People behind us swerved to change lanes. They honked. He wasn't the guy who had yelled at us about the noise. There had been a metamorphosis. He was in a bad spot. My mom was in a bad spot. My father had no idea how to cook for himself. His own parents were infirm. He had expenses: he was making $33,000 a year and owed a big chunk in child support and to my sister's private school, which later became three private schools. We lingered at the tollbooth, impeding traffic, in a stillness.

Fathers have a hard time quitting smoking.

He smoked Kents, a brand that doesn't seem to have the profile now it once did. He lit one then, in the car, fumbling with the lighter. I loved the smell of cigarettes newly lit in enclosed spaces, the perfume of sulfur followed by the ribboning of tobacco smoke, clouds lingering like halos around smokers, the meditativeness of cigarette paraphernalia. All suggested for me, as the New York City subway token once did, the seriousness and gravity of adults. The theatrical business of grown-ups. Ordering a *coffee regular,* putting on cuff links, lacing up wingtips, putting stamps on envelopes, presenting a credit card. This was the world I longed for when I was a kid, in the backseat of the car at the tollbooth. I didn't want to be a passenger. My brother and sister and I tortured my father by crushing whole cartons of his Kents, knocking the cigarettes out of his mouth, intoning quotations from antismoking propaganda we'd seen. Then all three of us became smokers. When my sister died, many years later, she was still hiding her smoking.

Fathers, unmarried, will pursue girlfriends.

The first girlfriend he presented to us was like an insoluble problem — like the existence of God, the location of the soul — upon which you founder in your undergraduate course work. My father arrived to pick us up one weekend, and the front seat of the red Firebird, the front seat over which we argued so relentlessly (only to cede it time after time to my sister), was occupied by *this woman,* this blonde, not our mother, our small, frail, indomitable mother, and this woman was going to treat us so well, in ways we never deserved nor understood, because it was so sad how much trouble we had been through, us kids, and we were so *cute,* and we would ignore her as a matter of course and we would constantly measure her against our mom, waiting for her to disappear so that we could move on to the art of making the next girlfriend feel just as miserable, holding all of these perfectly generous women in the dungeon of our contempt, inducing them to come to our Little League games and then upbraiding them for it, in our black, disconsolate moods, displayed for anyone who walked into the middle of our remorse and tried to soothe it with respect.

Fathers tell stories. Fathers are responsible for the very shape of story-telling; all stories issue from the mouths of fathers, and all laws about stories, including laws about the number of examples that will suffice to tell stories, how many times it is permissible to repeat jokes, and the role that rhythm plays in the deployment of anecdote.

For example, stories about working in the body shop, and how the one guy came in with the brand-new sedan complaining about an awful scuff on the hood, and how my father got up onto the hood to buff away the offending mark, to make the sedan shiny and new, only to leave a foot-wide circle on the hood completely free of its paint job. Or the stories about summers working in the psychiatric hospital, the catatonics, the hebephrenics and their laughter, the schizophrenic guy upon whom you were not to turn your back because he would pick up his lunch tray and attempt to break it over your head. Or the tales of Maine — my father's friendship, in Waterville, with the son of the driver of a Hostess truck, how they were allowed to ride in the truck and sample the baked goods, cupcakes, Twinkies, sweetmeats; how, after changing elementary schools for the fourteenth time, my father hid in a packing barrel to avoid going to school while my grandmother had the police combing the neighborhood looking for rapists, abductors, pedophiles. Or tales of army life during the Berlin Crisis, my father launching howitzer shells, my father, married with two kids (my brother wasn't born yet), getting ready to ship off to Berlin, where the Soviet and NATO tanks were parked headlight to headlight. Stories that were not always funny; stories that often had fear as an unstated dimension: my sister, outside Fort Bragg, North Carolina, swimming in a local creek, surrounded by water moccasins; my father, as a kid, deciding to take his skiff across a harbor to one of the islands off the coast of Maine during the preliminaries of a hurricane and getting lost, fogged in upon the water, so that he might very well have motored accidentally out to *Europe* — until he ran smack into some rocky Maine beach. Stories that got repeated until they acquired the mythological status of *shaggy-dog stories,* stories at which you smirked and cringed, so that in long car rides you would beg him to alleviate the tedium of unchanging landscapes with *the one about the guy who would break the tray over the orderlies' heads.*

Fathers appear to us to love us without condition if only we can interpret their complicated language. Fathers move over expanses of time, across abysses of generations; fathers move across impediments, opening out, softening, becoming unguarded, giving away the rules of fathers to younger, angrier men; fathers, over time, become solicitous and kind, regretful and warm, sensitive and, even, gentle.

We had five different addresses in five years. With my mom. I was shy to begin with, wary, disappointed by human interaction. I took *months* to get up the pluck to start a conversation. I refused to be photographed. I was sick a lot. After a couple of relocations, I gave up worrying about it all. I crossed off the days on a calendar, waiting to move again. My brother and sister were untroubled by this, or so they have said, but for me what was broken was irreparable. I hungered for company, and this famishment was my first perception in the morning and my last before bed, and I couldn't remember feeling any other way, though there were people who loved me all around and there had always been. I was the focal point of cheating scams and extortion schemes at my public schools — *Let's make Moody give us the answers!* I cried spontaneously, I plotted the murder of my brother, banter seemed impossible, kids pushed past me as though I were spectral. My camouflage was perfect. *But what I was good at was reading.* It started in the sixth grade with *The Old Man and the Sea.* I read through most of Hemingway that year. Complete disclosure: I also liked J. R. R. Tolkien and anything having to do with horror or science fiction. Where I found that one reliable thing, that other thing, that elsewhere, that space unavailable to me in contests for masculinity and prestige and social standing, was in books. And this was where I met my dad. Where I encountered a guy I had never before been introduced to, really, whose preoccupation had always been numbers, numbers, numbers. October in Darien, and my sister and brother were outside, in the urgency of a chilly weekend evening, and I asked my dad to explain the epigraph to *For Whom the Bell Tolls,* and he located somewhere in his house a copy of selected John Donne and we sat and went over it line by line on the couch where my mother had last slept when she slept in what was now my father's house, lines about being a part of the herd, the rabble, the people of whom I knew nothing. About lineage too, or so I thought, how we are of one substance with the past, with countrymen, with peerage, with all who went before us, even in the nomadism of the late twentieth century, when families were easily sundered and people moved away from one another. *No man is an island.* And Hemingway wasn't the only American writer my dad knew about. He'd been an American literature major. I wasn't sure what this meant, but it sounded formidable. There was Hemingway on the bookshelves, there was Fitzgerald; there was Salinger (I quickly consumed *The Catcher in the Rye* and *Franny and Zooey*), John P. Marquand, Stephen Crane, Thoreau, Frost. I'm sure that my father, with this additional time to spend with us, this time of *visitation,* was canny enough to search out areas where my sister and brother could bask in his attentions too — I'm sure my brother learned to make the football spiral properly, I'm sure my sister learned to operate a manual transmission — but I felt, as a reader, that the bright light of parental affection had been turned on me for the first time. I was good at something.

It wasn't long before my father urged on me his favorite book, the book on which he had spent most of his college years, *Moby-Dick.* Illustratively, he began reading aloud a certain passage annually, over Thanksgiving dinner:

> Wonderfullest things are ever the unmentionable; deep memories yield no epitaphs; this six-inch chapter is the stoneless grave of Bulkington. Let me only say that it fared with him as with the storm-tossed ship, that miserably drives along the leeward land. The port would fain give succor; the port is pitiful; in the port is safety, comfort, hearthstone, supper, warm blankets, friends, all that's kind to our mortalities. But in that gale, the port, the land, is that ship's direst jeopardy; she must fly all hospitality; one touch of land, though it but graze the keel, would make her shudder through and through. With all her might she crowds all sail off shore; in so doing, fights 'gainst the very winds that fain would blow her homeward; seeks all the lashed

sea's landlessness again; for refuge's sake forlornly rush-
ing into peril; her only friend her bitterest foe!

Know ye now, Bulkington? Glimpses do ye seem
to see of that mortally intolerable truth; that all deep,
earnest thinking is but the intrepid effort of the soul to
keep the open independence of her sea; while the
wildest winds of heaven and earth conspire to cast her
on the treacherous, slavish shore?

But as in landlessness alone resides the highest
truth, shoreless, indefinite as God — so better is it to
perish in that howling infinite, than be ingloriously
dashed upon the lee, even if that were safety! Take
heart, take heart, O Bulkington! Bear thee grimly,
demigod! Up from the spray of thy ocean-perishing —
straight up, leaps thy apotheosis!

A strange passage to read at hearthside at the celebration of our
nationhood. In which wonder and memories are unmentionable. In
which domesticity is repudiated and the wild call of landlessness is
celebrated in its stead. *Better to perish in that howling infinite.* After
some years of this, my brother and I both got much of chapter XXIII
by heart, and would quote from it while engaged in more pedestrian
activities.

And in the midst of this homely education in the American clas-
sics, which stretched out over my early teens, my father must also
have let me know about the coincidence with respect to Nathaniel
Hawthorne of Salem, Massachusetts. He was a good writer, of course,
not as good as Melville, but pretty good, Scarlet Letter *is pretty good,
except for where the allegory gets the best of the work,* but what was most
interesting about Hawthorne *was that he had written a story about a relative of ours,* a story about a Moody! Forefather of our clan. It was the
kind of thing you repeated on the playground. *I'm related to Davy
Crockett! My grandfather owns a newspaper! My father fired off a howitzer! Some guy called Hawthorne wrote a story about our family!* Dad had
a complete set of Hawthorne, a nineteenth-century edition, and he
therefore provided substantiation, produced the uncut leaf on which

the facts were to be found, the first page of "The Minister's Black Veil" in the *Twice-Told Tales* volume of *The Collected Works:*

> Another clergyman in New England, Mr. Joseph Moody, of York, Maine, who died about eighty years since, made himself remarkable by the same eccentricity that is here related of the Reverend Mr. Hooper. In his case, however, the symbol had a different import. In early life he had accidentally killed a beloved friend; and from that day till the hour of his own death, he hid his face from men.

He wore a veil? What did that mean? Hey, who cared? We were famous!

By the advent of the evening in which I sat down to discuss John Donne, my father had mostly retired from literature. He had responsibilities. He was a dad, clocking in and out, getting vested in the pension plan, writing the child support checks, taking the car to the shop, catching the 5:02, but according to my daydreams, maybe more than that too, maybe he was part of a great long line of dads, it seemed to me, extending back to intrepid religious protesters of the seventeenth century, to Carvers, Bradfords, Winslows, Brewsters, Allertons, Standishes, Aldens, Fullers, Martins, Mullinses, Whites, Warrens, Howlands, Hopkinses, Tilleys, and their ilk, the *trash,* as I have heard it put, that came over on the *Mayflower,* who wrote on their way to their New World, *Haveing undertaken, for ye glorie of God, and advancement of ye Christian faith and honour of our King & Countrie, a voyage to plant ye first colonie in ye northern parts of Virginia, doe by these presents solemnly & mutually in ye presence of God and one of another, covenant, & combine our selves togeather into a civill body politick, for our better ordering, & preservation, & furtherance of ye ends aforesaid; and by vertue hearof to enacte, constitute, and frame such just & equall lawes, ordinances, acts, constitutions, & offices, from time to time, as shall be thought most meete & convenient for ye generall good of ye colonie; unto which we promise all due submission and obedience,* and if not one of these, then part of some other wave of immigration, some other American flotilla, *part of something,* I felt, after learning about Hawthorne, even if lapsed, even if a television-watching, martini-drinking, sports car–driving, American cheese–eating dad, even if estranged from ancestry, even then part of something, and I part of his tribe, though I was perhaps a disappointment to the ghosts that hovered around me: *These stern and black-browed Puritans would have thought it quite a sufficient retribution for their sins, that, after so long a lapse of years, the old trunk of the family tree, with so much venerable moss upon it, should have borne, as its topmost bough, an idler like myself.*

What trouble we got into next. I'll have more to say about it. *The resistance to fathers is honorific, and resistance to fathers is always the last lesson in the instruction of fathers. Fatherhood knows that it is honored by teenage contempt.* My sister was expelled from Rosemary Hall for curfew violations and finished up at Pelham High. She crashed my dad's car and pretended that it had nothing to do with drinking. My brother crashed my dad's next car. We stole booze from my father's liquor cabinet and stayed out all night and we walked the beaches, or went driving, looking, searching among contemporaries for lessons calling from the past. A whole sequence of fathers and sons and their relations looking backward for answers, finding, ultimately, that the most impossible father, with the most draconian set of regulations, was not in the living room preparing to lecture them, but cradled inside and impossible to dislodge.

THE OLD PEOPLE OF THE VILLAGE
CAME STOOPING ALONG THE STREET . . .

My grandfather Hiram Frederick Moody, Dad's dad, from my first recollection, engaged my brother and me in disquisitions on work. On the theory, the application, the pragmatic essentials of labor. He was a mostly bald, cheerful older guy by the time I got to know him. He smoked incessantly. He wheezed. He looked a lot like the elderly Vladimir Nabokov, but friendlier. He never failed to wear chinos and flannel shirts and a sequence of beat-up sport jackets, one of which, a plaid, I still have. He hung around the house in Darien quite a bit, since my grandparents lived just a couple of towns over, in Norwalk, Connecticut. My grandfather and grandmother would show up on a Sunday, most often, spend a few hours, and vanish as quickly as they had arrived. They had two cars, a Cadillac sedan in royal purple that belonged to my grandmother and that never seemed to age, and my grandfather's car, known only as the *sports coupe.* This would have been shop talk, since my grandfather had been a car dealer in late life, and before that a middle manager for the largest of automobile manufacturers, General Motors. Cars were much in his thinking. My grandfather's *sports coupe* was so run-down, so battered by the years, that it looked as though it might have been a candidate for a demolition derby: it was full of trash, old wadded newspapers, cartons of cigarettes, tire irons, spark plugs, stray gloves, rags, and tarps. It smelled like a wet campfire. There was nothing *sporty* about my grandfather's trash-hauling Pontiac. It was the color of yellowing teeth. The engine sounded like a toolbox falling down a staircase.

The model must have dated back to the late fifties, and it had the homeliness of that period of design. Since my grandfather could barely see (glaucoma) and was mostly deaf, it was terrifying to imagine him actually driving his *coupe,* but he must have driven it, since he often parked it in our driveway on Sundays. Dad used to say that my grandfather was so attached to the *sports coupe* that when it breathed its last so would its owner. But Gramps impulsively traded it in, about 1970, on a model that was nearly identical — just as beat-up, just as run-down — except that the replacement was of more recent vintage. And indeed this new *sports coupe,* without tail fins, conveyed him just fine, in the style he liked, and it outlived him too.

Presumably, since my grandfather had a General Motors pension and had saved some money from the divestiture of *Moody Motor Sales, Inc.,* of Winchester, Massachusetts, he could have purchased a new car had he really wanted one, though there's the possibility that he was spending all available funds on my grandmother's sequence of Cadillacs. I prefer to think that he liked the *sports coupe,* liked its anonymity, its bland similarity to all other cars, the cars of his fellow Americans. My grandfather could go anywhere, slip into any bar or public space, and start a conversation with anyone (and this skill was unusual since the rest of my family was to varying degrees troubled by shyness), and I imagine him starting a conversation with the guy at the used-car dealership in Norwalk, in 1970, about the time of Altamont, trying to convince this guy that his *sports coupe* from 1959 or 1961 with its boxy design was a *darned sporty little car,* though it was rusted clear through the floor, such that in the backseat you could see the white lines of the avenues beneath your feet, and the guy at the dealership would stand there watching, and my grandfather, with his mesmerizing affability, would begin to recite the history of the model, the range of models and colors available, the way the assembly line works, *a marvel of modern technology, let me tell you, why this is the most reliable car Pontiac ever produced at the assembly plant, just look at this,* in his Down East bantering style, and the guy at the dealership would think, *How am I going to get this crank outta here?* and just as the conversation was teetering at the point of irritation, with repetitions and restatements, my grandfather would stick out his gnarled paw, offer a farewell, and be gone, until the next day, when he would start all over, until the deal was closed, such that he was driving another *sports coupe,* no better than the old one, just as full of detritus, though he got it for a song.

First and foremost, a *birthday party trick master,* with that standby act of legerdemain, honed over the years, involving the production of loose change from inside the ears of preschoolers. A good trick at birthday parties, and it had as part of its pyrotechnics a stream of exaggerated verbiage about how *it was probably not the best idea to be growing dimes and quarters in the ear canal, make you hard of hearing one day;* this was his first responsibility, party trick master, and didn't matter if it was the kid next door's birthday party or the dog's birthday, he would turn up just the same and do the trick, and we would marvel and applaud. Then he would dole out the small change to outstretched hands, change produced from the tympanic membranes and cochlea of juveniles. This change later became dollar bills. Any time he encountered anyone shorter than a certain height, any neighborhood child, he would produce some faded currency and give advice on thrift.

When we began to progress beyond the *party trick phase* of childhood development, my grandfather instructed us in the matter of work, through the application of our energies in backyard agriculture. He was not allergic to poison ivy, or so he claimed, and we used to watch him pull it out of his own garden with bare hands (to my grandmother's horror, since she had a list of powerful phobias, among them any variety of poisonous vine or shrub). And he did not confine himself to his own garden, from which he was perennially carting around tomatoes and offering them to strangers. He also worked in my mother's garden, and I think of him most often there: alone, in the backyard with a garden trowel, or a hoe, or a scythe, sometimes stooped over a row of seedlings, sometimes mopping his brow with a tanned handkerchief, sometimes spinning out his repertoire of fibs and outrageous lies to anyone who chanced to pass near. He could go for some time without really talking — there was reticence beneath the affability — but eventually he felt a need to repeat certain imperative questions: *What's your favorite subject in school?* Replies were never sufficient. No matter what you said, *he was off.*

The reason we needed to be instructed in work was that we were indoors watching the television most days or *engaged in pugilism* or trying to avoid the trouble around the house, the penetrating cosmic rays of trouble, and I imagine my grandfather knew this, though he never mentioned it, and so he would haul us out into the garden, the last place we wanted to go, to regale us there with his strange scholarly opinions about *the wax bean,* as it is called here in America, flagging us down, my brother and me, until we were standing by the garden with him, and he leaning against the scythe, reciting the history of the vegetable, which had assumed for him a tremendous spiritual importance: *Now, listen here, this bean, this is a great bean I have here. This bean was not always called the wax bean; that's what I want to tell you boys. Back around the turn of the century or thereabouts this bean was called the yellow bean. And back when it was called the yellow bean, why, it was one of the most popular beans in America. Absolutely the most popular bean around. A darned good bean. There's nothing like a yellow bean fresh from the garden like this, nothing like it. Good for you, tastes great, fresh, crispy. Now, the bean manufacturers decided that the name, the yellow bean, it just wasn't the right name for the bean, a change was in order, they wanted to distinguish this particular vegetable from other beans, so they changed the name, and this bean became the wax bean, and I don't know where they got that name at all. A big campaign was launched, advertising and whatnot. But that was absolutely the wrong name for this bean, by God, because people just didn't want to associate wax, you know, with a bean, and since then this bean, which is really one of the tastiest beans you ever could want to try, has fallen out of favor. A shame. A terrible shame. Nobody wants to eat this bean anymore. It's a godawful name for a bean.* We would nod and agree, although we couldn't stand wax beans, no matter what you called them, and any time he tried to get us to eat them, or any time my mother tried to get us to eat them in order to humor my grandfather, we would stifle the upsurge of vomitus, *oh God,* swallowing the wax beans with floods of milk, and we would try to deflect attention away from the cords of uneaten beans stacked upon our plates, or my brother would begin his bartering on the number of wax beans that would be required for him to procure dessert. *You're going to have to eat more than that,* my mother would sigh, and my brother would say, *I can't eat any more, they're horrible, I'm going to throw up, I can feel it coming up already, I'm going to throw up, I can't stand it,* and my mother would say, *You're going to have to eat some more, eat five more forkfuls,* and my brother would say, *Four more, four more forkfuls,* and soon the negotiation would devolve onto the actual number of beans in a forkful, the nature of a forkful, etc.; for example, since you could stab a bean with a fork and then load this perforated bean into your mouth, didn't that imply that *one bean* could technically be a forkful? Would four forkfuls be acceptable if they contained a certain minimum number of stabbed beans, one bean per forking or stabbing motion, or maybe even *halves of beans* or *little fragmentary bean portions, as these could technically load up a fork, could they not?* And eventually my mother would become exasperated, *I'm not discussing it anymore,* and my brother would eat one more bean, and clamp his hand over his mouth to keep the bean down, feeling the alarming gastrointestinal tempest, but he would keep it down, because the main thing was to be permitted entry into the paradise of desserts. At which point I would claim that I was being *discriminated against,* because now I had eaten all my beans (always on the lookout for political leverage against my brother) and had not complained, and my sister would tell us both to *shut up, we were bugging her.* You can tell from the effectiveness of my brother's negotiating skills how he most resembles my grandfather: the same charm, the same wicked smile.

There we were in the garden, inside the small chicken-wire fence that my mother had erected to keep out rabbits and raccoons but which kept out neither, and my grandfather was teaching us about work. *The idea here,* he told us, *is that you have to do the heavy lifting first. You have to do the hardest part of the job first, and then the easy part afterward. That way, by the time you get to the easy part of the work, it's easy, and you have a good feeling about what you've accomplished. Might as well just plunge into the hard part and get it over with, and you can look forward to that easy feeling later on.* The job in question turned out to be moving a certain large rock that was impeding the process of scything and tilling in the garden. It was sunny, and it was before all the new houses went up on our street, before the housing boom of the later sixties, and there was no traffic. Our dog, Trouble, was coiled at the base of a tree, and no child had yet that morning gashed him- or herself, no child had humiliated another nor run inside aggrieved, and it was before my parents had quit talking to each other entirely, and so it was a perfect morning, and my grandfather leaned down to pick up the large rock in the garden and paused. *Before we start, there's one other thing you have to learn about work. When you do the hard job, you have to grunt while you do it. You have to actually grunt. Make a noise. In your throat. You're going to have to learn how to make that noise, so let me hear you try it once before we try to move this rock, because I want to make sure you're going to be able to grunt properly. It's an important part of this work you're going to do.* My brother and I, with deadly earnestness, in squeaky voices, tried to imitate the low growl my grandfather was employing, as though we were Eastern Bloc weight lifters, as though we were day laborers, and when we had mastered this simulation of physical exertion, or when my grandfather was satisfied with our simulation, he at last allowed us to *move the rock,* to heft it over to one corner of the garden with elaborate grunts that were cosmetic but which had an efficacy you couldn't dispute.

Work is what I would ask my grandfather about if I had him around now, though big questions about life are infrequently asked among my family. When he was at General Motors, he was a successful corporate employee; he rose through the ranks of the corporate hierarchy, though this success in business had been costly for his small family. He and my grandmother and father had moved so many times, according to the needs of the General Motors chain of command, that my grandmother had put her foot down and refused to relocate again. My father was shell-shocked from his tour through a half dozen elementary schools. After years of putting the needs of the company first, my grandfather had eventually been promised the post of assistant general sales manager for the eastern third of the nation. He had overseen sales in the Boston area, in Philadelphia, Pittsburgh, D.C., Cleveland, all around New England, and now he would be located in Detroit and he would have a stable caseload of dealerships to manage in the east, and he would claw his way up toward some well-paying senior-management position. But instead of taking the assistant general sales managership, my grandfather left the corporation, in 1946, and bought his own GM dealership — and not even a large dealership: not the Boston franchise (he turned it down), not Portland, Maine, not Providence, Rhode Island. No, he bought the GM dealership in Winchester, Massachusetts. Why did my grandfather choose this bend in the road? A local newspaper article about him, from years later, observed the following:

> In 1946 he went into business for himself in Winchester, and during the years that lie between that date and the present [1963] he ran a successful business here. Moody well remembers the day when he first walked by, and then came into the Star office while this writer and the Editor, T. Price Wilson, were chatting in the front window as they used to in the "good old days." Hi Moody wanted to ask some questions about Winchester before he committed himself to taking over the Pontiac agency here, and he also wanted some advice about lawyers and banks.

Did my grandfather buy the dealership to appease his wife, my grandmother? To permit his family to settle in one place? Did he find, in himself, that resistance to and dislike of corporate superiors that other Moodys have felt? But why a dealership that was not terribly lucrative for General Motors? My grandfather had done the hard part of the job first, I think, had done the heavy lifting and grunting, and had determined that he was now going to content himself with *that easy feeling.*

His other subject, besides the theory of labor, was mathematics. He was a substitute teacher of mathematics in the public schools of Norwalk until he turned seventy. It got him out of the house. I found the fact of his dispensing discipline impossible to imagine. He was never hard on us. In my public school, when substitutes came to class, my peers normally exchanged seats with one another, so that the seating chart would be useless. We feigned ignorance. We concocted fibs and cheated on tests. We threw things at substitutes. Did my grandfather know to expect this from kids? Or did he treat kids with the jocularity that was so effective everywhere else? I imagined him getting up from his desk for a lecture on *the quadratic equation,* turning his back to the classroom, and then, because of deafness, completely failing to notice a hail of spitballs and several attempted rapes taking place in the back of the room. I imagined him beginning a discussion on long division and then getting sidetracked on the proper way to prepare and serve lobsters: *The best way, see, is to dig a pit in the beach right there, and then you go on and wrap some potatoes in tinfoil, set these right down there in the pit while you're boiling the water. You'll want some clams, some steamers, so you ought to bring the clam hoe along, and then you set all of these in the water there. The clams, the lobsters. Did you know you can hypnotize a lobster? Sure can. You can hypnotize them, they'll go right out like they're taking a long nap — you turn them head down, see, get the claws facing backwards, tail curled around, and then you stroke the back of the tail, it's true, every word I'm telling you is true, and that lobster, why he'll go directly to sleep, and then when you put him in the pot there he won't know what hit him. Allow the lobsters to boil or steam for twenty or twenty-five minutes or so, that ought to do her, and then serve them right alongside the steamers. The potatoes take a little longer, of course. Best part of the lobster is the roe. It'll take you a while before you like it, probably, but it's terrific. Have you kids ever had a lobster?* The hypnotized-lobster experiment was another of his routines, see. Whenever lobster was to be served there were two or three of them upended, like doorstops, on the kitchen linoleum. My mother and my sister stepped gingerly through the room as my grandfather worked his necromancy. A whole religion of shellfish consumption sprang up in my family in the wake of my grandfather's relish for these crustaceans. Disembowelment, with lobster forks, of the *bug* in order to produce the satisfying tail section was especially smiled upon among Moodys, as was Talmudic argument and negotiation on the proper construction and assembly of the sandwich called *the lobster roll,* which you might find at any curbside shack on Route One in Maine: leftover lobster meat (little shreds from inside the body section being especially useful), in the amount of two cups, and mayonnaise (two tablespoons), dash of mustard, dash of paprika, and, according to my own tastes, the highly controversial half cup of diced celery, served on a toasted, buttered hot-dog bun. Makes several sandwiches. In my grandfather's honor, new members of the family (spouses, girlfriends, grandchildren, etc.) are still subjected to instruction on the autopsy of lobster, as well as the crucial side dishes, viz., pickles, potato chips, mussels.

He was the family historian, whose comic tendency to exaggerate was so faint that it was the same shade, just about, as the truth. That seems to be how he liked it. As when he sat us down to enumerate the eminent Moodys to whom we were related. Moodys were present at all the important moments in Western civilization, and we were related to them all. Our occurrence, as acorns on this massive oak of Moodys, was foreordained. *Have you all heard the advertisements for Pepperidge Farm cookies? Titus Moody? Why, he's related to us. Comes down the Waldoboro line. A cousin, two times removed.* Sure, we had heard these radio advertisements, just as we were attuned to the varieties of TV dinners. That accent that my grandparents had, that Down East lockjaw, it was familiar to us. I told my mother, next time I heard Titus Moody on the radio, that Gramps had made clear that we were directly related to this guy. Maybe this implied that we were entitled to discounts on certain Pepperidge Farm products?

Well, actually, Titus Moody is fictitious, dear. So I'm sure your grandfather is bending the truth a little bit. Titus Moody is probably just an actor. He's just pretending to be this man from Maine for the sake of the commercials. Still, I told everyone at school that I was related to Titus Moody, in spite of a lack of corroboration, and in this way I proved my relation to my grandfather, that I too was an exaggerator. And I tried it all again when my grandfather told me that we were related to an actor, Ron Moody, from *Oliver!* Ron Moody, who played Fagin. He was a British subject, but we were related to him just the same, my grandfather said, because we were related to all Moodys, because we came from a line of humble laborers hiding out in ghost villages down the coast who were nonetheless bent upon *global eminence.* Thereafter, I said the immortal words *Please, sir, may I have some more?* with greater abandon, knowing that *Oliver!* had benefited the

Moodys and their global conspiracy. *Don't believe anything he says,* my grandmother advised, and since my grandfather had fibbed boldly in these cases, was there any reason to believe him when other fish stories emerged, like later, when we got to *Handkerchief Moody,* who had killed his roommate rowing on the Charles and who forever after kept his face hidden from men? My father had told us some variation on the same story, and its repetitions were eerie. But where did my grandfather get this rowing business? His own embellishment? A pitchman for cookies, an actor, a preacher who kept his face covered throughout adulthood. A tribe of dissemblers, these Moodys. And my grandfather was one of them. Loose with facts, rich in stories.

One summer he erected an assembly-required slide for us in the backyard. He put the steps in upside down. It never got fixed. Those steps always hurt, especially in bare feet, but we were enough moved by my grandfather's efforts on our behalf that we never complained. If you shined up the slide with wax paper, it worked like a charm; there was that instant of acceleration that hinted at the larger world of physics. In fact, while he was putting in the slide, my grandfather was explaining geometry to us, schooling us in *the Pythagorean theorem.* It was humid out, and we were mostly at Weed Beach in summer, at that torpid, crowded sandbox on the Long Island Sound where I was also engaged in a lengthy deceit about how much progress I was making in swimming class. But when we were home, my grandfather would turn up and quiz us some more: *The square of the hypotenuse is equal to the sum of the squares of the two legs. Repeat after me.* The word *hypotenuse* was so strange, so wonderful. A chimerical animal, a dinosaur, a mammal with wings, an eight-armed marsupial, a lizard capable of invisibility or spontaneous division or fire breathing, something animate, something dangerous, this *hypotenuse,* the impression of animation made more vivid by the presence in the theorem of *legs.* My grandfather tried to draw a right triangle on a piece of paper and explain the theorem to us, waving off mosquitoes in the half-light of dusk, but the measurements didn't work, not the way he wanted them to work. Much later, when I got to geometry, I had the theorem in permanent storage, like a commercial jingle. I repeated it to myself on the swings of grade school and ever after.

Soon it became apparent to me that my grandparents did not have a routine *marital arrangement.* For example, they lived on different floors. In their house in Norwalk my grandmother lived on the second floor and my grandfather lived in the basement. The first floor was no-man's-land. The kitchen and the breezeway were on the first floor, where we often sat with them, but no one used the living room or the den for anything. Throughout my childhood, these first-floor rooms accumulated dust and a complement of forgotten baubles and appliances, as well as the yellowing photographs of our infancy — my sister from the period when all her teeth had fallen out, my brother in kindergarten, the three of us wearing our matching naval outfits — displayed as though current. Almost everything in the house was pink. There were pink curtains, pink rugs, furniture upholstered in pink, or lavender, or mauve, and the furniture was covered with plastic wrap so as to protect the upholstery. My grandmother collected glass pianos, replicas, and every shelf or table in the living room had a small piano upon it, some of these dispensing melodies when you wound them up. Yet my grandparents never spent much time in these rooms, except perhaps on Christmas Day, when we were there to open gifts, and my grandmother's gift selections of *carob bars* or *extra scarves* were quickly tossed aside by us in search of more intoxicating fare, the new plastic Formula I race car, the doll, the suede jacket we had hoped for. The rest of the year, my grandmother cooked my grandfather dinner, and then he went to bed about seven or seven-thirty, woke with the first light, and spent most of the morning reading at a small desk *in his basement.* He used an old-fashioned magnifying glass. He had several dozen books, all secondhand, on the subject of Maine history, or by Maine authors: Kenneth Roberts, author of *Northwest Passage* and *Lydia Bailey;* Ben Ames Williams, of the classic *Fraternity Village.* These books were worn out by the meanness of my grandfather's room, the mildew and damp. They had broken bindings, flaking pages. (When it became clear that I was going to be a reader, my grandfather bought for me a half dozen of these Maine titles at various secondhand-book stores, and then looked disappointed in the months following when I never got more than ten pages into any of them.) My grandfather had a double bed in his basement, and across the room next to the boiler there was a sink where he washed his clothes by hand, and, bisecting the room, a drying line upon which he strung up sleeveless T-shirts and boxer shorts to dry. There were a number of photographs on the Sheetrock or paneled walls; for example, a signed photograph of Ted Williams, the last four-hundred hitter in Major League Baseball, to whom my grandfather had sold a number of Cadillacs, and also a photo of my grandfather wearing a Red Sox uniform, from the year he was invited to attend spring training as a guest.

This is where my grandfather lived, and where he had lived, apparently, ever since he'd owned the dealership in Winchester, ever since my dad had gone away to school. In Winchester, he'd been on the second floor, and my grandmother on the first; in Arlington, Mass., he'd lived in the basement, and it was basements from then on, in Rowayton, in each of their houses in Norwalk.

My grandmother, meanwhile, was a night owl. She stayed up late to *look at the television set.* Among her favorites, Lawrence Welk, the middle-American bandleader and polka expert; Merv Griffin, the middle-of-the-afternoon talk show host, and the fair-to-middling Johnny Carson. Since my grandmother didn't go to bed until a few hours before my grandfather woke, it's hard to imagine them spending much time together. How long can you live with someone before, driven out of your routine by loneliness, you venture endearments, just for a night or so? Once my brother and I were to dine with my grandparents on a weekend, and in the company of my grandmother we drove to their place in Norwalk. As we walked through the breezeway into the house, it became clear that my grandfather had attempted to fix the main course himself (chicken, in some unspectacular recipe), just to get the meal under way. But the chicken was scorched. The oven was smoking. My grandmother harangued my grandfather at greater length than I had ever heard before: *You stupid old man! How could you think to do this? You stupid old man! What are you doing trying to cook, for godsakes?* My grandfather said nothing, stood silently by. Oaths rained down on him.

She wouldn't be happy at the right hand of God, he used to say.

About then, my sister went off to school, so it was mostly my brother and I who watched his decline. Not long after the scorched-chicken incident, we were spending a day with the two of them at their house. My grandfather, who could scarcely make out a reply to any of the questions he now repeated over and over — *Any girlfriends yet? What are you studying in school? Do you like mathematics?* — seemed agitated and uncomfortable. He wasn't breathing well, and he was restless and bored, disappointed by his inactivity when schoolteaching finally came to an end. And my grandmother, whose main pastime was the amassing of small fortunes of cash at the contract bridge table, had very little to offer us in her house, excepting games that we had tired of years before. Parcheesi and checkers. The neighborhood kids of Norwalk were the progeny of union men and women and we should have known how to talk to them, but we didn't.

I wish I could remember more of this, that memory wasn't just a series of desires, a series of protective encasements for identity, like chain motels at the edges of canyons, *damned lies* of the sort my grandfather told: I can see the lights in the basement, and my grandfather, *not feeling well,* poised at the bottom of the staircase; I can see my grandfather collapsing and calling my grandmother's strange name, *Helena?* A single naked interrogative. My grandfather falling to the floor and my grandfather's face veiled in this terror, and my grandmother at the top of the staircase, and my brother and me standing by him like idiots, not knowing what to do, and my grandmother asking what was wrong, a panicky vibrato in her voice, and my grandfather saying, *Helena, there's something wrong with my legs.* Immediately amending it, *I can't feel my legs.* My jocular, charming, witty grandfather, geometer and salesman, sitting in a heap at the bottom of the stairs, and my grandmother flustered, terrified, *Lord, you boys, you're going to have to try to lift him up, we're going to have to try to lift him up.* . . . And the three of us, my brother, who was ten, and I, eleven, and my grandmother, seventy-five, tried to help my grandfather up the stairs from the basement, and I can feel the impossibility of this and I can see the feebleness of the banister there, a lacquered rail bowing out on cheap brass fixtures, my grandfather clutching at it, the dimness of light on the stairs themselves, twelve steps, my grandfather wordless in his exertion, my grandmother afraid of losing *the option of him,* that voice from the basement, and perhaps suddenly ashamed of what she had allowed to go on right under her nose, *the retreat of a man,* so that he might as well have lived in a coal mine, for all she knew of him, and my brother and I lifting, though we were just wisps, and my grandmother, despite her determination, not a strong woman. It seems impossible to get the door open and to carry my grandfather through it when he couldn't walk and we were desperate and afraid, and that's why in the dwindling light at the top of the stairs bearing up the helpless corpus of that family chronicler, the rest of this part of the tale is lost.

It wasn't stroke but some powerful infection of the lower half of the body, *a gram-negative infection,* probably starting as an asymptomatic urinary tract infection, causing either precipitous drop in blood pressure or infection surrounding the spinal cord, etc., and then pneumonia, or pneumonia *and* some powerful infection, or some extrastrength arrangement of illnesses featuring pneumonia and infection, and he was in the hospital in Norwalk. Outside the semiprivate room where we were visiting him, I could hear my grandmother and my father conspiring about *the Will,* words that I had heard before, because of the deaths of my maternal grandmother and uncle, but with this additional force, now, as my grandfather, who had lost weight in a dramatic way and was perforated with IVs and catheters, *was dying in front of us,* offering only a few observations himself, shouting at my father out in the hall, *Get me the hell out of here, I don't want to be in here, get me out of the damn hospital.* What was everyone trying to hide? Some arithmetic of life was intimated, beyond the decoration and construction of hospitals, beyond their reverberant corridors, their overused and uncomfortable furniture; some devastating series of principles was concealed in this sequence of days. Every time I edged within earshot, every time I began to make out the whispering outside of hospital rooms or to interpret the anguished expressions in the elevators of hospitals, or the footfalls of nurses and doctors, meanings of words disappeared before me, the message disappeared, and whisperers fell silent, and trees waved dismally outside the windows in the silences that ensued. If I knew already about the imminence of mortality, why was the lesson of uncertainty somehow worse? *A sense of something to come, something that had been waiting long, long to happen; an opening of doors, a lifting of heavy, magnificent curtains.*

My grandfather recovered from his sequence of illnesses, from pneumonia and the *mysterious gram-negative infection,* but he was never strong again, and his emphysema got a lot worse, even though he gave up smoking and converted to the chewing tobacco that was his solace in these last years. The house in Norwalk was fitted out with antique spittoons. My grandfather was deaf, he couldn't see, he couldn't drive, he couldn't breathe, with great effort he could just ascend the stairs from the basement. And he had become forgetful too, unable to concentrate. One morning, my grandmother made coffee and called from the top of the stairs, as usual. No reply. She asked tentatively if he was all right, and when there was no reply, she called for an ambulance. We sold off the *sports coupe* for scrap.

Which brings me to the last conversation I had with him, when I was home on some break from school (up in New Hampshire, where I had enrolled for ninth grade). Differences had opened up between myself and my grandparents; they didn't know me and couldn't know me again, couldn't know the complications of this modern life, intoxicants with alluring names, unclothed girls, girls with intoxicants, hallucinations, electric guitars, loneliness, my grandfather *couldn't have understood.* Or so I thought. That first summer vacation home from New Hampshire, I had intended to get a job caddying at the golf course in Pelham, where my mother lived then, though I had never played golf nor caddied. When I went out to the country club to ask for the job, I lied disgracefully about my inexperience and, though I had been offered the job, I couldn't bring myself to report for duty at the links. I just didn't show up. My mother asked me what I was *intending to do* for a couple of weeks, and I evaded, and then she stopped asking. My grandfather's final remarks to me were on this subject, and therefore his last remarks were *about work.* The three of us were there, my brother, sister, and I, with our long hair and our worn corduroys and our exaggerated *slack,* and we couldn't be bothered to talk to my grandparents. Instead, we argued among ourselves about whether Led Zeppelin was better than Pink Floyd or vice versa, or what about Traffic and the Allman Brothers Band, which of us could play the beginning of this song or that, bar chords, unusual tunings, etc., until we were interrupted by my grandfather, fixed like junk-shop statuary to a piece of lightweight porch furniture, wheezing, *You kids just live off your father's money. You're never going to learn anything that way. You have to go get yourselves some work and learn something about how to work and how to save some money of your own. You have to learn about work. You can't live off your father the way you do. It's not fair to him and it's shameful. Get out of the house and go do some work.*

THE TOPIC, IT MIGHT BE SUPPOSED,
WAS OBVIOUS ENOUGH . . .

Nathaniel Hawthorne wrote most of *Twice-Told Tales,* the volume that includes "The Minister's Black Veil," from which my father and grandfather got their disconcerting family tale of Handkerchief Moody, in an attic room in his uncle's house in Salem, Massachusetts. The *castle dismal,* he called it. By then he was long done with Bowdoin, where he'd gotten his B.A., where he had failed to prepare for the law or the ministry, where he'd already written a novel, *Fanshawe,* a novel he eventually self-published for a cost of about a hundred dollars. *Fanshawe* didn't register even briefly in the national consciousness, and a large portion of the first impression, as collectors call them, was eventually consumed in a bookstore fire. Hawthorne so disliked this piece of juvenilia that he never mentioned the novel to his wife during the entirety of their marriage.

His father, a mariner, also called Nathaniel Hathorne (the younger Nathaniel conceived of the *w* in the surname), had died of yellow fever in the line of duty — hauling fish, bringing back sugar — in Surinam, before his boy reached the age of four. Together with his mother and two sisters, young Nathaniel therefore came to impose on the charity of his maternal family at 12 Herbert Street, in Salem, in a house overlooking the cemetery where his witch-hunting Hathorne ancestors were buried (*No aim, that I have ever cherished, would they recognize as laudable; no success of mine — if my life, beyond its domestic scope, had ever been brightened by success — would they deem otherwise than worthless, if not positively disgraceful*). When Hawthorne returned from his years at Bowdoin, this is where he resettled. Excepting a few travel adventures around New England with uncles or with friends from college, and excepting a brief, disappointing stay at a Utopian community called Brook Farm (the setting for his novel entitled *The Blithedale Romance*), Hawthorne never left the house until, in 1842, he married his fiancée, Sophia Peabody, and moved with her into Emerson's former family homestead, the Old Manse of Concord, Massachusetts. He was thirty-eight years old. (Hawthorne's engagement to Sophia lasted four years, indicating, perhaps, some further mixed emotions.)

Or, to put it another way, by the time Hawthorne left Salem for his domestic experiment, he had spent all of his adult life, more than fifteen years, in the *castle dismal,* trying to write his way out of his circumstances. He had abandoned a couple of collections of tales, even *burned* one manuscript of stories, but then, in the early 1830s, he'd begun to publish a series of pieces of short fiction in a periodical called *The Token,* the aggregate of which served to establish Hawthorne's initial reputation. The stories, generally, had early American settings (in contrast to the more fanciful allegorical structures that characterized a later collection, *Mosses from an Old Manse*): prerevolutionary tensions, Congregational and Quaker conflicts, Puritan moral allegories, etc. Most of these early stories were included in *Twice-Told Tales.*

Hawthorne published the story called "The Minister's Black Veil" in *The Token* in 1836, while he was briefly serving as the editor for the *American Magazine of Useful and Entertaining Knowledge,* a job for which he was all but unpaid. *Twice-Told Tales* was, as he performed his editorial day job, assuming its initial shape. The publication of this book too was to be underwritten, through the largesse — without Hawthorne's knowledge — of a college friend and lifelong correspondent, Horatio Bridge. Despite *winning some fame* in *The Token* (as he wrote in his journal in 1836), Hawthorne was still hard up for cash and still living with his mother's family, and the strain showed, as when, in a letter, he referred to this phase of development as one of *dark seclusion — the atmosphere without any oxygen of sympathy.* Or, in another letter: *I have made a captive of myself and put me in a dungeon;*

and now I cannot find the key to let myself out — and if the door were open, I should be almost afraid to come out.

There must have been some light in the constricted space of the *castle dismal,* as during Hawthorne's renderings of his occasional sallies outdoors in the 1830s: *Old Haynes made a long eulogy on his dog Tiger, yesterday, insisting on his good moral character, his not being quarrelsome, his docility, and all other excellent qualities that a huge, strong, fierce mastiff could have. Tiger is the bully of the village, and keeps all the dogs in awe; . . . "But he's a good dog!"* And yet generally there's something fetid in the attic air, in the dozen or more years of Hawthorne's separation, something impervious to lightheartedness (*A recluse, like myself, or a prisoner, measures time by the progress of sunshine through his chamber*). Small wonder, then, something like a germinal idea for "The Minister's Black Veil" comes to Hawthorne in these years, in the context of his journals: *An essay on the misery of being always under a masque — A veil may sometimes be needful, but never a masque. Instances of people who wear masques, in all classes of society, and never take it off even in the most familiar moments, though sometimes it may chance to slip aside.* A similar image, an image of philosophical unveiling, appears in the pages nearby: *To represent the process by which sober truth gradually strips off all the beautiful draperies with which imagination has enveloped a beloved object, till from an angel she turns out to be a merely ordinary woman.* This is the complicated writer who breathes life into "The Minister's Black Veil."

The subtitle given the story in the 1837 edition of *Twice-Told Tales* is "A Parable." You can't help but wonder what kind of parable, what kind of *simple story with moral.* Maybe the sort that is found in the New Testament? The sort with which most colonial Americans would have been familiar? (*The kingdom of heaven is like to a grain of mustard seed, which a man took, and sowed in his field: which indeed is the least of all seeds: but when it is grown, it is the greatest among herbs, and becometh a tree, so that the birds of the air come and lodge in the branches thereof.*) The words "A Parable" also provide the initial home for Hawthorne's footnote about the Reverend Joseph Moody of Maine, and this footnote appears at the bottom of the first page of the story. The rest of that page is given over to setting the table in Milford,

Connecticut, where, in the first half of the eighteenth century, "The Minister's Black Veil" finds its locale. (These days Milford is a little homely blot on the interstate between two large, somewhat run-down New England industrial towns, New Haven and Bridgeport.)

"The Minister's Black Veil" begins with celebratory music, with the sexton of the Milford Congregational meetinghouse "pulling lustily at the bell rope" in the town's center. (Which reminds me of a very beautiful fragment that appears, unembellished, in Hawthorne's journals from 1836: *cannon transformed to church-bells.*) A procession of townsfolk in their Sunday best makes its way to the church, old folks of the village, children, "spruce bachelors" who gape "sidelong at the pretty maidens." When the parishioners have reached the porch of the meetinghouse, it is the sexton's habit to look for the minister, coming through the parsonage door, whereupon he rests from his bell ringing. The dramatic situation is effectively laid, and we're ready for Hooper's entrance — as in *The Scarlet Letter,* which opens with Hester Prynne on the scaffold above town, revealed in her punishment. The Reverend Mr. Hooper, like Hester Prynne, can only launch his heroic investigation of self *before the community:* "All within hearing immediately turned about, and beheld the semblance of Mr. Hooper, pacing slowly his meditative way toward the meetinghouse. With one accord they started."

Thus the dread garment is introduced: "Swathed about his forehead, and hanging down over his face, so low as to be shaken by his breath, Mr. Hooper had on a black veil. On a nearer view it seemed to consist of two folds of crape, which entirely concealed his features, except the mouth and chin."

No mention given, here or elsewhere, of Hooper's morning, his breakfast and vocational preparation, how he wrote Sunday's homily, whether he spoke to his fiancée, initially absent from the account, how he liked his toast, nothing prior to the moment at which he appears upon the footpath. What was Hooper doing, for example, *on Saturday?* Anyone see him on Saturday? Any wag of Milford have idle conversation with Hooper? Did Hooper discuss the weather on the day before *assuming the veil?* Did he call on any ill parishioner, on any *shut-in?* Were any kisses bestowed on his beloved? And where are we exactly on the church calendar? Ash Wednesday, with its dark iteration of mortality? Third Sunday of Lent? Advent? Is there an ecclesiastical occasion that causes Hooper to appear obscured?

Hooper has already made the decision and won't unmake it in succeeding pages, and that is just *how it is;* we're not privy to his prior life, his confidences, his doubts. What Hooper has evidently decided, through his own means, is that rather than wearing the veil to the butcher's shop or to the glazier's or to the candlemaker's or to his fiancée's house (for polite, supervised conversation), he will wear the veil in a professional setting first. In church.

A series of paragraphs follow on the public reaction to the revelation in the meetinghouse. "I can't really feel as if good Mr. Hooper's face was behind that piece of crape," says the sexton. "I don't like it," says an old woman. "He has changed himself into something awful." There is a "general bustle, a rustling of the women's gowns and shuffling of the men's feet, greatly at variance with that hushed repose which should attend the entrance of the minister." Things don't much improve when Hooper ascends into the pulpit: "Such was the effect of this simple piece of crape, that more than one woman of delicate nerves was forced to leave the meetinghouse. Yet perhaps the pale-faced congregation was almost as fearful a sight to the minister, as his black veil to them." Nonetheless, Hooper delivers the morning's sermon resolutely. His normal oratorical style is *mild persuasion,* and though his style is unchanged now, his new threads have a perceptible effect. "But there was something, either in the sentiment of the discourse itself, or in the imagination of the auditors, which made it greatly the most powerful effort that they had ever heard from their pastor's lips."

This is the terrain into which "The Minister's Black Veil" quickly moves. Hawthorne's story is not so much about the *meaning* of the veil; rather, the story is about *the impact of the veil* in the community. It's a descriptive fiction, not a prescriptive one; it's a story about life *before and after* the simple appearance of this fashion accessory. It's a parable. Though any Puritan or early American divine might, that Sunday, have given a sermon on *sin* (Jonathan Edwards: *Men in a natural condition may have convictions of the guilt that lies upon them, and of the anger of God, and their danger of divine vengeance. Such convictions are from light or sensibleness of truth: that some sinners have a greater conviction of their guilt and misery than others, is because some have more light, or more an apprehension of truth*), Hooper's sermon, given how he's trussed up, is much more dramatically relevant to the subject:

> . . . those sad mysteries which we hide from our nearest and dearest, and would fain conceal from our own consciousness, even forgetting that the Omniscient can detect them. A subtle power was breathed into his words. Each member of the congregation . . . felt as if the preacher had crept upon them, behind his awful veil, and discovered their hoarded iniquity of deed or thought.

The sermon fills the townspeople with irremediable dread, though Hooper is attentive, after the service, in his usual way, with kindnesses to the faithful and blessings for children. "Strange and bewildered looks repaid him for his courtesy."

Community speculation follows. Throughout the day. And it's not a routine Sunday for Hooper. He has chosen to wear his veil while engaged in many labors. After the late-day Congregational service, he is engaged to perform a funeral. In his new vestment. Suddenly, we see the veil in a different contextual light, as "an appropriate emblem." Its appropriateness makes this funeral passage the spookiest in "The Minister's Black Veil," a passage of dark implication. For example: the deceased, a young lady, gets the only unveiled view of the reverend in the story: "As he stooped, the veil hung straight down from his forehead, so that, if her eye-lids had not been closed for ever, the dead maiden might have seen his face." Next, some Gothic lore gets mixed in with the mortuary setting (reflecting the interests of a "superstitious old woman" on the scene): "At the instant when the clergyman's features were disclosed, the corpse had slightly shuddered, rustling the shroud and muslin cap, though the countenance retained the composure of death." Any number of commentators have taken care with this moment in "The Minister's

Black Veil" to insist that Hooper and the deceased young lady had *consort* or other relationship (Edgar Allen Poe, e.g., in his unsigned review of *Twice-Told Tales: The* moral *put into the mouth of the dying minister will be supposed to convey the* true *import of the narrative; and that a crime of dark dye {having reference to the "young lady"} has been committed, is a point which only minds congenial with that of the author will perceive*), and thus it's held by some that the young lady's shudder is carnal or ecstatic, upon perceiving Hooper, her ravisher, at the casket. But by the time we reach the end of the funeral scene, when another member of the funeral party goes as far as to suggest having seen "the minister and the maiden's spirit . . . walking hand in hand," it's clear that there's a danger in committing too much interpretive energy here. There's a more complicated story to tell.

Two services and a funeral would be enough activity for the first day of veil wearing, but Hooper, of course, has a marriage at which to officiate too. A marriage featuring the handsomest couple in Milford village. As with the church service and the funeral (in which Hooper's memorial prayer was considered "tender and heart-dissolving"), the wedding scene is given a before-and-after treatment with respect to the veil. In former days, Hooper was esteemed for his "placid cheerfulness" at weddings, and since he is himself affianced, that's admirable: he has a sympathetic understanding of the conjugal institution. But Hooper appears at this wedding wearing his black veil, and the prank doesn't strike a joyful note for the handsomest couple. The bride, for her part, is *mortified.* Contextually speaking, the narrator says, the veil "could portend nothing but evil to the wedding," and therefore, as at the funeral, rumors attach themselves to this unusual ceremony: "The bride's cold fingers quivered in the tremulous hand of the bridegroom, and her death-like paleness caused a whisper, that the maiden who had been buried a few hours before, was come from her grave to be married."

More gossip erupts. "The whole village of Milford talked of little else than Parson Hooper's black veil. That, and the mystery concealed behind it, supplied a topic for discussion between acquaintances meeting in the street, and good women gossiping at their open windows." Still, no one is able to *ask* Hooper about the veil, and this deepens the enigma: "It was remarkable, that, of all the busy-bodies and impertinent people in the parish, not one ventured to put the plain question to Mr. Hooper, wherefore he did this thing." The veil, in fact, is so persuasive that it not only subdues the parish, but it subdues readers too, it subdues *us,* so that we aren't preoccupied with credibility issues, with the logic of the mystery. Though an "imitative little imp" in town covers his face with an "old black handkerchief," there's still no boor forward enough to demand of the reverend why he wears the veil, likewise no veteran of Queen Anne's War or any other bloody Indian conflict who, with military bearing, dares come forward to demand that he remove the garment? Even when a delegation from the Milford congregation is sent by the town to ask Hooper about the eccentricity, they find themselves instead enchanted into silence. Language itself is suddenly complicit in the mystery. "Were the veil but cast aside, they might speak freely of it, but not till then."

This orphic, mutable aspect of Hooper's veil is amplified when his fiancée at last makes her entrance. Apologies for my delay in getting to her. She's been hidden until now, out of the loop, though we are told that "as his plighted wife, it should be her privilege to know what the black veil concealed." Elizabeth tramples the silence, the solemnity, that hovers around the controversy. She's a breath of fresh air in the narrative. She's able to launch forth, with a *direct simplicity,* and both she and Hooper are relieved by her directness. "Come, good sir, let the sun shine from behind the cloud. First lay aside your black veil: then tell me why you put it on." Hooper smiles but establishes the terms of the discussion: "There is an hour to come . . . when all of us shall cast aside our veils. Take it not amiss, beloved friend, if I wear this piece of crape till then." The reply is disquieting. Elizabeth feels that Hooper's words are as mysterious as his garb. She feels, in fact, that even his explanations are veiled.

Hooper would, in this moment of crisis, explain the mystery if he could. He tries again and again in different ways, in the next paragraphs, coming at it from different points of departure, using his rhetorical skills, his theological wisdom: "Know, then, this veil is a type and a symbol, and I am bound to wear it ever, both in light and darkness, in solitude and before the gaze of multitudes, and as with strangers, so with my familiar friends. No mortal eye will see it withdrawn." This first attempt, it seems, accounts for the general category of the veil, which is the category of *symbol,* but not for the meaning thereof. He gets a little closer in his next effort, but only in a conditional way: "If it be a sign of mourning . . . I, perhaps, like most other mortals, have sorrows dark enough to be typified by a black veil." The use of *if* here closes out any certainty for Elizabeth and for us. And to make sure we get the point, the same formulation occurs again: "If I hide my face for sorrow, there is cause enough . . . and if I cover it for secret sin, what mortal might not do the same?"

Might be a sign of sorrow, might be a sign of mourning, might be a sign of sin.

Elizabeth arrives at her own conclusion: "For a few moments she appeared lost in thought, considering, probably, what new methods might be tried, to withdraw her lover from so dark a fantasy, which, if it had no other meaning, was perhaps a symptom of a mental disease." Then comes the most rueful passage of "The Minister's Black Veil," and who can read it without an uncomfortable, blossoming perception that the veil might, at last, be a part of what it means *to hold conversation,* whether with self, acquaintance, friend, or lover: you can talk for hours, blue streaks of syntax, you can lie upon the couches of psychoanalysis offering up your dreams and your phantasms and your aspirations, you might spew monologues to yourself on unpopulated subway platforms, you might talk to yourself in mirrors, you might telephone home and update your mom, you might call that lover with whom you are pursuing the first garrulous weeks of new romance: you might talk all you want and never once get to the bottom of what drove you into *the arcade of chatter* in the first place; there's always leftover need at the end, a desire that exceeds its object, a way in which you feel known and remaining to be known, and at the end of all this language, shouted from rooftops, sung earnestly in choruses, whispered over the cradles of infants, *yearning isn't resolved;* there's always a remainder, thus the veil, and thus Hooper to Elizabeth, who begins to weep: "And do you feel it then at last?" What a gift to his betrothed. The recognition that their romance will always have its apartness. As she leaves the room,

Hooper, in the desperation of his position, offers her what it really feels like to borrow his robes; he offers to make the implicit psychology of the story explicit: "Have patience with me, Elizabeth! . . . Oh! you know not how lonely I am, and how frightened, to be alone behind my black veil. Do not leave me in this miserable obscurity for ever!" She asks him just to lift the veil once, and he can't, and, with a long last gaze at her beloved, Elizabeth departs.

He's *unable* to speak of his assumption, I think, just as he's powerless to change his circumstance; the density of the veil is such that it can't be lifted; it's impossibly heavy, cannot be dislodged, at least by the living. As Hooper shows no sign of having decided to put the veil on, he likewise seems to have no faculties for drawing back the curtain. And the townspeople, therefore, make no further attempts "to remove Mr. Hooper's black veil, or, by a direct appeal, to discover the secret which it was supposed to hide."

The reverend then does what any man or woman denied a community of fellows would do. He becomes very effective at his job. Hooper's veil and his postassumption ostracism enable him to "sympathize with all dark affections." The meetinghouse in Milford therefore becomes a popular spot both for tourists and for the spiritually desperate. Hooper's infamy grows to such a pitch that he's even allowed to preach an election sermon, one so powerful that "the legislative measures of that year, were characterized by all the gloom and piety of our earliest ancestral sway."

And finally, after a long, anguished life, it's time for Mr. Hooper to die. At which point we're in an interesting fix. As readers. Because, technically speaking, *nothing has happened so far* in "The Minister's Black Veil." Hooper appears at the beginning of the story wearing a veil and despite a number of attempts to divine the meaning of the veil or to see it removed, Hooper, at story's close, is much as he was at the outset. He's still wearing the veil. We still don't know why. Yet the possibility of his death offers us, and the villagers of Milford, one last chance to see the veil doffed. *Give us a happy ending! Warm the minister's heart!* We're implicated in the desire to get to the bottom of the matter, just like Hooper's neighbors. We want our social code, our order, our community values, affirmed.

As if to prove the possibility of a happy ending, Elizabeth reappears. Ministering to Hooper on his deathbed, she is among the circle of strangers there ("natural connexions he had none"). The veil that he has worn all his life has "kept him in that saddest of all prisons, his own heart," the narrator opines, but as he has endured so long in that prison, we should feel genuine doubt about the possibility of conversion during this extreme unction. Furthermore, Elizabeth, chastened by her early opposition to the veil, is now so loving toward the reverend that were he to be accidentally divested of his rag, "there was a faithful woman at his pillow, who, with averted eyes, would have covered that aged face, which she had last beheld in the comeliness of manhood."

Pillars of the community are gathered around, as are we, readers of "The Minister's Black Veil," to see the lunatic bared. The visiting minister asks if Hooper is "ready for the lifting of the veil that shuts in time from eternity," invoking a prior interpretation of the word *veil,* not sign of mourning or of sorrow, but of death itself. As in the prior funeral sequence. There's some back and forth, some ambiguous assent on Hooper's part, which wrongfully emboldens the Reverend Mr. Clark to attempt to reveal "the mystery of so many years," by folding back the crape. This gambit fails, as it must. Hooper rises up from "beneath the bedclothes" to hang on to the black veil, "resolute to struggle, if the minister of Westbury would contend with a dying man." Whereupon, having thwarted our desire for action, for reversal, Hooper at last pronounces his own deathbed interpretation of his plight:

Why do you tremble at me alone? . . . Tremble also at each other! Have men avoided me, and women shown no pity, and children screamed and fled, only for my black veil? What, but the mystery which it obscurely typifies, has made this piece of crape so awful? When the friend shows his inmost heart to his friend; the lover to his best-beloved; when man does not vainly shrink from the eye of his Creator, loathsomely treasuring up the secret of his sin; then deem me a monster, for the symbol beneath which I have lived, and die! I look around me, and, lo! on every visage a Black Veil!

Then Hooper gives up his ghost, smiling (he smiles a lot, as many have observed), and is soon buried *with veil upon him,* as, presumably, the audience that attends wears a quantity of veils both metaphorical and actual. The conclusion follows: "The grass of many years has sprung up and withered on that grave, the burial-stone is moss-grown, and good Mr. Hooper's face is dust; but awful is still the thought, that it mouldered beneath the Black Veil!" It is a summary from the point of view of an entire community, and it also connects this story from Hawthorne's *castle dismal* to his later masterwork, *The Scarlet Letter,* which likewise ends with the tombstone characterization of fashion victim Hester Prynne: "All around, there were monuments carved with armorial bearings; and on this simple slab of slate — as the curious investigator may still discern, and perplex himself with the purport — there appeared the semblance of an engraved escutcheon."

By the time he composed these later lines, Hawthorne was happily wedded, or so he claimed: *Thou art the only person in the world that ever was necessary to me. Other people have occasionally been more or less agreeable; but I think I was always more at ease alone than in any body's company, till I knew thee.* In the twilight of marriage, however, Hawthorne found another grim attic for himself, having had it constructed to his exacting specifications atop his house in Concord (ruining the roof line, as one biographer reports). Each day he trudged upstairs to remain undisturbed, writing, rewriting, and abandoning his later works, "Septimus Felton" and "The Dolliver Romance," and scribbling desperate letters and notes marked by the sorrowful tone he had favored in Salem: *We consider {Mr. Hawthorne} finally shelved, and shall take early occasion to bury him under a heavy article, carefully summing up his merits (such as they were) and his demerits, what few of them can be touched upon in our limited space.*

CUSTOMERS CAME IN,
AS THE FORENOON ADVANCED,
BUT RATHER SLOWLY . . .

---

*Every young man at some time or other wonders whether he can be a salesman.
Almost every man, when he is young, daydreams about making the big sale.*
Like I say, from salesmen have I sprung, of automobiles, of financial
planning, etc. From salesmen have I sprung, from that great religion, that American system of learning. Out of school in the early
part of the Reagan presidency, I was fixed on abandoning the East
Coast, abandoning lineage, abandoning the prying gaze of my sets of
parents, and so I conceived of a plan to go to New Zealand, or Down
Under, maybe, Auckland, or Sydney, somewhere where they spoke
English but that was otherwise remote. I was afraid of being stripped
of my tongue, of having nothing but awkwardness with which to
negotiate foreign lands. I made a few trips to the library to hunt up
facts on Anglophone countries. I asked friends at barside (digging
into our pockets for quarters to insert into Asteroids) if they knew
anyone who had ever lived in New Zealand or Australia, and did
they know anything about these regions? Did sheep really outnumber
people? Average annual rainfall? Principal industries? The Maoris,
the Aborigines, walkabouts, didgeridoos, great white sharks? Ultimately, I got as far as San Francisco. They spoke an English much
like mine. I had never been west of Philadelphia, except for a week in
senior year of high school when I was in Denver. San Francisco was
farther than Denver; it was set upon hills, draped in fog, there were
gay people in profusion, there were earthquakes. I was to have two
roommates on this adventure, both from school *back east*. One was a

director of theatricals, called Mark, the other a budding novelist, Jeff. Mark had journeyed west first and secured us an apartment. And I was to meet Jeff in his hometown of Detroit and make the drive to the coast with him in his used Volkswagen Rabbit, sorrel hued, a car that his father had helped him purchase. We would have as company on our adventure Jeff's dog, Bloom, a mixed-breed animal clearly *at wit's end* (the West Coast fleas, to which Bloom was unaccustomed, later drove her over the brink, and she could occasionally be seen foaming at the mouth and running in circles). In Detroit, upon the advent of our departure, we were faced with the difficult problem of how to get Bloom to sit in the back of the Volkswagen, under the hatchback, in a nook carved out among Jeff's modest store of possessions. She kept attempting to free herself from this confinement. Jeff's father, an affable and warm man, clearly Midwestern, *a salesman,* enlarged by a garrulity that put you totally at ease and somewhat balding for the purposes of this anecdote, stood beside me as we attempted to jam another duffel bag full of Jeff's outfits into the available space, next to the spot where there was, in Tupperware, a three-day supply of peanut-butter-and-Welch's-grape-jelly sandwiches. Next to Bloom's nook. I was trying to close the hatchback to keep the dog from escaping. The dog was escaping. Jeff's dad was squashing in a gym bag. We were trying not to crush the sandwiches. All these things at once. The outcome was this: I closed the hatchback on Jeff's father's head. And it wasn't a love tap, either. I forcefully smashed the hatchback of the Volkswagen down on the front part of Jeff's father's forehead, where all rational and abstract thinking was stored, where there was a reservoir of *sales strategies,* and there was a dull and vegetative thud, as when, for example, *you take a swing at a honeydew with an aluminum bat.* I was amazed that Jeff's dad wasn't prone on the driveway when I was through with him, but he was still standing by my side as the hatchback swung wide again and the dog took off up the road. He cried, *You're in a hurry, aren't you?* Fixing on me a stare that was suspicious and irate. There was something horribly lonely in all this. I didn't know where I was going, to what American city, I had only the name of the place, some town where I knew exactly two people and a dog, a state I had never even seen, a mythical state, a state of soft-rock renown, and I was going west for no good reason but that it was time to do something new, time to pursue uncertain prospects, great expectations. And my first performance of greatness *in the wilderness of this world,* as Bunyan puts it, in a period of rapid, unexplainable growth, was to inflict head trauma on the man who had taken me in for the weekend. Moving rapidly to add insult to the performance, I then reached out to touch the spot where a hematoma rose on Jeff's dad's brow, as if a laying-on of hands would help. This is what I would have done, anyhow, if it had been Jeff himself I had lobotomized instead of his dad, and I suppose I was trying to offer an apology, I was mumbling something *soothing and kind,* but Jeff's father recoiled from me, backing away toward his abode, through the front door, rubbing the front part of his skull. Some things *are* unforgettable, certain smells of infancy, lyrics to bubblegum Top 40 singles. I can't remember our address in San Francisco exactly, I can't remember most of the people I've met recently, but I will probably always remember Jeff's father's expression at that moment. *You're in a hurry, aren't you?*

Later, in the first two hours of our drive from Detroit to San Francisco, the Volkswagen succumbed to total electrical failure. It shut itself off, and we rolled silently to the shoulder. Waited for a tow. This took time. After paying the tow truck with some of our unimpressive cash reserves, we had the battery jumped at a filling station. Bloom sniffed around the rear of the building where the men's room was located. The mechanic could not explain the origin of our problem, but he had jumper cables. Mystery unsolved, we pushed on, with our carload of bare necessities, through Chicago, into Indiana, across Indiana, all the way to Iowa City that first day. When night fell, the headlights on the car began to flicker. I was tired. I thought I was imagining it. But I began to understand fully this *intermittency* two days later in the seventy miles between the exit for Salt Lake City and the next for West Wendover, Nevada. The Salt Flats. *No exits, no standing.* Seventy miles. After dusk, I was drinking from an open container and listening to King Crimson on headphones, and Jeff drove, and I noticed this ebbing and flowing of illumination from the front end of the car, like the saraband of dusk through autumn boughs, and at first my heart sank — there was something really wrong, we would be stranded, further misfortune ahead, and Jeff was tired of my company. I didn't say anything, and he didn't either, and I drank, and we drove through the tabula rasa of Utah. In this monotony, I faced up to the truth: the Rabbit might stall out at any time. At the side of the highway, Bloom would scare up poisonous snakes. Jeff and I would retreat into our discrete anxieties. On the other hand, everything was negotiable; it didn't matter much. *The world was our oyster.* The car could be retired here or it could survive to the Bay Area (where it would have its alternator replaced), but if we had to stay in Elko, or Reno, or Sacramento for a few days, if we had to sleep in the car, call home for money, buy a new car, kill each other out of despair and poverty, what difference did it make?

This is youth wandering carelessly into an era of responsibility. The *intermittencies* of the moment were general: a car that doesn't reliably work, two writers out of work with bad work prospects, arguing periodically, a dog about to develop epilepsy, unaffordable rent in an expensive city, drunkenness, all swelling like cactus blossoms in that moment in the desert, with the headphones blaring, with open containers. The music of King Crimson, I recognize, is the kind of *noodling, pretentious music* that no one should admit listening to, even on headphones in the desert, but the particular song that I would like to claim for the moment has appropriate resonances, namely "Neil and Jack and Me," a song about the Beat writers and their relentless crisscrossing of the nation's highway infrastructure, and maybe Jeff, the budding novelist, and I had some atavistic love for the myth of writers crisscrossing the nation's highway infrastructure, drinking, thinking somber thoughts, passing through the Tetons in a day, snowfall in the mountains one night, and the next in the desert, wasting quarters in a slot machine, eating peanut-butter-and-jelly sandwiches on the prairie with a skittish mutt. Parents everywhere, *fathers everywhere,* wish better for their children after the graduation of this progeny, a reliable source of income, a credit card for emergencies, but we had none of these things, or at least I did not, and there were times on the trip west when I was afraid to stop for what I might see, a land of struggles, a land of cruelties and dis-consolations. From Nevada across the Sierras we didn't talk much, and soon we were on the Bay Bridge, and trying to make it up the steep hills of San Francisco, when the car stalled at every red light and we attempted to roll it, and this was the moment of the announcement of madness, lurking around the edges of this story from now on.

Memory brings me therefore to the Lower Haight of San Francisco, California, not the part of Haight at Ashbury, where the Grateful Dead had lived, where the Summer of Love had its magnetic north, down the hill from there. In a gentrifying neighborhood. Two liquor stores right on our block, fine with me. There were always a couple of drunks weaving around on their way past. Our landlady was a psychiatrist. She let us repaint according to whim. The couple in the apartment below was a threesome, two gay men and a lesbian in *a committed loving relationship*. They were raising a child together. A daughter. They had the most violent fights I'd ever heard. Two of them would throw the third against a wall, the floor would rumble as if with the continental tremors of the Bay Area, glassware would tumble out of the cupboard. *You never loved me! You said you loved me, but you're out all hours of the night with other men! How can I live like this? You don't care about our child! You selfish person!* Two or three such altercations a month, during which you would hear bodies hurled against walls, doors slammed. Some years later, all three of them, the committed lovers, appeared on a television talk show, on one of the issue-oriented eighties talk shows. They boasted of their success with the child. They were articulate and calm. Their daughter would be a teenager now (as I write this), according to my math, just coming into the productive phase of her teen rebellion.

Our apartment was a three-bedroom, with a small living room and kitchen, and I lived in the main expanse of the apartment, next to the kitchen. Jeff and Mark were in adjacent rooms off the hall, at the top of the stairwell. Bloom, the epileptic hound, was locked in my end, where she was often looking for something to rip to shreds. She had a knack for getting into my inner sanctum — furnished only with a bed and a small shelf on which I kept my typewriter.

Bloom would climb up onto my futon to scratch her suppurating wounds while I was elsewhere, and for this reason my pallet, a futon on a discarded door mounted on milk crates, was both infested with fleas and streaked with the blood of our house pet.

I spent most of my commencement gift on rent and security deposit for the apartment, so I needed a job. My father did business in San Francisco and had old associates there, and he enabled me to get a number of *promising informational interviews* with successful practitioners of West Coast finance. They were kindly, but when they agreed to meet me they had no idea of how unmarketable my skills really were. I had no idea either. All of these people tried hard to help me (the periodicals director at a very large bank told me frankly that *I should do something that would challenge me,* and then he asked for my *birth sign*), but I was ill equipped for the burgeoning global economy, although I was good at arguing about the epistemological problems raised by French literary theory. I couldn't pretend, and therefore I couldn't get *a single decent interview* out of all these busy people in their office towers with astounding bay views. When I turned up in my outgrown Brooks Brothers pinstripe suit I would forget to bring a pen, so that I had to ask to borrow one to fill out the employment questionnaire. Or I couldn't get my hair to lie down flat. Or I got the name of the interviewer wrong, or even the name of the bank. It seemed I was the sort of wet-behind-the-ears job applicant who, though amusing, does not want the job and is therefore *a drain on your time, your good mood, your productivity.* After each prospect soured, I would feel that I had made my effort that day and that I could now repair to our apartment to read the paper or go for a walk in the park or drink champagne out of plastic stemware by the Pacific Ocean. After a month or so of this, when I was down to fifty dollars in the bank and getting ready to plead for help from home, I found an advertisement in the want ads of the *Chronicle* offering great rewards for self-starters who were interested in art. *A chance to work in an important city arts institution, unlimited museum admission guaranteed.* I was intrigued! Didn't I know a fair amount about art, because of my survey classes in art history, because of my courses in Marxist aesthetics and Continental philosophy, because of my close personal association with many promising studio artists from the Rhode Island School of Design! My enthusiasm implied that keen *salesmanship* was reflected in the wording of that advertisement in the *Chronicle*. As one practitioner has put it, *The salesman who bursts into the prospect's office and loudly asserts that he wants to sell some life insurance rarely walks out with an order. You have to apply suction, not pressure.* Dan, my eventual boss, sure knew how to use suction on a young art lover like myself, because soon I was working at the de Young Museum, a faux-Renaissance building in the Golden Gate Park, during the run of a traveling exhibition of art from the collection of the Vatican. The job in question involved *selling recorded tours* of the exhibition. It paid $3.25 an hour.

I was going to become a salesman! A salesman from a long line of salesmen. A persuader, a rhetorician. *Selling is believing, believing in what you have to sell,* as Edward Goeppner of San Francisco's Podesta Baldocchi Florists has said. My tenure at the de Young was at the dawn of the age of the portable cassette recorder. Technology had not yet entirely licked the bulky design of early portability. It was our job to overcome these design shortcomings. There we stood, in the front hall of the de Young, ready to sell. Behind us, behind this staff of capable and eager recorded-tour salesmen and -women, were several large varnished hardwood shelves in which the cassette players were housed, on their sides, for easy access. And at the end of each of the two rows of shelves, near the twin cash registers, were a pair of metal trees where there dangled several dozen green earphones, their cords tentacular beneath them. Like postindustrial willows. There were eight of us on a shift, four to a side of the great entrance hall of the de Young. And, using language honed by other successful recorded-tour salesmen in other cities, using a minimum of words, a mere incantation of language, we would approach *the premium exhibition customers* as they were herded in our general direction by the crowd-control personnel at the front of the museum. As they shuffled into earshot, our voices would ring out. *Hi! Can I interest you in a recorded tour today?* There was a moment while the violence of our ambitions sunk in. These patrons had erroneously believed themselves already separated from their cash. At which point they would

a) *start irritably* from their private aspirations for a fathomless aesthetic experience among the artworks of the Vatican collection, causing them to rush past without a word, or b) *agree or disagree immediately,* yea or nay, perceiving at once that our efforts involved getting them to part with more of their hard-earned capital, or c) *pause,* in which case we descended on them with merciless and scripted prose to persuade them that no apperception of Leonardo's unparalleled *Saint Jerome* would be complete without the remarks of the de Young Museum's director, whose voice almost exactly resembled that of a certain whimsical television news personality, and though none of us had ever actually *heard* the entirety of the remarks of this museum director — we couldn't be bothered, really — it was our considered opinion that this recorded tour would enhance the viewing experience, the aesthetic experience, *the total art experience* here at the de Young, and in fact this recorded tour constituted an important addition to the criticism of the late twentieth century. If the wavering art patron had gotten as far as our recitation of facts, he or she usually caved. We were young. We were earnest. If necessary, we would say anything. (It's the first impression that makes the sale, as Al Burns, vice president in charge of sales at Sterling Drug, once put it, *The first twenty seconds, when you come in actual contact with the prospect on any day at any time, are, to my mind, the most exacting, exciting, and important of all.*)

One reasonable concern of many of the de Young patrons to whom we pitched our product had to do with the earphones themselves, which hung on the ear, a single ear, suspended by a plastic frame, rather than being inserted into or worn over both ears as they are now. Customers wanted to be sure that the earphones were *disinfected* after each use. Well, we were happy to report to these compulsive hand-washers that it was the responsibility of one company runner (it was the task at the de Young that I most looked forward to, because it involved no contact with the public) to collect these earpieces at the end of the exhibit, along with the cassette players. At this juncture, he or she would scientifically *disinfect* the earphones with a squirt of industrial-strength antibacterial soap before returning both players and earpieces to the staging area up front. We could therefore, in the midst of our sales meetings with the museum-going public, assure these patrons that the earpieces were fully disinfected, after which we would *reach for their ears* and hang the little plastic flap over the top of the ear, having subdued them, having clinched the sale. *You're going to have trouble,* Dan the manager had assured us, *because people are territorial about their ears, but if you are polite and patient, they will allow you to show them how to use the earpiece.* I began to take a certain pleasure in this attention to ears. The way people would hop out of reach when you tried to probe for that cartilage. Only the very secure or the heavily sedated would easily consent.

The first important skill we had to learn, as members of the Acoustiguide sales staff, was to stand still without respite for eight hours a day. This was harder than we thought. The second skill was to negotiate long, concentrated stretches of soul-slaughtering indifference to our surroundings, to the events of daily life, and, indeed, to our futures. And the third skill was to endure the erosion of what few creature pleasures remained to us during the interminable days at the museum. Because, after a few weeks, Dan said *it didn't look good* that we were talking among ourselves during the early portion of the day, before the swarms. It violated one of the principles of good salesmanship, namely *sincerity.* When there was downtime, Dan suggested, we should be straightening the cassette players in the racks behind us and making sure the cassettes were fully rewound. And *it didn't look good* if we had our feet propped up behind us on the varnished shelving. And *it didn't look good* if we wore jeans. But before he was done with his new lecture, with whatever superficial correction he was after today, the hordes had descended on us anew, *a thousand potential customers in an hour* sometimes, more as we got nearer to the Christmas holidays, and then the museum was crawling with people, all of them irritable at the density of fellow art lovers, and the line would extend out into the hall, and they would be upon us, and we would recite the instructions — *Up is forward, down is reverse, and should you wish to stop the tape, just bring the lever to this middle position, and remember, the lecture is numbered to go along with the paintings, so you'll want to move in a clockwise direction as you pass through the galleries* — and then we would hasten to the next sale. In the midst of this grinding tedium, a customer would complain that I was *mumbling,* or that I had not completed the instructions, or that she couldn't understand how to operate the machine, or she would complain that I had attempted to *touch her ear,* while alongside another was sighing, and just behind him or her two or three more of them sighing, irritated that they couldn't secure their recorded tour and move on. *Business is more profitable when it is friendly,* or so it is said, but I remember Christmastime, when there was the whole line of them stretched out in front of me, hundreds of them, the thickest, densest crowd I had yet seen, each individual with his or her uncleaned ear, each with his ear flap and anvil and stirrup and auditory nerve, ear hair, ear wax, and into each of these ears I would have to whisper the same sales pitch, so close that I could have nibbled their earlobes, and at Christmas it seemed as if there was no dignity in the job and no relief, and the crowd pressed forward in its collective pique, and one guy ripped the tape recorder out of my hand because he was tired of waiting, and the crowds made me think of those factory farms where chickens, in low lighting, peck out the eyes of the weaker chicken beside them, and then the other chickens trample this weak bird and eat the remains, so that the next day the farmer rakes up feathers and nothing more, and the subsequent customer was no better than the last guy, so to her, the customer in front of me, I said, *We're having a really bad day here; do you think you might give us a little respect on the way past?* pleading, really, because my education had cost a great deal of money, and this was the only job that I could find in the Bay Area, to which the woman replied, *I'm having a bad day too, and I don't need your rudeness,* prying the tape player out of my hands, circumnavigating the line at the register, demanding to see the manager, probably because she'd been in crowds all morning, after which I *walked off the line,* leaving my colleagues to fend for themselves, the only time I did so during the months I had the job, and went into the dim, plain room behind the racks of cassette recorders where we were allowed to eat our lunches, and where Dan and his partner counted the lucre, and I punched the wall, in front of my boss, and said, *I can't take this shit,* a bit of drama, some gratuitous obscenity, but evidently I *could* take that shit, because soon I was back on the line, as I was every day during the three months in which I made $26 a day, or $520 a month, for a yearly pretax wage of $6,240. *It goes without saying that a salesman should always studiously avoid offending his prospect in any way, for a sale is always easier to make when the prospect likes you.*

Who were we, the indomitable sales force of Acoustiguide, Inc.? There was a woman named Mary who worked in the perpetually underfunded world of leftist politics, perhaps for the *Committee in Solidarity with the People of El Salvador,* and who was moonlighting at the museum until the organization could afford to pay her again. And there was a blond guy who always wore leather pants, every single day I was there, and brightly colored sweaters, and who had an unctuous style that combined honeyed vowels and menace. He turned out to be a drug dealer. There was an older woman, Estelle, whose husband was retired and who just wanted the extra income. She lived over on the good side of town, in North Beach, and she was kind and maternal, but in her company I couldn't think of a single thing to say. There was a young painter, a woman, with hennaed hair whose boyfriend was Japanese. She was strapped for cash and had animosity toward *rich people.* There was an older gay man — his lover drove a Jaguar, and one evening they gave me a ride home in their capacious backseat — who had been in the military, *deeply closeted* in the upper echelons of the American military. He seemed brilliant and ambitious, and not like the kind of guy who needed to work selling recorded tours for $3.25 an hour, and when I asked him about it, about how he got to this spot, he spoke of trysts in the park near the Pentagon, about the yearning and concealment, about the intimate relationship between *signifiers of force* and homosexuality, and, with a great seriousness, he concluded these remarks by observing that *everyone needs to be loved.* There was a Valley Girl named Lulu who hated *bad smells* and who often spoke of this antipathy; there was a guy who looked like John Lennon and who had all of John Lennon's albums. He gave me a ride on his motorcycle.

I read *The Confidence Man* over lunch. It would be gratifying to claim that after I had punched out at five o'clock, I was able to *throw the switch* on this sales job, that I could touch people's ears for eight hours and then go home to read Melville and compose short stories or whatever I was attempting to compose. But the facts were these: at night I did little but drink and watch the news. As a result, I don't remember much of *The Confidence Man,* or Foucault's *History of Sexuality,* or Heinrich Boll's *Group Portrait With Lady,* or *Juliette* by the Marquis de Sade, all of which I tried to read in San Francisco. But I did learn the hard way some of Herbert Metz's essential rules of salesmanship:

1. When you are lining up a dealer, go out with him and give him a practical demonstration of the market for your product by selling it to him.

2. There comes a time in many sales calls when you have to completely change your sales tactics in the same way that a fullback often reverses his field. It is foolish and very often disastrous to lower your head and keep bucking the line in the same old place.

3. In making a sale, no matter what you are selling, keep your eyes open all the time and be alert for the "break."

4. And finally, "know your stuff," and "know it well." Believe in it enthusiastically, whole-heartedly, and sincerely. Above all, realize how important selling is to you and to the country's economy, and glory in the work you are doing to the point that you get a greater kick and thrill out of it than anything else that you could do.

One incident at the museum made a lasting impression: the day that I saw my first blind art lover. He had the cane, the dark glasses, he had the outward signs of the disability, that system of styles that enabled us to tell him apart from the able-bodied. But he was here at the show like anyone else, and he had a friend holding his arm. He was bearded, in his forties. He was eager to rent our product. He and his friend passed into our domain, made their purchase, and later, while they were looking at Poussin or Matisse, I snuck in to watch. There was a crowd-control bottleneck around the blind guy and his friend, people were having trouble negotiating this hazard, but otherwise the blind man could have been any spectator. I flagged down one of the nearby security guards. *Lou,* I said, *there's a blind guy in the galleries.* Lou was trim, good-looking, middle-aged, and he had been at the museum for years. He'd made friends with all the docents, all the society ladies, and they were always to be seen regaling him, cornering him for gossip and art appreciation. With his most serious demeanor, Lou told me that there had always been *blind persons* who attended the museum, as it was *a place of reverence.* When they brought a friend with them, the role of that friend was to explain, describe, *embellish* the riches of the centuries. It was like a sales job.

I left the museum as soon as I could. I didn't last the duration of the Vatican collection exhibition, three months, at which point I would have been let go anyway. We were subcontractors, after all, and like all subcontractors expendable. January was torrential, and the combination of rain and drudgery blunted me further, and I felt lonely, as I almost always did in California, and so I took a job offered by my roommate Mark, building sets for an avant-garde theater company. In Sausalito. That job lasted only about six weeks.

I never had the affection my grandfather had for selling, I never felt what salesmen of his generation describe, I never thought about whether sales were good for the economy, good for character building, good for the community, I never had *the inner knowledge that marks every true member of the fraternity of salesmen: the knowledge that a successful sale can give you one of the greatest "oomphs" of your life.* My grandfather liked people, liked to be out on the floor, liked the associations of his car dealership, liked to ask questions about a young couple coming in to buy their first vehicle. When he bought his dealership, after the war, selling automobiles was a matter of taking names, because there had been no new cars for so long. After the war, people came to buy cars and you put them on the list and you treated them fairly, and they bought cars from you later. You were a reliable dealer; you were a thoughtful, decent salesman. Of course, in some dealerships it was possible to purchase your way to the front of the waiting list for new vehicles, but my grandfather was *disgusted* by his fellows in the fraternity of car dealers who would accept payoffs to bump people to the front of that line. He loved the product.

Here's P. Val Kolb, former president of Sterwin Chemicals, Inc., on automobile sales: *You can, and very often do, sell a passenger car on brand name, appearance, color, or comfortable upholstery. In such cases, women are the chief buyers. The appeal is emotional. But when you sell a truck, you talk performance. You marshal facts on dependability and operating costs. You assemble figures gathered from actual tests. That's factual selling.*

So the craft is about language, by which I mean that though my father and grandfather might have more completely welcomed me into the patrimonial lineage of Moodys had I become a bona fide salesman, maybe being a writer and being a salesman are not so different: *Selling is one of the subtle arts, which throws mind against mind, tongue against tongue, firmness against firmness. The salesman has much to accomplish with spoken words; and great things, as well as small, turn on these spoken words.* It's this language that I imagine my father overheard when he was working summers in the auto body end of Moody Motor Sales, Inc., banging out dents, watching my grandfather spinning a web of suasion. Maybe he passed the lessons on to me. *Suppose, for instance, you want a shotgun. You go into a store and there is a gun for $75 and another for $35.*

STOOPING SOMEWHAT AND LOOKING ON THE GROUND, AS IS CUSTOMARY WITH ABSTRACTED MEN . . .

The foregoing quotations on rules of salesmanship came from a book I stumbled across later in my short, unsatisfying professional career. Back on the East Coast, after my frontier adventure. I had managed to pack in some troubles, periods of very heavy drinking, periods of bad hangovers, periods of cocaine abuse, periods of promiscuity. I fled from one of these compulsive enthusiasms to another. At graduate school, at which I enrolled six months after returning to NYC, I began to break my unwritten rule about always waiting until five P.M. to start *hitting the bottle*, began hitting it at four, then earlier. The woman I was living with at the time, Jen, was observing a like schedule, the schedule of harm, so that we were well-suited to each other. There was a predictability to the months. Our habits were reliable. In autumn of 1985, not long after Jen and I had moved in together, her mother died suddenly, in her late forties, from drug addiction and anorexia. Cardiac arrest. There were complicated lives in Jen's tribe. Both of her aunts, back in Newport, Rhode Island, were *in recovery*, narrating their ordeals in detail to those who would listen. Nevertheless, in the months after Jen's mother's death, quiet months in our place in Hoboken, I would find, in the middle of the night, that Jen had gotten up from bed and gone into the kitchen to drink and *snort lines*, to drink and do lines and weep. In our railroad flat across the street from the old Maxwell House factory. We could smell the freeze-dried coffee they were concocting there. The stylized neon precipitation that poured from the *Good to the Last Drop* sign ornamented our neighborhood. I was young and I didn't understand *it,* her grief, I didn't understand that a mother who was as taxing as a mother could be could leave such torrents in her wake. I was under the misapprehension that the end of her money problems, her romantic failures, her laxative addictions, could in some way be a relief. But the scene of loss was replayed again and again in Jen's recollection, as follows: Jen was making coffee. She said, *My mother has been missing for three days.* The radio in our kitchen broadcast weather and national news. Then her mother was dead and *everything changed,* the interior decorating of our moods and habits. I was smart enough to keep my mouth shut, but no smarter. I would hold Jen when she wanted to be held and would look the other way when she wanted to be left alone, and I did my best to offer something, some reliability, when solicited, all of which was a hard program to maintain, since we both were doping ourselves. Even occasional efforts at getting unraveled from our clothes were half-hearted and sad.

Here's a portrait of her. Jen's hair was maroon, she had a ski-jump nose, she wore sweatshirts inside out with black pedal pushers, she was an aggressive driver, she didn't have hips, she was always enraged and always forgiving. She would announce her hypotheses in the middle of conversation. We unpacked Chinese take-out, our single-serve mustards, our fried rice and soy sauce, and talked about whether or not Chinese food was really as *fattening* as made out to be, staring emptily at the cork bulletin board that lined the wall in the kitchen — stippled with cartoons and with reminders and appointments — and then she would begin to ask if I thought *relationships were any good at all, if there were any promise to this love stuff,* if it didn't all end in disappointment, if love and *peeve* weren't synonyms. In the most theatrical way she would say these things, and of course she wanted the promise of the amorous, the long-term payout, she wanted things symbolized in the popular entertainments by gardens and lapdogs, and I was not providing these things, and therefore she was pretending she didn't want them. When she drank, which was every day, there was an uncivilized look she got, *a dilation of pupils,* a disarrangement of propriety in her, but it was even more psychologically rich than that: this incivility was the only way you could tell she was *wasted, potted, blacked out;* she never fell over or slurred her words or got into car accidents or lost jobs (I did those things); she engaged in maudlin subjects over Chinese food, or in cheap restaurants with vinyl tablecloths. She became free-associative. She became fierce. *Sir* (she used honorifics), *you have to do something about getting some exercise, sir, you look bad,* and then off on some tangent that she had not exactly thought out, her diatribe about the president, maybe: *He's a liar, you only have to look at him to see that he's a liar, I bet you can tell from the way Nancy talks too, there's a way she talks, you can see how she purses her lips, it's all in this pressure in the way the lips meet, I've met lots of women who have these kinds of lips and these smiles and you can tell that they're all liars, I could point out a couple on the street and you'd see.* Just as easily from this line of inquiry she might leap onto something serious, something having to do with *us,* the implication being, across all subjects, in all tongues, in all weather, that I had failed the fealty test of American romance, *I had failed her.* I had *shown up,* had attempted to dress becomingly, but conversation had dwindled, and she went through her convolutions, *Please turn that horrible music off,* or perhaps she simply turned the television up, as a sort of combat, because it was *always on,* and she needed to tell me something, she had a plan in mind, we had come to the end, her mother had died, and everything had changed, and she had made this decision to march herself off to a *rehabilitation center.* There was an abrupt quality to the announcement, as if she had been thinking about it for a while but hadn't told me while thinking, and yet it was almost certainly announced in the morning, in a rare period in which we weren't actually drinking or planning to get drunk (*we could put on first-rate simulations of young artists or media professionals, but they were truly simulations*), and maybe we were driving, because after her mother died we spent a lot of time driving back and forth to her mother's vacant house. It was during the early days of videotape, and there were whole weekends where we watched two and three movies in a row, at her mother's haunted ranch house, with Jen's kid sister hanging around, home from boarding school. I was on my third W. C. Fields film when she announced it, or we were in the car, and the sun was shining on the hamlet of Greenwich, Connecticut, as though that town would never be far from God's blessings, town of silver birches and maples, Greenwich, her ancestral homeland, and then Jen said, *Sir, I'm thinking that I might go to rehab.* I don't believe I said anything at first, it was just the *crisis of the month,* and I was more acted upon than acting, but maybe I stalled for time, maybe I stared blankly out the window, *What?* To which she said, *I'm thinking I might go to rehab. I think I'm going to get sober.* It was the work of the aunts, with their cultish beliefs! With their totalitarian schemes! Or let's say it was the evening, and we were drinking, we were in one of those soft landings where we were making less and less sense, and it didn't much matter, we weren't anywhere near any heavy machinery. *Uh, when exactly are you thinking of doing this?* She affected a pensive exterior. *I don't know, depends, maybe the spring,* and I didn't ask about her strange forecasting, because at least I had six more months with things as they were. Then I got into bed next to Jen and lowered my face close to hers in order to try to fix upon her a kiss.

In the weeks after, she gave up hope of *controlling herself,* a control she'd never much exercised anyhow, and I'd come home from my job, where I was now a postgraduate M.F.A.-holding *typist and filer of memos,* a reader of manuscripts by the very lonely, to find her already *lit,* drinking in front of the television with a glassy look, sitcom turned up louder than appropriate, wearing her *wild kingdom* expression, draped in the same clothes she had worn for several days, she would remember nothing of this exchange, would not remember if I said, *Don't you think you could try to control it just a little bit? So I don't have to take you to the E.R.?* I was trying to generate control, because she was drinking all my bourbon, she was cleaning me out, I had spent my minimal wages on *sour mash,* and I was going to different *package stores* each night, worried that they were taking note of how much I was purchasing, how many beers, how many bottles of wine, how many pints of the *hard stuff,* everyone was adding these things up, calculating sums, tallying up the results of my purchases, there was a mathematics around me. She was drinking it all, Jen was drinking it, and it was impossible to maintain an adequate supply, and when she opened her mouth, it was for some incoherent tirade, she'd tipped over the Christmas fern on the end table, was too lazy to pick it up, was mad about it, *really mad,* and I asked her one night when we were out if I could drive the car in her stead, since I thought she was too drunk to drive, and she showered abuse upon me: *Who do you think you are, sir, and what makes you think I even want to spend the next twenty-four hours with you, anyway? I never said I did.* I was thinking, *How many years can I do this,* how long until I too am just a swollen drunk, preoccupied with my opinions, fighting openly with my irritating, drunken wife?

In this arduous expanse of months, Jen also announced that she was going for a trip to some warm Caribbean island with her family, to Jamaica or Antigua or Aruba. I was not invited, unless I could pay for my ticket myself, which I could not, since I could barely pay rent and owed her thousands of dollars besides. *And I had to work.* I had only Christmas Day off, and New Year's. We were in our railroad flat. The wall in the bathroom was caving in. You could see clear through the Sheetrock. The smell of coffee wafted up from the street. I thought it might be a help to her to be in the company of her living relatives; I thought it might ease some of her oppressions, if these provoked her sequence of drinks. She had been pregnant. We had ended the pregnancy. Her mother had died. We were worn out from our carelessness. I could get some time to myself. I could shed my worries for a few days. She flew out of Newark, I think, on the twenty-second of that December.

I started drinking around the clock on the twenty-third. There was a company Christmas party, of which I remember nothing, not where it was held, not to whom I spoke, not what music was played. I took a woman from the office, an attractive nihilist from the sales department, Kira, redheaded, who knew every song ever recorded by Los Lobos and Wall of Voodoo; we drank libations first at a Japanese place, perhaps, or maybe at the Korean place Jen and I had frequented back when we were first together. When I think about it now, the night resembles *a colossal bruise.* The interior was dark, as all those interiors feel dark to me, interiors of bars after work; the walls were black, the paint jobs were flaking off, guttering candles neglected on tables, and we were dipping our fingers into the wax; we were bitter about how things weren't going our way in the office, and there was melodrama in that, *The editor who made her assistant pick up her new diaphragm for her,* and the head of the department had slept with a happily married regional sales manager and then with her best friend too, and the marketing guys were going to do profit-and-loss statements on the new titles, which would slay the art in the business; we breathed a few new adjectives into old stories. *Mel saw Lance reading the mail on his boss's desk?* The retractable dome was closing over us. Whatever was good about the job wasn't happening fast enough, our rise to the top wasn't fast enough, the confetti of talk and flirtation, certain bands and certain gigs at CBGB's, certain movies, a catalog of travails and disappointments to be negotiated; Kira had just broken up with the intravenous-drug-user boyfriend, and we were lonely, and loneliness was like *a bad taste in the morning before brushing;* Kira and I kissed, I can recollect it, even if I don't know exactly where she is now, I can recollect all such kisses, whether stolen suddenly or of such duration that time is insulted in them, *kisses are the exposition hurtling toward resolution;* nevertheless, Kira and I saw the writing on the wall, as they say, and it wasn't good, it was a mess. But we kissed anyway, and then we went to the Christmas party, and I lost Kira there, to sales department cronies, to more virtuous people, and I can't remember the festivities, can't remember being parted from her; I drank more, and next I was stumbling toward Port Authority, going back to Hoboken. Evidently, I'd left the party. Holy Port Authority, transvestite bars, strip clubs, Times Square; enterprise zone of abasement and self-destruction financed by guys going into the bus terminal, hookers, XXX features, financed by the husbands of Teaneck and New Brunswick and Montclair, *Honey! I'm home!* Why did Times Square seem more genuine, more true, more noble than the office towers that surrounded it? No different from these other abusers of Times Square, I was soon back in our place in Hoboken, ashamed. I called Pelham, where my mother lived with her second husband, talked to my brother, who was there without his girlfriend; I was on my way, to celebrate *the holiday,* the dread Christmas holiday, and my brother said, *Move your ass,* because he was meeting one of his friends at the Mexican place, Zapata's, and I could meet him there, right across from the train

station, short ride on mass transit; then the packaging and bundling
of stuff, a bag full of gifts — books that I had liberated from the
shelves of the publicity department at work, books my family would
not read — all while carrying around a tumbler of bourbon with ice
cubes in it, spinning my narrow playlist of records, drinking, *checking my look in the mirror,* worse for wear, then out into the night before
Christmas Eve, lavender sky above Hoboken dotted with the last
traffic-reporting helicopters of the evening, through the park with
the gazebo, weaving a bit, onto the bus, then onto the subway, across
town to Grand Central, the Metro-North train for half an hour, the
befouled linoleum of those train cars, the desperation of the commuters, nodding into rail travel, the flickering of lights, inconsistent
electrical lines, the trains rattling and drifting to the edge of the
platform. Zapata's was *packed,* and my brother was there with a congress of stewed friends, his locals, and my sister turned up, ready to
extend the night's merrymaking; yes, the moment of meeting fellow
tipplers, the moment of that encounter, the moment when the orders
were placed, so exceptional, so unquenchable, better than when the
drink arrived, you *began* the drink, and then it suddenly seemed
possible that no prior good moment ever existed, your heart had
always been constrained, and there was a free fall, no one understood,
trouble was rising, there was a *flood,* conversation was trailing off,
what did I have to say to my brother's friends, nothing, and I went to
call my college acquaintance from the next town, *Come on over! Bring
reinforcements!* And Irv brought his friend the philosopher, Gideon;
we were all at Zapata's, we were all drinking, and soon it was early
morning, there were no ribald jokes going around, no one was saying
anything, there was stern, pragmatic drinking, and that's when I
noticed that there were bookshelves about us, books that Zapata's
had apparently bought *by the yard,* books about cats, gardening, your
golf swing, complete works of O'Hara and Cozzens, three copies of
Glenway Wescott's *Apartment in Athens,* some Marquand, and beside
all these, the one that caught my eye: *How I Made the Sale That Did
the Most for Me: Sixty Great Sales Stories Told by Sixty Great Salesmen.*
Head shots of the sales promoters on the chapter titles, each salesman
with a head shot. My sister thought this was as funny as I did; we

took turns reading out passages about these *salesmen,* we took turns declaiming passages, though the time of night had passed in which such jokes can sustain themselves, at that hour irony begins to degrade even the ironist, Zapata's was closing, time to go home, I *stole* the book, though no one was counting, because the crate in which they came had been marked, *Books, two dollars,* who gave a shit, I had a right, because I had such burdens, I had maudlin thoughts, *Someone should hold me in their arms as I drift off tonight, someone should play me forty-fives on their bedroom Close-n-Play, someone should listen to the last sensible words I say before passing out, someone should remind me to drink fluids.* Though it was unlikely that any encircling of arms would take place, as Jen was in the Caribbean, and Kira was wassailing and caroling in the company of people who wished one another well, and I was a shade, I could barely talk, and then we were home, at my mother's house, somebody had driven us, the windows were dark, Irv and Gideon were mumbling farewells, getting into their car, we had tuned the cable television in the library, my brother and his friends, we were watching the commercials on MTV, we were drinking, my brother's friends were gone, here were the vanishing footfalls of guys in their twenties who would die young or get jobs that didn't work out, guys who lived over the dry cleaners, guys who would drive taxis and harangue you from the front seat, out into the night, across the golf course with their joints and bongs, I was alone, suddenly, watching *music television,* drinking, *Where there is a reflex, there must be a desire,* these advertisements were very edifying.

The deep pause of flagging spirits,
that always follows mirth and wine . . .

My hangover was bad (*One by one,* Hawthorne says, *by means of the association of ideas, the events of the preceding night came back to his memory; though those of latest occurrence were dim as dreams*), though how could Mom have known, in the kitchen, my small and devoted mom, as I had nothing to say on the subject of my hangover. My conversations with my mom had the qualities of position papers, other subjects being unspoken. I would say to my mom, *I'm certain that a Marxist-Leninist revolution is the solution to the situation in Nicaragua,* though I had arrived at this belief in a bar. What I was really saying was that I was afraid I would always be a filer of memos, a reader of manuscripts by the brokenhearted, and nothing else. My mother would nod sagely, ask questions, and six months later, I would observe that *the Sandinistas, by enlisting support from Cuba, have ruined the one chance for a true socialism,* though I didn't know if they had really enlisted support from Cuba or not, had no idea, and she would nod in the same fashion and politely ask questions. On Xmas Eve, it was about noon and I had just woken, never having made it back in to work, and I was staking out a position instead of saying, *I'm really lonely and no one on earth has ever been able to do anything about it and it makes it hard to do anything constructive with my life,* sitting in the kitchen clutching at my head, drinking cups of coffee, making pronouncements about the office now, about the state of book publishing, as if I were more than a ghost in that machine. She was organizing for Xmas Eve dinner, on which night, historically, I had vomited *four out of the past four years,* because we started with the rum and eggnog in the afternoon, and I couldn't figure out if that was the part of the equation that needed to be eliminated, the rum part, or if it was the relationship of the rum and eggnog to the bourbon, which usually came next, or to the wine, maybe red, maybe white. When I became worried that there wouldn't be any *room* for dinner, you know, from the five cups of rum and eggnog, then I would make the transition into spirits, talking to my stepfather and my stepbrothers, as my tongue had been loosened by rum and eggnog, and with it came some diminishment of the long-standing grudges that are frequent to those of us from broken homes, and then there would be the wine with dinner, copious wine, and we would jockey to avoid sitting next to certain family members, and we would drink, and then there were the after-dinner brandies or cordials, and then, later, midnight mass, at which all knelt to sing, in triplets, that one hymn best sung in candlelight. Well, I wouldn't be at mass, because I would be at home throwing up violently. Stumbling back to bed, with holiday cheer running from the corner of my mouth. My relationship with my mother was such that I never mentioned that I had been ill on Christmas Eve four years running, and I'm sure my mother wouldn't have told me if she had either, although we each would have felt sorry for the other and completely sympathetic. In addition to pondering the fact, just then, that I was almost certainly destined to *puke* in the coming hours, I was thinking, in the kitchen that morning, about having kissed that fellow employee, Kira, the night before. I was almost sure I had kissed her; I could remember the sensation of it, not the actual thing but the sensation, and in recollection this sensation seemed to be of *unsurpassed magnificence,* as if kissing and rock and roll were the same thing, or offered the same rewards. Nevertheless, my pulse scampered over particulars of the kiss as they returned. Maybe the instant just *before* the kiss was best of all. I liked when you knew that the kiss was imminent; kisses made me want to use names of *parts* of flowers: inflorescence, pappus, calyx, anther, pollinator, corolla. While degradation and remorse made me want to use the names of flowers themselves: phlox, geranium, sunflower, marigold, zinnia, chrysanthemum, bougainvillea; and I imagined Jen in the Caribbean, enduring the difficulties of her dad and his wife, Jen in a black leotard, missing me and forgetting about me by turns. I watched my mother organize a pile of themed Christmas napkins and Christmas glasses and Christmas flatware and Christmas china, and amid the distances integral to these conversations, imaginary conversations with Jen, conversations with my mother, my family, I found myself asking, *How long till rum and eggnog are served?* Next, I finished wrapping presents, I suppose, or I gave myself over to the unquiet waiting that is a fixture of holidays, by which I mean I was *in the basement,* with the television on, dumb with infantilism, in that indeterminate part of the day between coffee and beer. Perhaps it would be best if these two beverages could be admixed, maybe you could have an intravenous drip of this coffee-and-beer beverage, in order to pass the part of the day into which no foreign substances could be ingested according to rigors of polite society. In my agitation, the mild, agitated withdrawal of early afternoon, I took a shower, I put some fixative gunk in my hair, I donned a tweed jacket that belonged to somebody else, and then I drank rum and eggnog, I drank bourbon, I drank beer, I drank wine, I drank some more beer. I sneered at traditions of the holiday. It was Christmas itself that had made me spill my humors most years, the tinsel on the same tree every year, the waste and excess, the sorrow, the burden of a guilty conscience. Christmas was an odometer for the mileage *between* people. Why did people go to church at midnight, anyhow? *To pray for an upsurge in growth stocks?* There was booze awaiting me under the Christmas tree, I knew, because the people to whom I was related knew I liked to drink, and they didn't know enough else about me. I didn't give them much to go on. Of dinner, I remember only the moment in which I boasted that I would not be alive on New Year's Day 2000, and if that wasn't the year that I made this particular boast, then it was some exactly identical year during which I also had drunk and also had thrown up; this was a boast my mother had to endure, to which she responded by mumbling about the *phase* I was going through. All of us, the six of us, my three stepbrothers, my brother and sister and me, we were looking for ways to get away from the dinner table, from the predictability of the conversations; we were all bursting out of our antique chairs, we were fleeing the side dishes and courses, *Oh, here comes the part when they set the dessert on fire;* I walked out, with a glass of wine, and ensconced myself with a step-brother in front of *It's a Wonderful Life,* never liked the part *after* the angel arrived, and then I was sprawled somewhere, some bed, the one in the basement, the guest room, and somewhere my mother, solitar-ily, was filling Christmas stockings with pieces of chocolate, with new pairs of socks that had Christmas trees on them, and her hus-band was asleep, and my brother hadn't come home yet, and the house was quiet for the plight of those who had passed out, and my consciousness narrowed to a point, like on an old black-and-white television, my dull youth going backward from three dimensions to two, to a simple point in oblivion.

I woke early. Like I'd never slept. My musculature worked on strychnine or on some base metal, which was coming to the surface of me; the convertible bed was crafted with three-quarter-inch nails, and I was spindled on it. *A duel must have taken place the night before, and I was not its victor.* I climbed out of the bed in search of water. Threw on a couple of layers of clothes. It was about six, although I'd gone to bed after midnight. My balance wasn't good, objects were closer than they appeared, everything in the house, every surface, the stuff in the basement, the banister leading up from the basement, the doorjamb, the knobs on the cabinets in the kitchen, the kitchen table, the hanging lamp, the pots in the drying rack by the sink, everything had rusted slightly, had accumulated a layer of decay. I insisted, in my deeper interiors, that this wasn't so, selected an old plastic cup, filled it at the tap, drank. The water wasn't clear. With plastic cup half empty, I walked the first floor of the house. Some layer of myself that had been sealed tightly a couple of days before — when Jen drove off to the airport — had been pried up from me, the causes less important than the details. What was I doing up? Was it Saint Nick, whoever that guy was, whatever multinational he stumped for, who was responsible for my being awake, wasn't it the sound of hooves raining down on the rooftops of Pelham as he headed up the road to where a kid had been arrested for gun posses-sion, as he headed to the house where my mother's friend had just died of cancer? There was a disappointed way that the Christmas stockings hung, and I was uncertain if I should be opening one, if I should be sitting on the couch, if I should turn around, if I should go outside, if I should wake someone and explain. When I reached out to put my cup down, the perception of the cup wasn't right, as if a different term should suddenly apply to that container (*antimacassar,* or *curiosa*), and the rusty edges of things in the house seemed like occasions for bacterial infection. *This was fine,* I thought. *This was all fine.* Have coffee. It was the time of day in which you, the guy walking around with the cup of water, normally had coffee, and a wise strategy under the circumstances would be to proceed exactly as though all this were routine. I attempted diagnosis in front of a mirror in the half bath downstairs. A couple of mauve soaps laid out on the margins of the basin. My hair was ridiculous, my eyes were inflamed, but whereas, with a couple of drinks under the belt, I'd looked fine yesterday, boyish, today I looked roughed up, like somebody's mutt. Eventually, though, my body drove itself in another direction, my hands did the job, located coffee in the freezer, opened and closed cabinets, used the plastic scoop to empty grounds into filter, made liquids perform as liquids will perform, but there was an efflorescing of disquiet throughout this ritual. Then I took up a book that I had left nearby, Olivier's *On Acting,* though I was no actor. I sat on the couch in the glassed-in porch and read the same paragraph over a half dozen times. The sentences broke down into words that wouldn't reassemble into anything at all. I checked the clock. Relations would soon rise, gladness in their hearts, and this was both fearsome and welcome, yet a new problem had developed in the meantime, while I was attempting to think straight, which had to do with the physics of light, with quantum electrodynamics, dawn, mixed clouds and sun. I still needed the lamp beside the couch if I was going to read. But in switching on the reading lamp, some equal and opposite switch was flipped in me, and I began to struggle with the fact of light, with its imperial and merciless rule. Too many of these *quanta* everywhere. These particles, these waves. They got into everything. I turned the lamp off. I felt a devastation forming in my chest. I felt it begin to flow, corpuscularly, outward. If I left the light off, it implied that I wasn't there at all, without shadow; it implied that I no longer possessed mass and volume. If I turned the lamp on, an interrogation seemed to be under way, a Latin American military interrogation that would end with electrodes or kneecapping or the forced enumeration of *my secrets*. I began to sweat. The coffee, rather than opening up the blood vessels in parts of me, was now *disabling*. Turn the light on, the seventy-five-watt long-lived Sylvania, begin to feel the skeletons stirring in the closet; turn it off, feel like the last carbon-based life form cartwheeling toward nothingness.

There was precedent for this mix of uncomfortable sensations, from my *wild teens:* about the time my grandfather was dying, I'd undertaken some brief experiments with hallucinogenic drugs. In escalating doses. There had been a flicker of difficulty in the early phase of these experiments, evidence that maybe I wasn't the sort to mess with my cerebral hardwiring, in that a couple of the lower-dosage events had resulted in panic; for example, a night in which I wept in the arms of a friend, Liz, telling her that she was the only person I had ever trusted. Also periods when I was certain there were telepathic communications going on between people, most of which involved plans to exclude, humiliate, or torture me. The culmination of the experiments: an afternoon one December when I tried to take about six times the recommended daily allowance of this particular hallucinogen. I was in a dorm room with friends, in New Hampshire. An hour and a half normally elapsed between ingestion and derangement. The onset was normally a paroxysm of uncontrollable laughter. But I knew something was amiss if the walls started to *respire,* as they did, ahead of schedule, in twenty minutes, say. On the afternoon in question, I got immediately into a tactical battle with a peacock feather that my friend Locky was displaying on his desk. The center of this peacock feather's design was *an actual eye,* it was revealed, and I was condemned to attempt mastery over this eye. I was fencing with a peacock feather.

The real trouble began when the peacock feather began to talk to me, when its low, mean voice, something like that of a Turkish jailer in the moment of erotic transport, began to belittle my efforts to prevail in this dance of veils I was attempting. Furthermore, having been admitted to the world of imaginary voices, I realized that there was also a person or persons unknown *behind the walls* of Locky's room, as there were also gears and machinery back there, nineteenth-century engineering, and certain *perverted dwarfs,* and these people too were talking about me, and the news was foul and rude. The feeling of psychosis, however artificial, was like being submerged, slowly, in a windowless room. I could feel things getting worse. I tried to stay calm; I went to gaze at myself in the mirror downstairs, as though remonstrative language would alter what was happening: *You're on drugs, you're a kid at boarding school in New Hampshire, and you're on drugs, no reason to panic, the drugs will wear off in some hours, and the large questions of who you are will recede under waves of sweet calm;* no, it was clear that I was schizophrenic now, that I had accomplished what I had often worried about in my case, *madness,* with the same distrust of the diagnosis that the schizophrenic has, *It's not the drugs, it's that you have lost your mind, and there is a good reason why you have lost your mind, and that is because you are unworthy of your friends and the advantages you've had, and your friends are now conspiring to get even,* and I splashed water on myself, because the routine perceptions of reality, moisture on skin, calmed me. *It's hot in here.* If I could grab hold of these perceptions on the steep face of this terror, then maybe I could relax. But unfortunately the way the water beaded on my forearms revealed a truth that I had so far misunderstood, namely that my skin was composed of polystyrene or some other *large synthetic molecule.* In fact, I went upstairs to where Locky and Julian were sitting and I said, *I'm afraid I might be made out of plastic. So I think I have to turn myself in,* meaning that I would have to alert school officials that I was not in fact carbon based.

The remark got their attention.

The walk to the Reverend Flanders's apartment, where I was headed to inform on myself (I had selected the reverend for the honor because my difficulties seemed *religious*), was only about five minutes long, and it was characterized by numinous silences among the firs and hemlocks and pines that adorned our campus, as if all flora, sentient, of course, verbal, of course, were giving me a wide berth. Julian and Locky went the whole way with me, attempting to get me to rethink what I was about to do. (I would be expelled from school, *and therefore I would definitely fail the upcoming geometry test,* and this would make it more difficult to get into a good college, which would make it more difficult to get a good job, which would make it more difficult to make money, to attract a suitable bride, to afford good drugs, to get fully vested in the company pension plan, to buy a fast car that would be heavily insured, to get my children into our boarding school, and this would in turn affect their future, their ability to procure their own drugs; indeed, the entire course of human events, upcoming presidential elections, foreign-policy initiatives, all seemed explicit in this momentous decision.) Locky and Julian whispered in the most compassionate ways, *Moody, do you really want to do this? Moody, do you know what you are doing?* The silence of our forested surroundings was oppressive, the worst sort of evidence; *God knew,* I believed emphatically, even though I was a professed atheist, *God knew,* generally, and I believed in *everything,* in echelons of deviltry and witchery (*Accordingly, The kingdoms of* Sweden, Denmark, Scotland, *yea and* England *it self, as well as the Province of* New-England, *have had their Storms of* Witchcrafts *breaking upon them, which have made most Lamentable Devastations*), in all things that can't regularly be seen by the senses, because my senses now apprehended these forces (*That there is a* Devil, *is a thing Doubted by none but such as are under the Influences of the Devil*), I was a mystic, I was eternal, and *most fallen,* and as I rounded the last corner and proceeded down the wood-paneled corridor that led to the door that in turn led to the apartment that led to my confession to the reverend, Locky and Julian turned back, like nocturnal wildlife at the margins of a conflagration; they watched me throw myself forward, toward that imperial door with its door knocker. I made the last twenty paces by myself, *A human eye, growing out of the floor of a padded cell, at the end of a vine, a floral eye, a peacock eye, attempting to communicate, though in no common tongue, through the mouth of its eye, speaking through its pupil, myself in a padded cell with a carnivorous vine growing out of the floor, a vine apparently contortionistic, an urgency in its posture, as it attempts to communicate with me, and then I am standing in an impossibly large assembly hall, an* infinite *room, to which none has access but me, where an army of circus clowns thinks and speaks in perfect unison declaiming on the subject of my madness, I ask for help, and the word appears as an object, a thing, a series of balloons drifting above the scene, and this army chants the phonemes of my name and makes clear that I must die, the end of each of these filmstrips is that I must die, I must die, I must die, in every account I must die, yet I am afforded one last appeal to an intercessor, and a chapel, a religious sanctuary on the grounds of my school, is his mouthpiece, his body on earth, and I say to this intercessor, I need* help, *but this sequence of letters is no more than a jumble under the circumstances, and the clouds are vanished above the chapel and a voice calls out, "Beyond help."* For a second before I knocked on the door, in a cold sweat, the precipitation of hallucinations slowed, and I looked around and saw that it was just a night in December, a night featuring recent snowfall, and that I didn't need to be so upset. Then, as though I had crested a hill and was headed back down (*The Sins of men in this Generation, will be* mighty *Sins; men will be more Accurate and Exquisite and Refined in the arts of* Sinning), I began to experience the terror again. Then the Reverend Flanders opened his door.

The difference in 1986, years later, was that *I hadn't taken any drugs.* The sensation was familiar, the malfunction of inner organs was familiar, the pinprick of the ulcer. But when I started to see myself as traveling down into this microscopy of panic, when I began to observe its crystals and formations, I knew that I no longer had the immediate excuse of drugs. The last few floorboards that supported me were giving out. My hands were trembling. I was clammy and moist and alert, but to what? I couldn't sit still, couldn't concentrate long enough to do anything. My mother appeared, wearily, in the kitchen, asking if I wanted anything to eat, *some fruit tart, perhaps.* The repast awaited in the fridge. I believed I would be able to feel the food all the way down my esophagus, past pyloric constrictors, into my roiling gut, large intestine, appendix, bowel, and therefore food was *obscene;* I turned down my mother's offer, looked at her plaintively, wanting to talk but dammed up in the matter of language; what was the thing that I wanted to say? There was no trauma, no Hollywood origin for this sensation I had, except things that people went through every day. For no reason, I had woken on Christmas Day with a hex on me. A bad spell. *What are you reading?*

my mother asked, and when that didn't get a response, *Did you get a few little things in your stocking? Did you look?* I mumbled evasively. The coffee pot refilled. My stepfather appeared, silent, repentant, as upon most mornings. *Missed a nice service last night,* my mother observed. She felt that it was her job to draw out reserved persons. Panic inside me began to throw off more elaborate theories and prognostications. The accumulation of *seasonal gifts,* which I had managed to ignore on my earlier wanderings in the house, now emerged as the locus of dread. The gifts had obligations attached to them, and performances. Every gift, shucked of its wrappings, was a performance, and as my various stepbrothers and siblings and their spouses appeared, a conspiracy of obligations was upon us all; surely they felt as I felt, that whatever I had bought was unacceptable, that I was operating below the level of *minimum acceptable participation,* as their bodies collided merrily around me, fruit tarts everywhere, as they laughed, celebrated, with knickknacks from their stockings. How enormous their mouths were, with perfect dentistry, how enormous their appetites, their ambitions, their intentions, their inventions. I sat off around the corner, and periodically my brother would come by and attempt a joke, some bit of levity, and I would smile halfheartedly, unable to drift up through these binding agents to respond, and he, conscious of mild failure in these jokes, would return to the fold, to the larger organization of family, and then it was time to open the presents.

By prearranged moment, according to western civilization, Christmas. In towns to the left and the right of you, in streets busy and serene, people moved to this expression of their relationship with fellows, and it seemed it was only me (this was a vain thought) who was veiled at Christmas, who was covered over somehow, and thereby unacceptable to the huddle. Still, I flittered at the edges of affiliation because it was even more frightening to renounce it. Until we were all in the living room, with those nineteenth-century Japanese paintings of my grandfather's on the wall around us, mismatched with the modular sofa, the upright piano, the stereo, and I sat at the piano, meandering through improvisations that had no beginning and no end; I plinked on a couple of keys; and people began to open their gifts, as though the display of gifts would reveal other meta-phorical concealments: *Oh, hey, thanks a lot, how did you know?* Or: *Yeah, you know, I was at the store and it just called out. Your name all over it.* A slow-motion approach to a traffic accident, and I could see the stationary object, could feel the front end of my car flattening in front of me, but then I would loop around to approach the accident site again, each time the language of disaster consistent and pre-dictable, and then my brother brought over what was clearly a book, *Must be a toaster oven,* he said, handed it to me; it was from my par-ents, and I could see everyone was looking at me now, this was the moment for performing the dancing-bear routine, and my hands shook, but I got my index finger under the lip of the wrapping paper, which revealed a minor biography of a somewhat obscure literary fig-ure from the early part of the century, and I looked nervously up at my mother and whispered some confection of gratitude. They sus-pected there was something wrong, I knew and they knew, *One Christmas he assigned seats at the holiday repast by lottery because he didn't think the patriarchal seating arrangement was acceptable; once he got every-one cans of Del Monte vegetables because he thought the labels were really beautiful.* There was precedent for erratic behavior on Christmas, to be sure, but I had fallen below the level of *minimum acceptable behavior,* and there was an uncomfortable silence around me, and at last it seemed unbearable, as though yellow jackets were going to fly out of my mouth, and when the general attention moved on to the next gift, I grabbed my mother by the arm, *Can I talk to you for a second?* And she followed me out into the library, and disorder cascaded from me, what would no longer be put off: *I think I might be having a heart attack, will you take my pulse, will you tell me if I have a pulse, I think I might be having a nervous breakdown, I don't know what it is, I woke up, and something was wrong, and I can't calm down, and I don't know what's happening, but I can't catch my breath, and I can't think straight, and I think I'm having a heart attack or I might be dying, or I'm having a nervous breakdown, and I don't have time for a nervous breakdown, I don't have time, what's wrong with me, do you think there's something wrong with me?* and so forth; of course there was sobbing, of a sort that rarely came from me, even after my *bad drug experiences,* when for months I was *afraid,* of anything synthetic, of any plastic anything, of any concentration of objects made by man, industrial architecture, all of these malefic, *the Serpents of the dust are crawling and coyling about us, and Insulting over us.* One night, eight or nine years prior, I had sat with her in her room and tried to explain it, how bad everything around me had become, but *never got the message through,* and here I was trying to explain again. My mother held me on Christmas, nervously, with that effort that comes to those who themselves have been through many difficulties.

—You need to go lie down for a while. Why don't you go upstairs and lie down?

—I can't do this, I said. —I can't.

—Can't do what?

—I can't open the presents. I can't go to Dad's. I need your help. Do you think maybe you could call him for me? Could you tell him that I can't come?

—Go lie down. If you can't go later, you can call him and tell him.

—Can't you do it for me?

—Go lie down. You'll be fine. You just need to rest.

As a member of the society of persons with multiple sets of parents, I was still experiencing Christmas as a contested day, see, a day of *visitation,* a day negotiated by lawyers, as I have said, and when we were done opening the gifts, we were bound for my father's apartment, my brother, my sister, and I, where we would repeat the whole performance with his tree and his gifts, until all presents had been opened, and then more food, more gourmandizing, more excess. Nevertheless, in the centrifuge of anxiety, I did what my mother told me, that is, I went up to my brother's room, lay down on his bed, and tried to read the biography of the minor literary figure, of which only one fact indelibly remains, namely that this writer was so disgusted with himself that he would occasionally dig in his yard and force himself to *eat dirt* as an expression of his feelings of self-regard. This seemed plausible and even dignified. When I closed my eyes on my brother's bed, malevolent clowns had reassembled themselves, the clowns from my *wild teens,* as though their legion, underemployed in the intervening years, had waited around for another trip to my Slough of Despond, so that they could faithfully discharge their harrowing responsibilities. Eventually, I was driven up from my brother's bed, unable to find peace there, and I padded slowly downstairs, where I skulked back into the living room. Some low conversational tones had been given over to the subject of *me* in my absence, it was obvious, but I sat in a corner and tried to read, tried to watch them all as they left gifts with my name on them to accumulate at my side. My sister came over, gave me a hug, and I tried to say something to her, only to find that even the simple locutions were now impossible. An aphasic crudeness characterized my efforts to describe what was happening. My distressed language grew more unmistakable. I tried to call my father to tell him I wasn't going to come to his house for Christmas, and this interview concluded with my father advising me to *do whatever the hell I wanted to do since that's what I was going to do anyway.* So I went along with my brother and sister, shivering in the back of my sister's Honda as she took the Bruckner Expressway into the city. When my father opened the door to his apartment, he bestowed on me a dismissive glance and said, *What are you doing here?* When I had no sensible reply, he said, *Have a drink, for godsakes.* So I did. I drank. I had some wine first, and then some bourbon, and then some more wine, and at the end of all this drinking I had to admit that I didn't feel *so terribly bad.* In fact, words were coming back to me.

IN HIS CASE, HOWEVER,
THE SYMBOL HAD A DIFFERENT IMPORT . . .

As you might suppose, Hawthorne's story "The Minister's Black Veil" and its symbology have generated innumerable critical papers and allusions. (And I read and reread it myself, throughout the whole of my youth, in college, in graduate school, feeling myself drawing nearer to it.) Whole forests' worth of pine, spruce, cedar, cypress, hemlock, fir, have been defoliated, scavenged, and bleached for the purposes of supposition and departmental infighting on the subject. This criticism is the subject of the next few pages, and I urge readers who might skip to the more narrative chapters nonetheless to heed this brief interlude, this ligamentary passage, the better to understand the way in which an unresolved image, *the veil,* hangs around in history. Like a trauma incompletely forgotten.

At least one illuminating catalog exists of *all* the criticism pertaining to "The Minister's Black Veil," by Lea Bertani Vozar Newman, of North Adams State College, this contribution assembled according to the rigors of a school called *reception theory.* Newman's catalog includes a listing for every single article written on Hawthorne's story from the date of its serial publication (in 1835) up to 1987, a span of more than a hundred and fifty years. The list enfolds within it, however, an awesome fifty-seven-year gap between a survey (by Leslie Stephen) written eight years after the author's death and Newton Arvin's excellent *Hawthorne,* published in 1929 (in which the Reverend Hooper is said to exhibit *a misanthropy that outPuritans the Puritans*). On either side of the gap are divergent analytical tendencies. One in which the critics respond affectively to the work (according to dictates of something close to the Romantic tradition), as in Charles Fenno Hoffman's review of *Twice-Told Tales,* in which "The Minister's Black Veil" is *pregnant . . . with pathetic thought and profound meditation,* or in a review by Elizabeth Peabody (later Hawthorne's sister-in-law) in which certain stories are deemed *dangerous for his genius.* This very passionate responsiveness exemplifies the nineteenth-century approach to Hawthorne and to criticism in general, and it endured to the author's death in 1864, when, for example, a critic named Richard Hutton compared the late Hawthorne to the Reverend Mr. Hooper: *{Hawthorne} seems to speak from a somewhat similar solitude. Indeed, we suspect the story as a kind of parable of his own existence.*

After publication of Newton Arvin's critical biography and following another lengthy silence on the subject of "The Minister's Black Veil" (this one lasting until after the Second World War), American criticism begins to militate generally for a more exacting and scientific approach. At which juncture, as Lea Bertani Vozar Newman remarks, academics begin to find support for a stunning variety of interpretations in "The Minister's Black Veil." Mark Van Doren, for example, finds the story filled with *irresolution;* Gilbert P. Voigt finds Hooper's conduct *capricious* and yet sees Old Testament analogues for it, while William Bysshe Stein believes "Hooper is the Devil's agent and his behavior is a perversion of Paul's second epistle to the Corinthians" (e.g.: *As God hath said, I will dwell in them, and walk in them; and I will be their God, and they be my people. Wherefore come out from among them, and be ye separate, saith the Lord*). One critic argues that *Hooper hides behind the veil to escape the sexual demands of a normal life,* while another observes that Hooper is *one of Hawthorne's narcissistic characters who is isolated by his egotistical individualism;* yet another says that Hooper makes a sacrilege of the theological mysteries of the Gospel According to Mark (*Unto you it is given to know the mystery of the kingdom of God: but unto them that are without, all these things are done in parables*), and so forth. There is mostly silence, in these postwar years, with respect to the fact of the veil itself, its symbolism. *As if the veil itself were veiled* from the critics and their diverse strategies. Rather their analysis is principally on the matter of Hooper and his motivation, a rich subject, of course. The essentially theological conjecture of this period, in which a single correct answer to the question of the character's motivation is possible, a hermeneutics of Hooper, abruptly gives way, however, to the New Criticism of the later forties and fifties, in the person of one Richard Harter Fogle, who introduced into the discussion of "The Minister's Black Veil" a word from which the story has never gotten free since, namely *ambiguity.*

Fogle's argument begins with a hypothesis suggestive of earlier critics: *The veil is the visible symbol of secret sin, suggested by Hawthorne's reading in New England history and legend,* but he soon digs beneath this superficial layer: *The explicit statement, however, leads to more than a single possibility. The self-imposed martyrdom of Father Hooper must correspond with some deep necessity of his nature.* Fogle invokes F. O. Matthiessen's term "ambiguity device" to describe the application of the veil in the story: *The purpose of this device is to suggest a meaning while simultaneously casting doubt upon it, or to offer two or more interpretations at once of the same incident.* Or, as he elsewhere says, *The veil has varying effects upon different minds and different levels of society,* and though Fogle is speaking here simply of the secondary characters in Hawthorne's story, the townsfolk, etc., he could just as well be predicting the reaction, ever after, among critics: *The minister himself believes the veil to be an emblem of the secret sin that poisons the souls of all mankind, but we are not compelled to accept his reading of the matter.* After which Fogle brings readers to the alarming summation of his important broadside: *We conclude, then, without arriving at a clear decision as to the meaning of the tale.*

Though there are those critics after Fogle who attempt a certainty of the quaint, old-fashioned sort on the matter of the black veil (Glenn C. Altschuler, e.g., writing in 1974, in a transcendentalist journal, *The veil was one of separation: of that there was no question*), protestations of uncertainty become the norm, as in Robert E. Morseberger's essay from 1973: *It is a mistake to concentrate too much on the veil itself. Aside from Mr. Moody, no one wore such a veil, and the possessor of it is merely an eccentric.* Or Raymond Benoit, in 1971, from *Studies in*

Short Fiction: Straightforward analyses of Hawthorne are hard to come by for the simple reason that he was not straightforward; he was fully aware that the world of human affairs is indeed a round one.

By 1988, Norman German, writing in the same periodical that featured Benoit's essay, can feel compelled to admit to exhaustion on the subject: *The anatomical workings of "The Minister's Black Veil" have so long been under the incisive explicatory knives of every type of critic that one might think the story, by now, scraped to the bone.* Since the ambiguous reading of Hooper's motivation (and of the veil itself) has grown so powerful as to be unavoidable, the readings of the seventies and eighties — as Lea Bertani Vozar Newman points out — have concentrated most prominently on historical contextualizations: *What underlies the bulk of criticism published in the 1970s and 1980s, however, is not a new science or a new philosophy or a new biographical approach, but a very traditional discipline — history.* The bulk of this historicist reading concentrates on the Great Awakening of the Puritans in the middle of the eighteenth century (of which Jonathan Edwards, for example, was an eminent voice), in the very period when Hooper would have led his flock. This historicist analysis reaches its acme, according to Newman, in a study by Michael C. Colacurcio, in which he *provides the comprehensive results of what an informed researcher can deduce by reading the election sermons given during Governor Belcher's administration (one of which Hooper is credited with delivering).* Later historical readings apparently travel similar latitudes. Among these, I liked best Frederick Newberry's interpretation, which includes mention of Joseph "Handkerchief" Moody, and which observes of Hooper's use of symbolism, *Ultimately, the Puritans' reified use of typology presupposed the advent of the millennium foreseen by St. John the Divine in the Book of Revelation,* or, to put it in my own tongue: Hooper is one of those believers looking into the tea leaves of the Holy Bible's most recondite daydream, *Apocalypse,* and coming up with bad ideas about how to conduct his daily life, which makes him, for me, an ideal American literary character.

After the historicists, Newman begins to close out her catalog with a list of readings of the Hawthorne story that *do not yet exist:*

No archetypalists, of either the Northrop Frye or the Jungian strain; no Structuralists, applying the linguistic concepts of Ferdinand de Saussure or the grammatical poetics of Jonathan Culler or the lexies and codes of Roland Barthes; no Deconstructionists, quoting Jacques Derrida or J. Hillis Miller or Paul DeMan; no Speech Act theorists, and no Reader-Response critics, emulating Norman Holland's "identity themes" or Harold Bloom's influence-produced "defense mechanisms," or Stanley Fish's "affective stylistics."

Newman concludes: *When readers look at "The Minister's Black Veil," the text becomes a mirror wherein they see reflections of themselves, of their concerns and their preoccupations.*

A babble of competing theories. No particular theory more right than any other. And one can therefore select from these voices for any such analyses that delight or amuse. An existentialist reading, say (*The basic contrast, then, is not between a damning isolation and a saving sympathy, but between death and life, or more exactly between death-in-life and life-in-death*), a reading informed by pragmatism (*The veil is merely the external emblem of that condition that William James, in* The Varieties of Religious Experience, *labels "The Sick Soul." For victims of such profound melancholia, "evil is no mere relation of the subject to particular outer things, but something more radical and general, a wrongness or vice in his essential nature"*), or, if you like, a psychoanalytic reading. How about a psychoanalytic reading *in which the critic later renounces psychoanalysis?* For example, Frederick Crews's fascinating monograph *The Sins of the Fathers:*

> In declaring that Hawthorne's "innermost concerns" are "invariably" those highlighted by psychoanalysis, I was egregiously begging the question. Who is to say which of an author's themes are "innermost"? What this meant, I am afraid, is that my love affair with psychoanalysis had reached the point where a given theme would be considered preeminent in Hawthorne's mental

94 • Rick Moody

economy precisely by virtue of its correspondence to
Freudian theory.

Never has a critic more embodied the ambiguous psychological
motivation of a Hawthorne character, perhaps of the Reverend
Hooper himself, than in Crews's self-lacerating exposé:

> When I could finally bring myself to ask what objective
> grounds [Freud] had produced to warrant acceptance of
> his system, all I could find was a cloudy tale about a
> heroic self-analysis; a series of artfully composed case
> histories about patients who, one could make out, had
> been brow-beaten by the therapist without experienc-
> ing lasting relief from their symptoms; and many suave
> assurances about imminently forthcoming or previ-
> ously supplied proofs that are nowhere to be found in
> the record.

Like Hooper on his deathbed, Crews, in his afterword, argues about
hypocrisies, about verities, about limitations of systems of thinking
here on earth. Yet despite his later need to recant (*that a critic might
want to renounce his influential theory and release his followers has come
to seem incomprehensible; it smacks of self-destructive mania*), Crews the
younger, the unreconstructed analyst, remains one of the most passionate, convincing, and human critics of Hooper and "The Minister's
Black Veil":

> Thus, the world of "The Minister's Black Veil" is one in
> which a man can reasonably be "afraid to be alone with
> himself." The real struggle in the tale is not between
> Hooper and the others but between conscious and
> unconscious thoughts within each individual. Total
> repression is restored in everyone but Hooper, and in
> his case, as in Goodman Brown's, the truth is permitted
> utterance only in the form of symbolism and accusa-
> tion. Hooper has sympathy with "all dark affections"

but he lacks the courage to confess their hold upon his own imagination. He too is one of those who are frightened by the veil, and understandably so, for he has had clear intimations of what the fore of civilization must contend with in its effort to remain the master. Hawthorne leaves us with the Swiftian idea that a little self-knowledge is worse than none, and that the best approximation to happiness rests in an ignorant, busy involvement with a society of unconscious hypocrites.

Since candor is imperative in my history of the criticism of "The Minister's Black Veil," I should admit, however, that I was trained in the very *guilds and schools* about which I am skeptical above, the psychoanalytic criticism that bedevils Crews's Hawthorne monograph and its even more voluptuous stepgrandchild, *deconstruction.* And perhaps this is a sort of parable about how people grow and learn. I was at Brown University in the late seventies, and I had a brush with Marxism, because to say I was a Marxist-Leninist was the thing that *most irritated my parents.* I read *Capital,* the first volume, anyhow, and the *Manifesto,* and some of Lenin, and was very interested in Stalin's argument about how *all children should be raised by the state,* and I went from Marxism to existentialism, where I wobbled around for a while, not understanding that there was more to existentialism than Sartre and Camus, until I wrote a term paper on Satan (in *Paradise Lost*) as existentialist hero. Then, in junior year, I took a couple of film courses in the department known as *semiotics,* in particular "Introduction to Film Analysis," and these idylls in the film program brought me, at last, to "Foundation of the Theory of Signs," or Semiotics 12. Where the school of deconstruction welcomed in its fresh prospects.

This was near upon my twentieth birthday, and a number of crises were in the midst of their germination, which crises conspired to make me susceptible to argument and anxiety in general. Over the summer, I had *broken up* with my girlfriend since boarding school, a lovely, well-mannered, and brilliant young woman of the sort you definitely brought home to meet the folks, and in her stead I had put not one but two mercurial, dark, undependable women who had mixed feelings about me: a cocaine-abusing employee from the brokerage firm where I'd had a summer job, and a stained-glass-window maker from RISD called Isabella. The latter of these unrequited targets worked the night shift at a Store 24 in Providence, on Thayer Street, where she sold a lot of pornography to hapless residents of the city's east side. Barbara, the cocaine abuser, had encouraged me, after a night at Danceteria, to chop lines of that fell drug with her on her parents' Roy Lichtenstein print. After which she refused me and I slept on the couch. Back at school, a friend from my teens had begun hawking, on campus, examples of a prescription medication that he referred to as *Australian quaaludes.* They were probably strong antihistamines, not much more. Taken in large enough doses, though, or combined with beer, they made my friend's customers, myself among them, thoroughly confused. I experienced my first regular blackouts on these pills, and whole days were lost. Or I came to at some party having shredded articles of my clothing and talking like a reptile. Or I awakened alone on some distant corner of the campus and struggled back toward my dorm room though my locomotion was impaired. When Isabella, artisan of stained glass, told me that *she couldn't see me anymore* because her boyfriend wouldn't allow it, even under the most chaste circumstances, I returned to my cell block, where my roommates were five extremely tall members of the Brown basketball team, and I decided to take *all* the quaaludes, with some Jack Daniel's I'd bought, my total stock of *Australian quaaludes* being about fifteen. I took twelve, I think, some number in the double digits, but even this wasn't enough, as I suspected it would not be, so, instead of being relieved of my adolescent love trouble and the cares of the world, *I slept,* a sleep more like precipitous unconsciousness than sleeping, from which I woke twelve hours or fourteen hours later with an anxious lurch, to gaze myopically at the bedroom clock. *I was missing my discussion section of semiotics.* Dragged myself out of bed, wearing last night's outfit, a mostly black outfit, grabbed the assigned book, Foucault's *Discipline and Punish,* wobbled down to the List Art Building, where our discussion section met. Before class I offered some probably mostly incoherent and oddly boastful description of my *unconvincing suicide attempt* to my friend Josh or others, and then we filed into the room, and I put my head down on my desk and went to sleep. I didn't wake again until the stirring of the rest of the class at lunchtime. You'd think a *conversion,* a battering of the heart, couldn't possibly have firm tread on such lassitude, but sometimes conversion is like pines that grow on glacial outcroppings, sometimes conversion is like the grass forcing its way up through the cracks in the paving stones, or like the brisk moment of self-knowledge that dawns on the most impervious adolescent; therefore, when I had expelled the quaaludes in me, *Discipline and Punish* looked entirely new, looked like the glimmering saber of the revolution, opening as it did with an incredibly violent description of the execution of a regicide, *drawn and quartered in public,* this assassin, in order to make an argument about the imposition of political order, from which Foucault went on to construct his extremely artful and generous theories: *The body is directly involved in a political field; power relations have an immediate hold upon it; they invest it, mark it, train it, torture it, force it to carry out tasks, to perform ceremonies, to emit signs.* The theories of Foucault were more like manifestos, more like exhortations, and, as such, they seemed to have qualities in common with the novels that I'd been reading (Borges, Genet, Burroughs, Beckett), more in common with novels than with the dry social theory that I had found in my philosophy classes. And it was this novelistic dimension that kindled in me the *zealotry of the newly converted,* leading me thereafter to such documents as *I, Pierre Rivière, Having Slaughtered My Mother, My Sister, and My Brother . . . ,* an eighteenth-century case history edited by Foucault:

> I therefore took this fearful resolution, I determined to kill all three of them, the first two because they were leagued to make my father suffer, as to the little boy I had two reasons, one because he loved my mother and my sister, the other because I feared that if I only killed the other two, my father though greatly horrified by it might yet regret me when he knew that I was dying for him . . .

Since this work was novelistic, and since it had resonances of Hand-kerchief Moody's bloody deed, and since I had come to it in my period of *love trouble,* I realized, as only the newly converted might, that this new faith was indeed about *love,* was about finding in the orthodoxies of the semiotics department only those interpretations that cohered with where I was already situated, in disorders of love and mood. Everyone in the semiotics department was in love, there was a *venereal affliction* making its way around the semiotics depart-ment, love was in the air, and the boys were pretending that they liked the other boys (except in the instances in which they *did* like the other boys), same with the women, including a pair of sisters, in the semiotics department, who were sometimes seen to dance sug-gestively together, as if to intimate that *they too were in love with one another,* or perhaps merely in league, and there were rumors about various professors in the semiotics department, that they too loved the students who studied there, loved them both metaphorically and actually; notwithstanding frequent denigration by these professors of all intellection that depended on the despicable excesses of *roman-ticism,* they too were romantics, lapsed utopians, and thus in their tutelage, I found everywhere in Semiotics 12 the language of love, *Discourse on love though I may for years at a time, I cannot hope to seize the concept of it except "by the tail": by flashes, formulas, surprises of expression, scattered through the great stream of the Image-repertoire; I am in love's* wrong place, *which is its dazzling place: "The darkest place," according to a Chinese proverb, "is always underneath the lamp,"* as Roland Barthes's love was boundless, immense, and encompassed even tourist attrac-tions, movies, plastic, and wrestling. But maybe this is how you talk about your conversions after the fact, you romanticize them. So: I threw in with a revolution that had *romance* as part of it, and this was especially true as we in Semiotics 12 turned our attention at last to *Of Grammatology,* by Jacques Derrida. I remember a guy in the class, an older guy who had come back to school after being a drug dealer in Boston, I remember the look in his eyes when he said he had *thrown that book out the window,* I remember reading some of *Of Gram-matology* to my mother, who pronounced it nonsense, I remember sitting in the library, spending an hour on just a page or two of it, diagramming and rediagramming the sentences over and over, trying to decipher the words, *difference, trace, supplement,* trying to figure out what Jacques Derrida was trying to say, and when I was done, I was *converted.* I loved a Derrida who spoke of *le jeu,* the *game of criticism,* who started every essay with a question, e.g., *Is it certain that to the word* communication *corresponds a concept that is unique, univocal, rigorously controllable, and transmittable: in a word, communicable?* Even in a circumstance in which he might deny the validity of these games, I loved him, because then he would go and play these games regardless, he would toy with the philosopher John Searle, even addressing him only according to the French acronym for a limited liability corporation. I loved him when he refused rigor: *But let's be serious. Why am I having such difficulty being serious in this debate, in which I have been invited in turn to take part?* I loved him when he tangled with Lacan, when he composed an entire book out of postcards, when his radical skepticism involved installing brackets and quotation marks around every word and even *crossing words out* in the printed versions of the texts, when he wouldn't admit to knowing his own motivation exactly, or even if he, the author of the books, was an entity whose motivation was perceptible. Back then I supported the fashionable *death of the author,* I wanted to get rid of the author, to get rid of authorial claims of unique status, to get rid of the trappings of traditional scholarship. And so I favored Derrida, the lover and lyric troubadour, Derrida the prankster, Derrida the poet.

> Each time that a multiplicity of voices has imposed itself on me in such a form that I tried to present it as such, that is, to distribute the voices in some way, to act *as if* I were distributing voices in my text, there were always women's voices or a woman's voice. . . . I do not write *about* these voices — you ask me if I am tempted to write about the multiplicity of voices in music — I never write about them. In a certain way, I try to let them take over — and keep — speech through me, without me, beyond the control that I could have over them. I let them, I try to let them speak.

I took *Australian quaaludes,* I wrote all my papers in one draft, because in the semiotics department you had to write your papers on one side of one page of typing paper with no margins, no title, and no footnotes. You had to put all of that housekeeping on the back side of the page, but the professor wouldn't read the back side, in all probability, if there was additional text on the back side; the length of papers was arbitrary, I wrote them in one draft, I was converted, I had seen the light, which was a stylized announcement of light, not an actual light, *I had no self, self was an arbitrary shifting, just a tendency toward certain gestures, as structured by institutions of power in order to secure permanent exclusivity of power among the few, and it had always been this way, the instability of language was always concealed, the failure of writing was always erased, the selflessness of self was always effaced, and the riot of feelings remained, the loss, the desire that exceeded the object,* I was converted. I remember the special handshakes of that halcyon time, the secret greetings of the gang of semioticians, and I could mumble the secret greetings, and I can mumble these greetings still, when I see my fellow semioticians from afar, these white tigers of the past, out in the world making their independent feature films, winning their National Book Awards, teaching in the universities, writing their screenplays, performing their performances.

So: when Lea Bertani Vozar Newman, in her catalog of writings on "The Minister's Black Veil," remarked that thus far there had been *no Deconstructionists, quoting Jacques Derrida or J. Hillis Miller or Paul DeMan* among Hawthorne commentators, I was pleased, because, had there been, I would have had to travel back into the Dark Ages of my own education, and I did not want to revisit these orthodoxies because I had forgotten what certain words meant: *oneiric, ontological, phallogocentrism, aporia, catachresis, hypotyposis, prosopopoeia.* It was devastating, therefore, when I discovered that Newman's catalog was out of date, that, indeed, the deconstructionists *had* visited "The Minister's Black Veil," had collided completely with Hawthorne's text, in the person of J. Hillis Miller himself. Miller had, in fact, devoted an *entire book* to the subject, namely,

Hawthorne and History, and therefore I needed to familiarize myself with it, with sentences like *The reading of the story culminates in the double proposition that the story is the unveiling of the possibility of the possibility of unveiling,* in which I encountered again that euphony and nonsense of the tomes of my youth. Or: *"The Minister's Black Veil" is put by Hawthorne not under the aegis of the opposition between allegory and substantial realism, but within the space of a somewhat different contradiction. This is the opposition between the genres of parable and apocalypse, on the one hand, and true history.* But, hey, where's the *romance* in this? J. Hillis Miller did deliver in part on *le jeu* of his deconstructive method, including a pun that I used to hear often in elementary school:

> Names may be significant. The Reverend Moody of York had reason to be moody, though this was in fact just the name into which the historical Moody was born. He had accidentally killed a beloved friend. The name Hooper doubles or folds over the name Moody. It repeats the double "o", already doubled itself in each name, like two round eyes in the middle of each name. The change "M" to "H" moves the name in the direction of Hawthorne's own name. A "hooper" is either "a craftsman who fits the hoops on casks, barrels, etc., a cooper. Also a maker of hoops," or "one who hoops or cries 'hoop'; only in *hooper's hide,* an old name of hide-and-seek."

But thereafter, J. Hillis Miller finds that much in the story has to do with Hawthorne's tendency toward *blasted allegory,* and Henry James's critique of same, and thus we naturally find many allegorical readings here in *Hawthorne and History* itself, e.g., *This makes the veil, so it seems, an example of what Hawthorne has been seeking unsuccessfully in all his writing: the material embodiment of a spiritual or allegorical meaning,* which analysis amounts to the kind of anaerobic, utterly cerebral interpretation that I associate with the later work of deconstructionist critics, a tradition that negates or evades the Real in favor of a tidy, schematic reiteration of some epistemological sort that will *save no lives*. Miller seems closer to the flame, to the source, in discussing the sexual ambiguity of the veil, but he leaves that theme behind quickly, from which he turns back toward metaphysical readings such as, *Hooper's sin is the sin of irony,* in the process casting "The Minister's Black Veil" as a failed historical reading of the life of Joseph Moody, or a story that both narrates history and allegory: *In the case of the minister's black veil and "The Minister's Black Veil," as my reading has attempted to demonstrate, the veil and the story are undecidable in meaning. They may mean this or they may mean that.* Which, of course, is exactly the *ambiguity* that Hooper himself affects: *Thus, from beneath the black veil, there rolled a cloud into the sunshine, an ambiguity of sin or sorrow, which enveloped the poor minister, so that love or sympathy could never reach him.* It is not only that the veil itself is *valent,* reflective of the interpreter. The Reverend Hooper also confers his own motives on whoever turns the leaves of his pages, as (J.) Hillis Miller, whose name has the same initials as Hooper and Moody, as "Handkerchief" Moody, the same initials as my father and my father's father, turns out to resemble Hooper, in just the way Frederick Crews does, in imponderables and undecidables. But this reader grows weary of mock-conclusive perceptions while looking instead for a criticism that purveys a more credible and honest *fun* in its pages.

However, *what is unresolved lingers,* fun or no fun, and therefore, the time has come to point out to readers well versed in anagrams and palindromes that the word *veil* is an anagram of both *live* and *evil,* an obverse of both states, as Norman German observes in his very stylish essay "The Veil of Words in 'The Minister's Black Veil.'" After this debate and argument, I for one am certain mainly of uncertainty, couldn't tell you even *a pair* of the seven types of ambiguity, couldn't tell you a spondee from an amphibrach; I am incapable of dramatic irony, all my leitmotifs are uncontrolled and unintended, and the only valuable thing I know about the veil itself is that *you can see through it.* It *does not* conceal, not perfectly, not eternally, except that it announces the possibility of concealment. As Carlysle says, *In a symbol, there is concealment and yet revelation.* Or, as Shelley remarked, *Poetry lifts the veil from the hidden beauty of the world.* Sure, let's get to a sunnier impulse, neglected in the song of Hawthorne's guilty conscience: a wearer of the veil may be concealed, but the artist, though likewise veiled himself, brings us to a spot *behind* the veil, into the ambiguously flavored condition of *insight.* Now, that's a romance.

My dad first took me to *the fatherland,* to the ragged, fierce, melancholy coast of Maine, six months before *all this,* before the Merry Xmas that I've described. I was in my mid-twenties. I had never been. The junket was billed as genealogical, but I couldn't have cared less. I had little money, no plans to travel, no ideas about travel, no real ideas at all. I'd flop in the corner or play tennis at the country club. Either way. I was happy to get back to the land if there was a car stereo involved, the possibility of a motel bed, preferably with *Magic Fingers,* at end of day. Some drinks. In the meantime, the hardscrabble dirt where my ancestors had farmed, the estuaries where they had fished, the homely churches where they had prayed, sure. Give me the moose striding across the coastal roads, slaying the local convertibles. Give me the empty roadside stand with its promise of lobster rolls, its New England clam chowder; give me the islands of the bay.

It rained the entire week.

We shivered in one locale after another, in front of all the houses of my forebears, evergreens our cover, of the phylum Pinophyta, those trees that survived merely to spite the shore and its brutalities, those trees that seemed to cackle at the difficulties of the landscape. We drove on county roads, in and out of the fog, over frost heaves and through mud puddles, and in front of us there was always a pair of guys with crewcuts in an old brown pickup with a shotgun rack — in Ocean Point, in Warren, in Waldoboro. They drove five miles per hour *slower* than the speed limit, in order to see if we would pass, thereby to consign us to their system of classifications. We were from *away*. My father had a long-standing need to try to find a party or parties on whom he might blame the rain. He assigned responsibility in all weather-related cases, wherever weather inhibited his progress, especially on important weekends, family gatherings; someone must have been the *rainmaker,* someone must have caused it. And the culprit was often me. Concealed in this effort was a sense of his guilt with respect to precipitation, I'm guessing, or a sense that he ought to have been able to fix the rain, or a feeling that the weather was constantly *against us,* though clearly by giving it so much attention he only amplified its menace. Still, the citizens of Friendship, Maine (my father and I had each read the Ben Ames Williams stories, collected in *Fraternity Village,* and so we wanted to see the place where these stories were set), hailed us just the same, mentioning in passing that the weather wasn't *too darned good.* You couldn't see more than twenty yards in any direction! Later, in Lamoine, just past Bar Harbor, we actually narrowly escaped *driving into the Atlantic Ocean.* The road abruptly ended, a coastal road, and we hadn't noticed until the waves were breaking against the whitewalls. Perhaps this is to tell the story in the local style. Yet the gauze of so much fog and rain was appropriate for acts of memory, for my father's mnemonic reveries. This was what it looked like when Haynes Huzzy and Big Red and the other reprobates of his summers in Ocean Point crept up through the accretion of contemporary distraction. They were striding through heavy fog, with their tennis rackets, wool sweaters, jackknives, fly-fishing gear, to compromise the morals of one another. The house my father was born in, in Waterville, the ramshackle farm my grandmother's family had owned in Millbridge, a pestilence of blackflies, steamers out on the harbor at low tide, everywhere in these Maine scenes disrepair, enclosures of fog, as if it were a function of Maine that it existed *only* in memory.

That first trip back to *the fatherland* culminated on the island of Vinalhaven, in Penobscot Bay, after a ferry trip of an hour or so, during which we had our one ephemeral glimpse of blue sky, a glimpse that did not last. On the far side, we docked in a genuine fishing village, amid a scaffolding of slips and pilings, homely powerboats, cottages on the hill. We were in the drizzle again, among locals, men and women of few words. They trudged past us in mackintoshes, and we stood in a small dirt parking lot, where an ancient station wagon with a soon-to-be-missing tailpipe served as the island's only taxi. We had no idea where we were staying. We were operating on the assumption that we were to be met by the hosts from the wedding party for which my father had come, but this host never materialized. Instead, we came after much waiting to the Tidewater Motel of Vinalhaven, where a laconic front-desk attendant remarked, *Foggy enough?* The Tidewater Motel was a hundred paces from the ferry dock, and as advertised, the ebb and flow of the coastline's tidal activity occurred directly under the Tidewater, directly under *my room,* like an auditory hallucination. Back and forth, every six hours. Meanwhile, my father had located the address of the rehearsal dinner — in a town of this size, everyone knew — at a nearby restaurant, and while he went to the rehearsal dinner, I looked for a convenience store, or a grocery store, or a package store, anyplace where distilled beverages might be obtained. Nothing doing. Finally I asked at the video merchandiser and was told that the island was *dry.* No liquor store anywhere. I'd never heard of such a thing, or rather I'd heard of it in southern counties, but not here in the pragmatic northeast, where men drank and that was that. So a night of mild detoxification was added to bad weather, to days spent in the car, to the rush of the tidal pools filling with their salty Atlantic overspill. The sound of the ocean was an intolerable din. I watched network news. There was a series of foghorns competing in the bay, each signaling the problem brewing in me. I woke without the shakes but irritable and impatient. Next day, after the clambake, we made off for Portland, for civilization, for home, for drinks. So much for *fatherland.*

All this had changed by 1998, in pursuit of lineage, in pursuit of Handkerchief Moody, my ancestor. There would be *research,* the taking of notes, the consultation of locals, though this was always a hurdle since I'm uncomfortable with strangers. Nonetheless, I met my father in Boston, in Back Bay, on Mass. Ave., where he was parked in his Jaguar, having conducted business downtown during the week. His Jaguar, a four-door in a champagne hue, was about as ostentatious a vehicle as we could possibly select for the trip. It was a complete embarrassment to me. My father had a Jaguar in college, had used some of his money from his employment at Moody Motor Sales, Inc., for the purposes of buying a Jaguar, and there was an obsession with cars in my family, so perhaps there was continuity to his current choice. As he had pointed out during the casual planning of our mission, if you had to put in a lot of driving *you might as well be comfortable.* I couldn't argue with the logic, but this was not the car that would make me comfortable. What would we look like in the towns where our agriculturalist relatives had lived, with our Jaguar rutted in a ditch in front of a mossy graveyard?

The beginning of the journey: I always make it a point to know where the state mental hospitals are. I have long been a lover of the facades of Harlem Valley Psychiatric, for example, better known as Wingdale. Coming over the lip of the hill on Route 22 and seeing those buildings, the ones with concertina wire draped around them, home for the *criminally insane,* that bygone brick architecture, it always invigorates me; it suggests that the cruelty that I imagine *secreted away under the impeccable fairways of civilization* is fact. Some people aren't suitable for our company, or so it is said, and we are willing to pay to have them stowed away, we are willing to use some minimal resources to that end, even though by and large we would prefer to save money for frivolities. In New Hampshire, where I went to boarding school, we were located near the state hospital, and our dining hall, at least the dishwashing part of it, was staffed by people who resided in that institution. In New Canaan, Connecticut, where I lived as a kid, we were next door to a celebrity psychiatric venue, where stars of popular music and wives of business moguls went to work through their collapses. I have also occasionally made charitable visits to the inpatients at the detoxes of Bellevue, which has the best and most ominous facade of any psychiatric hospital. All this to say that I happened to know that Danvers, Massachusetts, was the site, in that state, of a public psychiatric facility. And as my father and I passed it, going north, this brought up my father's stories from his summer working at McLean Hospital, where, over the years, a number of writers did their time. I managed to prevail on my father for more stories; for example, the story about Horace, who said only three things: *Yes, Sure,* and *You're having a time for yourself.* These were his three remarks. Yet the day apparently arrived when Horace finally said *No.* For reasons long forgotten. The head of the ward was charged with describing each patient's conduct in periodic reports, and he described Horace that day as *negativistic.* After months, years, of the same three responses, Horace was suddenly *negativistic.* Long after Horace had reverted to his affirmations, the story was still being told.

It was the violent ward, my father's workplace, the high-security ward, and there were fewer effective treatments then for psychosis, so one of my father's responsibilities was to secure the psychotics for *electroconvulsive therapy.* He strapped them down and then, after, helped them back to their beds. I imagine Horace might have said *No* when faced with the option of shock therapy or another treatment of that period: lobotomy. Dad said he *didn't have as much sympathy for the men of the violent ward as he needed to have,* the catatonics, the schizophrenics, the hebephrenics. And this was why he never became a psychologist, as he had thought to do. Instead, he went on to sell investment strategies.

Danvers was just an exit, signage on the interstate, but not without symbolic importance as a starting point on a trip in search of a guy who elected to wear a veil in public for much of his adult life. Next, on the interstate, was Exeter, New Hampshire, home of Clement Moody, of the Exeter line of Moodys, born in the second half of the seventeenth century or thereabouts, *parents unknown.* Also the home of William Moody, son of Caleb, brother of the Reverend Samuel Moody, and uncle, apparently, of one Joseph "Handkerchief" Moody. Exeter was at the time of their habitation, the later seventeenth century, only recently governing itself, only recently out from under the jurisdiction of the Massachusetts Bay Colony, which had engulfed its neighbors during the English Civil War, while imperial attention was elsewhere. *Though the population of the town must have been about three hundred, the number of qualified voters at the first election was but twenty; there being in the entire province only two hundred and nine,* according to Charles H. Bell, the official Exeter historian. This is why the conjunction of two Moodys in such a location at such a time is unlikely unless they were somehow kin.

One source gives the following about Clement Moody:

> It is supposed after years of investigation that Clement was a new immigrant from the Isle of Jersey in England. He settled in Exeter, NH, and was known as a member of the Jerseyman Colony there. . . . He was born in 1661, he had a brother, Nicholas, who witnessed an official document in Exeter on 6/20/1679. Clement was in the French and Indian War in 1712, a member of Capt. James Davis's Company of Exeter. Clement's first wife was Sarah Clark. . . . He was an inquest juryman in Exeter in 1696 and the member of a scouting party that same year. . . . In 1729, he left a widow, Alice.

Elsewhere, the *Genealogical Dictionary of Maine and New Hampshire* has Clement born in Exeter in 1692, *possibly a Jerseyman,* not much else. No record of his immigration exists; his name is not on any passenger list from the period. About William Moody of Exeter, on the other hand, there is the following unfortunate information: *Twice taken by Indians in 1709 and supposed to have been roasted to death.*

Here's a more complete account:

> In 1709, on the sixth of May, William Moody, Samuel Stevens, and two sons of Jeremiah Gilman . . . were surprised by Indians at the Pickpocket Mill in Exeter, and carried away as prisoners. Moody was taken to Canada, and while his captors were traversing French river with him in canoes, a few days later, they were attacked by a party of English. . . . Several Indians were killed, and Moody was left alone with one savage in a canoe. The English encouraged him to despatch the Indian, which he attempted, but in the struggle the

canoe was overset, and Moody swam to the shore. Two
or three of the English ran down to the bank and helped
him to land, but a number of the enemy attacked them,
and Moody unhappily yielded himself again to the savages, who afterwards put him to cruel torture, roasted
him alive at the stake, and devoured his flesh.

There were occasional attacks by Indians, of course, throughout
the region, as there were wherever we were busy *dislodging them,* so
that every town history is fated to display the ramifications of colonial conflict: *Timothy Cunningham, as he was traveling from Hilton's
garrison to the Village of Exeter, was shot down by a party of Indians. He
was a shop keeper in Boston, and left a wife and four children, and a
respectable property there.* The natives who lived on the land that the
colonists seized are implicit in any history of the region, *never forgotten;* where a stake is being driven in the woods, a party of natives is
being relocated inland, where a church is being raised up, the wor-
shipping habit of natives is being profaned; *savages* being the pre-
ferred endearment for these local residents in most accounts of the
Puritans. Or, on occasion, *heathens: They were wont to be the most cruelest
and treacherousest people in all these parts.* War against them was appropriate and justifiable: *It is lawful by war to defend what we have
lawfully obtained and come by, as our possessions, lands and inheritance
here, to which we have as far a title as any ever had, since Israel's title to
Canaan.* As the minister Joshua Moodey (William Moody's great
uncle) says in "Souldiery Spiritualized," *A Christian must be a Souldier.
That which I mean by it is that there is a great Harmony, Likeness, or
Similitude between the work of a souldier and that of a Christian.* Clement
Moody, the son of the initial Clement Moody of Exeter, went on to
serve in Exeter's regiment during the siege at Louisburg (of 1745),
also devoted to *vanquishing the savages* (and their allies, the French),
and Samuel Moody, father of Handkerchief Moody, was chaplain of
that very Exeter regiment. Can it be but that the ghosts of all this
slaughter were heavy on the fire-and-brimstone consciences of old
New England?

My father and I stopped in the town of Exeter just to see if we
could get a look at the local historical society. After, we made a quick

tramp around the campus of the Phillips Exeter Academy, a boarding school, which happened to be my father's alma mater. Exeter,
where the students were *treated more like men, and less like children.*
They were taught that in their conduct they were to be governed by the
unwritten code of propriety and honor which is recognized as the fundamental
principle of every moral and enlightened community. Exeter, where my
father went, and where my brother managed two years before trans-
ferring after a bad spring of mononucleosis and failing grades. My
father's stories of Exeter also feature grave illness (he and a friend
were referred to as the *Tubercular Twins*) and appalling marks. Dad
arrived at Exeter having been educated publicly, or mostly publicly,
and he was surrounded by an aristocracy from the private schools of
New York, Philadelphia, Boston, etc. He was, he claims, one of the
worst students of Latin the school had ever known. I imagine my
brother working through this gauntlet of difficulties in his own history, coming home (I remember him that summer, wan, silent) in
the fullness of *his* inheritance.

In 1973, my mother and father and I drove together to Exeter to
see about my applying there (I was two school years ahead of my
brother, and so I was first). This would not have seemed unusual to
the admissions people there, a nuclear family in its usual configura-
tion, except that my parents had been divorced three years earlier
and were not on particularly good terms. It probably added a layer of
discomfort to the visit that was perceptible in an interview setting. *Is*
he going to say something horrible? I wondered about my father. *Is she*
going to have that pinched, melancholy expression? Is this particular sentence
coming out my mouth incredibly stupid? Are they going to argue about it
later? Having my mother and father in the same room, anytime, was
disconcerting for me, for me and my brother and sister. One night,
after their divorce, when my mother and father threatened to take us
out to dinner, my brother and I walked out of the house and kept
going. Where? We didn't know, we just walked, out on the main
roads at dusk, on a Friday. It was a wet day in spring when the leaves
had just emerged from their buds. Caterpillars, on pendants, swayed
above us. We spent most of our adventure *looking behind* for familiar
cars, for the navy blue of an imported sedan, the green of a multiply
dented station wagon. What protest we imagined we were making is

impossible to reconstruct, and my brother and I didn't discuss it, we just walked, alongside cherry blossoms and dogwoods; our rage, which had been so motivational when we strode out of my mother's house, began to dissipate, until it was more sepia toned, more like regret. My father pulled up, somewhere near the border of Darien, and shouted, *Get in the car!*

One of my psychosomatic complaints from those junior high school years, the time of this boyhood visit to Exeter, involved a constant need *to swipe at the corners of my eyes,* how else to say it, as though I were afflicted with some occluding agent, some flyspeck, at which point, after I had been rubbing and scratching at the corners of my eyes trying to eliminate this imaginary object, it really did feel as though there was something *in there,* the skin was raw, there was hyperemia, such that I would have to busy myself further, abrading and scouring. It was probably as exhausting to watch as it was to undertake. This odd compulsion prompted constant remark from my parents: *What's wrong with your eyes? Is something wrong with your eyes? Why don't you stop that?* Of course, where the events themselves were strenuous, as they were during a boarding-school admissions interview, with the Exeter alumnus on the other side of the desk smiling a discerning smile, I was even more likely to embark on a round of my eccentric habit. At Exeter the practice reached a dramatic zenith. Even the interviewer got involved: *Is there something in your eye? Do you need a moment to compose yourself?* Would a moment repair the detonated nuclear family that was so apparent to me then? Furthermore, I was in a logical bind here, because if I agreed that there *was* something in my eye, then that difficulty itself would need to be treated (we would have to go find eyedrops, or we would have to position ourselves under a lamp, as the admissions guy and my father and mother angled around me, probing with their thumbs at the whites of my eyes), but if I admitted that *there was nothing in my eye,* then *why was I rubbing my eye constantly?* Either possibility subjected me to a scrutiny that I didn't want. So much so that my eyes really started to bother me all over again. And I began rubbing them again.

I didn't end up attending Phillips Exeter Academy.

Of his years at Exeter, my brother remembers best, besides academic probation, *the crater,* a purported unidentified flying object crash site out in the woods. It had been a sleek saucer-shaped Thing. Or *it was as big as or bigger than a house,* or *it had no motor and came through the air like a leaf falling from a tree,* or it was a *giant lens-shaped flying object,* or it was *shaped like a dinner plate,* all these descriptions according to eyewitnesses in John G. Fuller's landmark investigation from 1965, *The Exeter Incident.* Fuller's hard-boiled column inches are perfect for a narrative about the collision of old New England with crackpot science:

> Autumn here is brilliant; it hurts the eyes. You approach the town from the east through a colonnade of burnt orange and russet maples, past the Old Harrison House on Water Street, a historical relic of the eighteenth century. . . . Just past the Academy is the Exeter Inn, a sleepy and docile hostelry, and haven for elderly gentility as well as for well-heeled parents when they come to visit their sons at school. . . . The townspeople are either of sturdy Yankee yeoman stock, varied racial groups who settled in Exeter during the Industrial Revolution, or the academic cluster at Phillips Academy.

Further, *The Exeter Incident* brings workmanlike prose to a discussion of the Thing, and its elaborate and reliable appearances over town in the middle sixties, in a way that must have been incredibly satisfying to the potheads and stargazers of my brother's acquaintance a decade later. Here's an alleged incident from a heavily populated part of Exeter, as Fuller describes:

> At approximately 2:30 in the morning, sometime in September of 1965 . . . Mrs. Mazalewski was awakened by a brilliant light illuminating her first-floor bedroom. At the same time, she heard a loud humming noise, which startled her. Her husband, asleep in another

room, was not aware of it at this time. She sat up and was able to see out the window from her bed. A large cluster of different-colored lights approximately 20 feet away from her bedroom window were blinking in indefinite patterns.

The Thing then landed, or had already landed, in Mrs. Mazalewski's backyard, by a *now leafless tree,* as Fuller puts it. Here's another account from patrolman Bertrand of the Exeter police force, as reconstructed by the author:

> It hovered there, 100 feet above the field, for several minutes. Still no noise, except for the horses and dogs. Then, slowly, it began to move away, Eastward, toward Hampton. Its movement was erratic, defying all conventional aerodynamic patterns. "It darted," says Bertrand. "It could turn on a dime. Then it would slow down."

Soon the accounts develop into a *constant, steady flow,* with people even parking at the edge of a certain field with coffee and doughnuts, waiting for the Thing to make its appearance. Finally, even Fuller himself is treated to a display: *I looked and saw a reddish-orange disk, about one-fifth the size of a full moon. It was about three or four plane lengths in front of {a} jet, which appeared to be a fighter. The plane was moving as if in hot pursuit. The disk was perfectly round, dull orange, more than red. It was luminous, glowing, incandescent.*

In the years since Fuller's sensational account, debunkers have had their way with the Exeter stories; the current conclusion seems to be *weather balloon,* and if so, it would be hard to imagine any actual landing crater in town. Nevertheless, the crater was a place of local renown; when my brother lived in Exeter, everyone went to the crater to get high. The crater afforded a conjunction of woods and technofuturistic mythology, the sort of arrangement of things that always *augments a buzz.* And once when my brother was there, he remembers, inexplicably, there was a *Scottish kid, out there in the woods, at the crater, playing bagpipes.*

The Exeter, New Hampshire, of Clement Moody, the Exeter of my father, my brother, my own Exeter, didn't seem to have much to do with the sleepy town we drove through, with its humdrum strip, its Wendy's, its Burger King. Just another New England locale with a colorful history in which only certain bifocals-wearing women with time on their hands were interested. The same was true of Portsmouth, New Hampshire, next spot on the map, except that my sister had lived there for a time. Well, Betty and Barney Hill of Portsmouth also claimed to have been pursued one evening *by the Thing*, or some similar Thing (it looked like *a huge pancake*), after which they both experienced two hours of amnesia, during a possible *abduction* by the crew of the unidentified flying object: *Always the same curtain of darkness for Barney after the critical moment at Indian Head. Always the blind veil for Betty after the strange series of beeps as they drove frantically away from Indian Head, with Barney, apparently in great emotional distress, at the wheel.* Portsmouth has its share of stores specializing in crystals and herbology and hemp products, its share of countercultural searchers, and maybe that's all I need to say about it, except that the place name *Portsmouth* invites morbid thinking, partly in the imagining of Handkerchief and his travails, partly in my sister's story, *for here she is in Portsmouth, onetime resident thereof, with her husband, and their house on the water, and their promise of children.* A better, simpler, more innocent Portsmouth than the one I drove through. After you passed through the nineteenth-century brick of downtown, you ascended over the homely girder bridge of Portsmouth, over the Piscataqua River, in light traffic, to find yourself in Kittery, State of Maine. The honky-tonk, the lobster traps, the fishing boats, the shacks on the inland roads; my grandfather saying, *I'd like to go Down East and see Maine one more time before I die,* my sister's death, onward onto the bridge, into the legends of Handkerchief, where he strode, dismally, among derisive townsfolk.

Perfect midsummer, bright sunshine surfing on the crests of the river, a ferryboat coming in where the drawbridge had just been raised, the traffic brought to a standstill. Out into the water bordering New Hampshire, as you crossed the bridge, you could make out the islands, the beginnings of those coastal islands, as if the State of Maine were a layer cake, partly consumed, and these were the crumbs trailing behind it. In particular, here were the Isles of Shoals, mainly uninhabited these days. Hawthorne visited in the 1850s, according to the last of the natives, Oscar Laighton, who wrote of these events ninety years later:

> Nathaniel Hawthorne came to visit us, bringing a letter of introduction from General Franklin Pierce. Mr. Hawthorne was greatly interested in our islands. I sailed with him to White Island Light and Star Island in my whaleboat. . . . He mentioned me in his *American Notes*. Mr. Hawthorne would pass the evenings with the Thaxters.

Laighton's book, *Ninety Years at the Isles of Shoals,* is, in fact, a midsummer night's dream of a book, riddled with idylls like, *Our island was a paradise for young lovers. There was delight and romance in the very air, in the sparkle of water and magic of the star-lit nights. Hardly a summer passed without an engagement, and one season there were five.* Apparently this destination was once packed with tourists: *Our islands, far at sea, held unusual attraction for visitors from the busy cities of the mainland. The bracing air came over miles of water, pure and invigorating, and there was perfect quiet, except for the murmur of the ocean about the shore, or the darling shout of the song sparrow.* Physicians also found the archipelago helpful for nervous disorders.

Not surprisingly, however, Hawthorne's account of the islands frequently dwells upon darker material:

> After dinner some of the gentlemen crossed over to Gosport, where we visited the old graveyard. [The graves] were of red free-stone, lying horizontally on piles of the granite fragments, such as are scattered all about. There were other graves, marked by the rudest shapes of stones at head and foot. And so many stones protruded from the ground, that it was wonderful how space and depth of soil enough was found between them to cover the dead.

This account, and a subsequent sequence, which finds Hawthorne in the company of a *drunken town clerk* of Star Island, leads directly to an extraordinary moment in the notebooks:

> He [the town clerk] led us down to the shore of the island, towards the East, and showed us Betty Moody's Hole. This Betty Moody was a woman of the island, in old times; the Indians came off on a depredating excursion, and she fled from them with a child (or children) and hid herself in this hole, which is formed by several great rocks being lodged so as to cover one of the fissures, common along these shores. I crept into the hole, which is somewhat difficult of access, long, low, narrow, and might well enough be a hiding-place. The child, or children, began to cry; and Betty, fearful of discovery, murdered them, to save herself. Joe Caswell did not tell that latter part of this story; but Mr. Thaxter did.

Oscar Laighton's version differs, as others have noted:

> I have often heard a story of a widow, named Betty Moody, who lived with her three small children near the Cove at Star Island. Her husband had left her the house, a good sized fish shed, a cow and a few hens. . . . Sometime before George Washington was born, there was a tribe of Indians camped on Breakfast Hill, in Rye, New Hampshire. These Indians, looking across towards the Isles of Shoals one still morning in September, decided to make a raid on the islands. Launching their canoes at Wallis Sands, they sped out to the Shoals, eight miles away. They were seen by the islanders, who rushed for safety into the fort — all but Betty, who was delayed in hunting up her children. The Indians were landing in the Cove, and Betty, seeing that she could not reach the fort, hid with her children in a cave on the other side of the island. While the Indians were

hunting for her near at hand, Betty's youngest child began to cry, and poor Betty held her hand over the child's mouth so long that it was smothered before she realized her terrible misfortune. The Islanders commenced to fire on the Indians with their cannon, and the savages were finally driven off. Betty Moody's Cave can still be seen on Star Island. If you will visit us this summer I shall be very proud to show it to you.

Hawthorne's account is the work of a gothic romancer, in that the possibility exists that Betty, *fearful of discovery,* commits a murder, as opposed to a manslaughter, simply to avoid detection. His Betty Moody puts her own escape above the lives of her progeny. Laighton's Betty is an accidental killer. I like some of the warmth of Laighton's version (*All but Betty, who was delayed in hunting up her children*); how he can't restrain himself from advertising his tour business at the bottom of the paragraph. Hawthorne, the thanatologist, of course, has to get down into the cave himself (*I crept into the hole, which is somewhat difficult of access, long, low, narrow, and might well enough be a hiding-place*), and this paradoxically proves his mettle as a realistic writer — as one who needs to know how plausible the story is — and also suggests his identification with Betty Moody herself. He wants to get into her spot in the tale, and the way his recitation is worded supports such an interpretation, because right after Hawthorne descends into the cave, the tragedy resumes (*The child, or children, began to cry; and Betty, fearful of discovery, murdered them, to save herself*), hastening to its unhappy conclusion. By the time of his trip to Star Island, it's worth remembering, Hawthorne already had two children — Una, born in 1844, and Julian, in 1846. It may be that his domestic situation, and its attendant fiscal woes, engendered in him some complicated feelings about fatherhood. Of course, this is the author who had already written, in 1835, an entire story based on another Moody, Joseph Moody, whose domain lay no more than twenty miles from where Betty had descended into her dark afterlife of conscience. Another murderous Moody whose tale the author had renovated to suit his own needs. Is it possible to avoid the surmise that Hawthorne apparently had dark suspicions about the Moodys, found in them a singular collection of murderers, eccentrics, mesmerists, enough so that he was willing to engage in his own pilferage, looting, sacking, to get at their veiled truths? These were my thoughts as my father steered his *champagne Jaguar* over the river from Portsmouth to Kittery, and we headed up the interstate, bent upon York itself, to walk in the very footsteps of Handkerchief Moody, having crossed a bridge of ghosts.

MR. HOOPER, FACE TO FACE
WITH HIS CONGREGATION,
EXCEPT FOR THE BLACK VEIL . . .

Back when I was working in the canyons of the city, back when I knew my time professionally speaking was not going to last, when I was living in Hoboken, by myself, spending more money than I could afford to take the ferry each day from New Jersey into the Battery Park area, because it was ennobling, because I loved to stand at the rail watching the way the skyscrapers of lower Manhattan moved in space, because I loved the relationship between the digits of the World Trade Center, because I loved the ribbons of stilled vehicles around the lower part of the island, because I loved businesswomen in freshly pressed suits and nylons and sneakers, because I loved listening, at a volume that resulted in hearing loss, to the Ramones on my *portable cassette player*, because I loved these minutes of absurd beauty before getting to the office and the discomfort of working for a guy who was contemptuous of me, *back then, I happened one day to take a certain literary agent to lunch*; by reason of shyness I found the prospect of this lunch difficult. I disliked all lunches and all pleasantries. Yet among my other professional disabilities, I had been told that I didn't use my expense account enough, and so I called a few *literary representatives* and took them to lunch, and I worked hard at making conversation, though such conversation wasn't very productive, as I wouldn't be acquiring for my firm any of the clients of these hardworking and ambitious *literary representatives;* my termination was assured in the not-too-distant future. Nevertheless, I liked cheap restaurants around Union Square, dives where I wouldn't have to overhear the bonhomie of powerful editorial personnel who, like the remaining individuals of an endangered species, lurched exotically from the buildings around the park into four-star joints for drinks and broiled fish. On the day in question, I was taking out a literary agent of my own vintage, a young-and-hungry type, whom I had met at the salons of a certain quarterly periodical noted for its parties and benevolence toward people like me. She was very kind, this particular agent, as well as generous, skeptical, and competitive in a way that boded well for her own career. And I was worthless to her, though I felt that way about many people, that I wasn't worth much to them. That evening I would be going home to a manuscript of my own that had gone unpublished for more than a year, and to the certainty that I would soon be fired. A correct belief, as it turned out.

The conversation with Sally the agent limped along, it's fair to say. No fault of hers. Accomplishment in the small, demoralized world of books was more avoidance of failure than success, it seemed to me, and the desperation of all involved derived from this point: how rare, how singular, an avoidance of failure in the marsh where we plied our trade. He who avoided failure, for an interval, was indeed the last of that species to be plucked from creation when his rainforest was clear-cut. I didn't pay enough attention to the conversation until somehow we were doing brief digests of our autobiographies. *Hey,* Sally said, *my mother's family had some Moodys in it. My mother still goes up to the homestead sometimes. In Maine.* I said something about how many Moodys there apparently had been in Maine, Moodys as numberless as weeds, like my father's cousin Linwood, he lived up there, probably, or his kids did, or how about old Levi Moody or Zephediah Moody or Scribner Moody? There was Moody Beach, I pointed out, Moody Mountain, Moody River. Sally nodded good-naturedly. Lots of Moodys. Then she said, as I reconstruct it now, *We're related to this crazy minister in York who apparently wore a handkerchief, across his face, because of some misdeed or other.*

There was, on my side of the cramped lunch table, a stunned silence.

The conversation had reached an important turning point. Maybe I seized her wrist. *Oh, isn't that interesting, Handkerchief Moody, yeah, my grandfather used to talk about him.* In any case, before long the story was tumbling out on my side, how Handkerchief Moody had been in my family the object of much lore and conjecture, etc.; I warmed to the telling, I began embellishing, I couldn't keep my mouth shut, though I didn't have very much substantiation for my embellishments. I was making it up. Then Sally trumped the entire display by delivering the following memorable interrogative: *Do you have a copy of the diaries?* The implication was immense. *Diaries?* I wasn't even sure, really, that my grandfather had not himself contrived the entire Handkerchief business, had not somehow snuck a footnote into all modern editions of Hawthorne's tales in order to impress his grandchildren. Diaries? Actual composition by Handkerchief? Sally admitted that her mother and her grandmother didn't talk very much about this particular Moody at all; they were a little embarrassed by him, and in fact Sally was, unless I missed my guess, a little embarrassed too, or maybe bored, but the more impressed I became at the unfurling of details about the diaries, the more she seemed amused by my contortions of delight. *They were in Latin. I think, or maybe they were in code or something, I can't remember exactly, but I think my mother might have a copy. I'll let you know.* I had no business card to offer her. But I made sure to get hers, and then I went back to my grimy, roach-infested office, where I had failed to turn in certain flap copy, or I had turned in substandard flap copy (I had used *brilliant* too often), and instead of correcting my flap copy I telephoned everyone in my family: *There are diaries!*

They arrived in the mail, not long after, in a softcover edition, probably one of fifty or a hundred copies. Self-published with introduction and notes. They were *translated,* but not because they were in Latin or in code. Rather, they were in Latin *and* in code, a code that apparently hadn't been very difficult to break. The translator and editor, I learned, was in his nineties and was evidently passionate about the subject: *For the more than merely respectable stature that his own people accorded {Moody}, their descendants and successors have substituted a misguided historic freak worth to them hardly more than a semi-derisive smile and a byword. This was not the "fame" which, without aiming for it, he so justly earned in his own day, and so grievously paid for.* This particular editorial project, I realized, was a labor of love. It was a rectification of perceived slights against Handkerchief Moody. A recalibration of the historical record. My father, for whom I copied a set, plunged into the diaries immediately and announced that they were mostly about *weather and masturbation,* and this did seem to be a valid first impression:

> *Sab. 9 {July 1721} Rainy, misty.*
> *Last night I lodged with Stephen Hews. In my sleep I defiled myself. Restricted in public and brief. Sam Emery kept me company for seven miles. I reached home in the twilight. I saw Kingsbury's vessel, which, yesterday, fully laden, had been cast upon the beach.*

Or:

> *Sab. 19 {February 1721}*
> *Dull, Galatians 3:32. But in some degree uplifted in the Society. Black and Edward prayed here excellently. A Brother and I went up together and I prayed in the fields with him. Enlarged, although restricted at first. I was defiled twice this night in my sleep.*

Or:

> *Mon. 28 {January 1723}*
> *Mr. Starret was here and had breakfast before I got up. The better pupils learned 25 verses. — Although awake, I defiled myself.*

Here's a two-day stretch from November 1722:

> *Tues. 27 Warm. Fresh S. p.m., thick*
> *I saw the beginning and the end of the eclipse. It was dark in the middle (of it). I had supper with Elder Parsons, who is bearing the death of his son in a most Christian manner. I went to bed very late, and half awake, I defiled myself.*

Wed. 28 Seldom saw the sun
Mr. White talked with me about the state of my soul and
prayed with me. We called on Captain Allen. I sat quietly
with my beloved. Certain people were here at midnight. I
defiled myself.

There were fifteen hundred entries in the extant diaries of Handkerchief, ranging over a period of four years, and not much, at first
glance, beyond weather and self-abuse. And so my father failed to
finish the diaries, initially. Likely, he did little more than skim them.
I didn't do significantly better. I stuck my copy of the diaries in a box
with a bunch of my grandfather's spotty genealogical documenta-
tions, and I went back to getting fired, and to riding the ferryboat at
dawn and dusk.

Yet as I began to awake, much later, to the understanding that I
was going to *pursue* Handkerchief, that indeed I had been driven to
do so and that much of my life had narrowed toward this particular
theme, the diaries were again on my mind, as was Handkerchief's
relation, Sally the agent, *whose family still owned Handkerchief's son's*
farm in York, Maine. Sally, in our subsequent phone calls, offered to
loan me the keys to the ancestral homestead. The premises had been
robbed several times, were depleted of antiques, were noteworthy
more for memorabilia of Sally's family these days than for anything
relating to Handkerchief's son's tenure there, or so she told me. Most
of this memorabilia dated from the period when the road to York
Beach and Cape Neddick went right past the front door, with a heavy
volume of sightseers, with people from *away,* recreational vehicles,
fishing boats in tow. This was a past not long past, and mostly without the flavor of the Puritans and their difficult garrisoned lives
among *savages.*

When my father and I arrived in York, therefore, on our second
trip to Maine (begun above), we had a crumpled piece of heavy white
bond with the directions to the Moody Farm of Ridge Road, York,
and a set of keys, and we made the turn off of the interstate, onto
Maine's gridlocked Route One, from there onto the back roads of
York. It wasn't hard to find. The farm was right out on the route to

the beach, as advertised, with ten or twelve acres, mostly overgrown, on both sides of the thoroughfare, through which we came to one of those colonials fashioned of clapboard, freshly white, in which the carriage house and a smokehouse had been added on or remodeled or adjoined until the structure had assumed a casual shape. It rambled. It was like the oldest oak in the arbor, long giving of shade, that had upstretched boughs in competition with its neighbors, and had out-lasted them all. I was nervous, upon attempting to fit the key into the front lock, because the house belonged to this more established branch of Moodys.

I had no right, and yet I made the key work just the same. We were inside.

The bouquet of the centuries. There's a specific science involved in that musty *parfum,* some carbon molecule, but I don't think it's so much a compound, an agent of decomposition, as it is recognition of what creation is, bacteria, termites and moist lumber, mildew, apples, ancient towels, chowders, wet dogs on the carpets, the spit-up of brats; all this variety of things is the material of time and memory in elderly houses, more so than Pine-Sol or lemon oil on chamois rags. Rankness and decay have *life* as their unuttered nickname. We worked our way around the interior, with its warpage, with its mat-tresses of straw, its crumbling masonry. But so much of the interven-ing years had been repainted over the plastering of Handkerchief's son that we couldn't make it out, even in the poster beds or the old wickers. We tried the outdoors, plodded across the property from one corner to another, back to a stream meandering in the forest, to the fields that had been mown down once in spring and now would be left to seed. Then we started back through the house again, this time locating the door, hitherto concealed, that led to the root cel-lar and to the smokehouse. Inside, there was an old sign propped against the wall, *1690–1790, Home of Joseph Moody, Son of Handkerchief Moody,* hand-lettered. This was a section of the house given over to *shorter people,* to those attempting to heat with woodstoves. It was un-heated, therefore, unwired, and it was now connected to the carriage house, in modern parlance *to the garage.* Down into the narrow root cellar, the refrigerating unit, just as it was in Handkerchief's time.

I felt like Hawthorne attempting to fit himself into Betty Moody's cave, *where the killing was done.* The root cellar's floor was of dirt, was cool and neglected in contrast to the narrow, blackened walls of the attic upstairs, the smokehouse.

As Sally's grandmother had been the last full-time resident, the Moody house was marked by the afterimage of her presence, and by baby books and spy thrillers, some tennis balls rolled into corners — the property of retrievers — and yet the mattresses were from a time before bedsprings. And the old brick oven still existed, though its mouth was crowded with a potbelly stove. It was a house emptied of its inhabitants, finally, and the enumeration of architectural details — a dormer here, a gable there — did nothing to convey what was or was not still apparent in Handkerchief's son's residence, the Moody Farm of Ridge Road, and it was only later, in confronting the diaries and their biographical material, that I knew what was missing:

> Moody's internal disquietude, without much doubt as active as it had been during the early days of the Diary, was not in any way relieved by a tragic event of 1736. In mid-February he lost both his wife Lucy, who died in childbirth, and their new-born child, also named Lucy. Moody was thus left with four children, Samuel, ten, Joseph, seven, Hannah, five, and Thomas, three. There are no records to keep matters straight, but this loss, sad as it was, would not seem to necessitate the breaking up of a family.

Yet within a couple of years, the editor of the diaries goes on, this very breaking up took place: *The ultimate date for the removal of the children was 1740 or 1741, for in 1741 the Moody house was empty. Whatever the precise dates, Joseph Moody needed sanctuary, the children better guardianship.* With the following result:

> As to where the children found homes, inferences can be drawn only from the tenor of their lives. The oldest, Samuel, aged 12, probably went to his grandfather's in

the village. He was prepared for Harvard, entered there in 1742, and was graduated in 1746. At thirty-seven he was made Preceptor of Dummer Academy in Byfield. Joseph, aged 9, must have gone to a farm, since he grew up as a farmer, and during his older brother's tenure at Dummer Academy, managed the farm which partly supported the school.

And so forth. It occurred to me at last that we had been looking at the home of an orphan, since Joseph *fils* never again went to live with his afflicted father. The house established, if nothing else, a credible legacy of upstanding domesticity. A home for he who was without a home. A house that would pass through generations unperturbed, if possible, by the remorse and morbid thinking that had resulted in the younger Joseph being separated from his father in the first instance. The editor of the diaries defensively argues that *this arrangement has traditionally prompted the disparaging charge against Joseph Moody that he "abandoned" his children. "Abandoned" is hardly the word to apply to a father who could not make the decision and was physically and mentally unable to care for his children properly.* Yet one wonders what the children themselves felt about it, if it did not feel like an abandonment to them. And what must Handkerchief Moody have thought about it afterward? This was the sort of father who wrote of himself, *Now I have spent another year, God knows, wholly in sin, surely in the worst manner.* Or: *My heart goes astray in the worst manner from God who has shown me his kindness again and again.* Or: *I neither know, nor (horrible to say) am I very much concerned what shall be done about my miserable soul. I go on without repentance, oppressed by the unspeakable burden of the damned.*

My dad and I stayed that night in an inn overlooking the York harbor. In the dining room, there was a twentieth high school reunion reaching the peak of its mnemonic harvest. The service wasn't great, therefore, perhaps because of the scale of conviviality around us. But the view from inside the dining room was dramatic, with crags and cliffsides all about us. We were mostly concerned with housing our bags, with having a place to rest, after our journey.

That night I lay awake reading about Handkerchief's intransigent horse, who never, in all his many citations, is graced with a name:

> *Sat. 8 {September 1722}*
> *Six of us hunted for my horse and for that of Mr. Wise. I myself after vain attempts caught the former, and expressed my thanks to myself only. The horse, therefore escaped.*

> *Sat. 15 {September 1722}*
> *Captain Moulton with three soldiers and with me looked for my horse in vain. We found it, but after a long straggling chase, it escaped.*

> *Wed. 19 {September 1722}*
> *We chased my horse as far as New Town, but in vain.*

> *Fri. 21 {September 1722}*
> *Six men looked for my horse with me without success. Father made out a deed of his farm to me. I did not express thanks, wherefore in the evening Father made his displeasure manifest. In the evening, I, with ten others, found my horse.*

Elapsed time in location of the horse: *thirteen days;* total number of men (excluding Handkerchief) needed for the search: *twenty-six.* And yet the struggle with that steed is not over:

> *Sat. 13 {July 1723} Pretty Warm. Fresh S. P.M.*
> *My horse strayed out of the way.*

> *Sat. 27 {July 1723}*
> *I and others looked for my horse in vain, for it has not yet been brought back from Wells, although three of us thought we had seen it.*

> *Tues. 27 {August 1723}*
> *In the evening I crossed the river after hunting with pupils for my horse, which is bothering the neighbors.*

And so forth. (There's a fair amount of searching here for other people's cows too.) With my own father a room or two away in the hotel, the poignancy of these entries did not escape me, how in the middle of Handkerchief's first struggle with his horse, he comes into his inheritance, his deed, his primogeniture, and isn't suitably grateful. Moreover, the specter of Samuel Moody, Handkerchief's father, is everywhere upon the diaries; if Handkerchief's unquiet life is ample reason for him to haunt the bluffs of York, his father's ghost must trail just after him, dispensing advice and correction, and urging him on to greater ghostly renown. In 1721, for example, there's the following: *At noon my father grew very angry, at first, perhaps, in my absence, for a cause known only to him; for I did ask whether I should dismiss the pupils, but I cannot be charged with having been negligent.* A couple of months later: *Father was angry with me because I would not confess guilt whether I knew it was just or not.* And, next day: *My mind is still in turmoil because of the irritation of my father, and I do not honor him, as I ought in my mind.* Later, in 1724, overworked and depressed, Joseph Moody writes thus: *In the evening I asked my father whether he thought I would be able to sustain my official duties and the care of his congregation in his absence. The good man scarcely showed me any commiseration.*

If masturbation is the sole entertainment in the diaries (*I stayed up late with my love not without pleasure, but I indulged my desire too freely, and at night the semen flowed from me abundantly*), followed close upon by weather obsession and trouble with livestock, it's what's underneath — the sorrow of patrimony, the burden of filial responsibility — that is revealed when one's father is slumbering down the hall.

Next day, having established ourselves at our lodgings, we located the First Congregational Church of York, which, according to legend, had a portrait of Handkerchief Moody. No, it turned out, it was his dad, and, when we showed up at the nave of the church — a lovely, unadorned New England chapel, all in white, perched on a hill in the town square — the truth was that the painting was not Moody at all but a *dramatic reconstruction of him* by some later minister, part of America's recent fad for historical simulation. He wore a reasonable approximation of a *fire-and-brimstone expression,* this impostor, and he was gesticulating in a way that would seem to suggest ardent belief or some performance of belief, but he was a little too handsome for the job. He was a Samuel Moody for the television age, robust, self-assured. Not the sort of whom his son might say, *In the evening Father considered himself to be in the worst state of health, and said he had for a long time been weary of his life.* That they had painted a portrait of the impostor (in oils) was nicely graven, unholy, idolatrous especially, in the confines of an austere Congregational church. The ladies of the parish office had got up from their desks to show us the portrait, and later they gave us postcards. Reproductions of the reproduction.

And across the street, in the village cemetery, we found Samuel Moody's gravestone and his wife's, and even that of Handkerchief's wife, Lucy, among old stones that lined the main street. These did nothing to call attention to themselves. The plentiful traffic hastened past. And our picking through the names, our kneeling before them, went unnoticed, as if we were simply part of a dull flood of genealogists, which we were, and thus unworthy of attention, with our pens and our cameras and our notepads. Like many of the gravestones from this early colonial period, the Moody graves were fabulously ornate, with renderings of skulls at the top and much marginal carving. But it was a disappointment that we couldn't find Handkerchief in this initial attempt, though I suspected from having glimpsed a printed compendium of York graves that he was somewhere nearby. We did, however, find the stone for one Thomas Moulton, died age ten. Since I didn't yet have the details on the *victim* of Handkerchief's notorious gunplay, I proposed, pro tem, that Moulton was the victim. The dates were close, and he was from an old colonial family, one mentioned occasionally in the diaries. Some sad narrative was also connected to his going hence, as Handkerchief's time was punctuated constantly with deaths, with losses, with illnesses, with the violence of genocidal slaughter and warfare, e.g., *Tom Bragdon brought a honeycomb. Sam Grover died. Lunt dined with us. Arthur Bragdon's son died in his 10th month.* Who was there to care about it now, three hundred years later, but the genealogists with their myopia, their insect repellant, their maps of graveyards?

After a quick tour of a historical museum shop in town, a half dozen plausible Handkerchief manslaughter theories were suddenly in play. My dad, displaying an admirable morbidity, had taken up a pamphlet on "Dying, Death, and Burial in Early York," and this not only gave the name of Handkerchief's shooting victim (*Mr. Moody's son of York, a lad of 8 years old, firing off a pistol childishly, shot Capt. Preble's son, a lad of 12 years, through the temples and killed him*), but likewise summoned up the familial history of death in that time:

> As we approach the [burying] ground more closely we are able to perceive that the ornamental motifs changed over time. Perhaps the easiest way to distinguish the different motifs is to examine the gravestones of a single family line — the Moodys. In July of 1705, the Reverend Samuel Moody buried his infant daughter Lucy in the burying yard. Her gravestone bears a Death's-Head. There are also Death's-Heads engraved upon the stones of her grandmother . . . and of her mother, who died in 1728. When the Reverend Moody died in 1747, a stone bearing a Cherub was erected in his memory at the yard. Fifty years later, Samuel Moody, his grandson, was provided at his death with a stone which combined the style of the Cherub with the newer style, a Classical Urn.

It was very satisfying to find that the Moodys were a model family for an investigation of local burying customs. But, more urgently, my father and I had never before considered Handkerchief's *weapon* with much attention. If the hunting-accident version of the story that we'd heard was true, then the murder weapon would have been a musket, either a matchlock or a flintlock. For these were the hunting weapons much in use in the colonies at the time. The muskets were quite large. For example, one 1717 design, as described by Charles Winthrop Sawyer in his *Firearms in American History,* was thus: *length about 5 ft. 2½ in.; barrel about 46⅞ in.,* or probably longer than Handkerchief was tall at the age of eight or nine years. Could he have lifted such a weapon? More likely the gun was a *general-purpose flintlock pistol,* as re-created by Robert Held in *Age of Firearms,* with its *touches of gold leaf on the barrel and a little silver wire inlay on the stock*. This firearm boasted *practical features such as stout iron butt cap, rugged over-all construction, large compression-leaking but sure-fire touchhole. Thousands of these weapons gave reliable service to generations of owners*. Of course, Handkerchief would have needed to prepare the flintlock in order to fire:

> Shooter pours desired quantity of relatively course-grained propellant powder into muzzle from large main flask. Then he starts to load the patched ball, and rams it down until it is seated atop the powder firmly but without crushing grain. The charge loaded, he returns the ramrod, opens the flashpan, and half-cocks the gun. Then he primes the fine powder from his priming flask, not too much nor too little. Lastly, he snaps the pan cover shut, tilts the gun slightly to the left for a second and taps it lightly to ensure that a few grains of priming have entered the touchhole, and when ready to shoot, cocks to the full-cock.

At last, he pulls the trigger. Pretty complicated, especially if you're about to shoot your best friend accidentally. Though maybe it was part of growing up. Because of the danger of the *savages,* firearms were probably left around the garrison for emergencies. Still, it's unlikely one of these flintlocks could just *go off.*

This fresh account of the shooting made us keen to see Handkerchief's grave, and the historical society personnel, especially the excellent head librarian, whose laconic style and attention to detail (we were required to wear white gloves while reading period manuscripts) made her a memorable character in the trip, gave us the details, sent us down to the other side of York, known as Scotland for its concentration of immigrants from that region. It was here that Handkerchief, succumbing to pressure from his father, accepted a post as minister to the Second Congregational Church of York. According to directions, at the margin of a field that ran down to river's edge we found a small cemetery, no more than a dozen or so headstones, right across the street, we were told, from where Handkerchief, *having assumed the veil*, passed his last days. Here was his marker. Like that of his poor sister, lost in early childhood, Handkerchief's gravestone had the death's-head design at the top. The death's-head, from its perch at the summit of the stone, rose above the ornamented text with its fell wings.

> Here lyes interr'd ye body of ye Revnd Joseph Moody, pastor of ye 2nd church in York, an excelling instance of knowledge, ingenuity, learning, piety, virtue & usefulness, was very serviceable as a schoolmaster, clerk, register, magistrate & afterwards as a minister, was uncommonly qualified & spirited to do good & accordingly was highly esteemed & greatly beloved. He deceased March 20, 1753, aged 53 years. Altho' this stone may moulder into dust, yet Joseph Moody's name continue must.

Across the street — like many spots in York, now the site of an *antiques business* — sat the residence of Handkerchief's dotage, where, as a ward of the church, he lodged in the care of a Deacon Bragdon, a former parishioner of Handkerchief's and an acquaintance from earlier days (*Fry. 27 Snow and damp rain A.M., but few drops P.M., N.E. Not many pupils being expected, I went down through the snow and the rain. Deacon Bragdon gave me advice about the Registry. I thanked him and answered that I would not refuse*). One account of this period is found in Charles C. P. Moody's biography of Handkerchief, in his *Sketches of the Moody Family*:

> After the death of his wife, he boarded with Deacon Bragdon, who was naturally a man of hasty temper. The Deacon had been out one morning, and had had some difficulty with one of his neighbors, about bad fences and breachy cattle. He made out to keep his temper tolerably well, while conversing with his neighbor; but after he had left him, reflecting on some circumstance, *old Adam* got up to a pretty high pitch. . . . As soon as he had entered his own house in a great perturbation of

spirit, he called out to Mr. Moody, "O Mr. Moody! You must pray for my poor neighbor; he has got *terribly* out of the way." Mr. Moody replied, "And does not Deacon Bragdon need a few prayers too?"

Yet this congenial, good-natured Handkerchief doesn't square with a later account by the Reverend Jonathan Greenleaf, also quoted by Charles C. P. Moody:

> After the death of his wife, he ceased to keep house, and boarded with Deacon Bragdon. It was supposed that he always maintained secret prayer; but for many years he would not pray with others, nor hold any conversation, unless it was drawn out of him. The first time he was known to pray with others, was under very pressing circumstances. The person whose duty it was to lead the family devotions, was, from some cause, quite out of humor, and the service was likely to be neglected, when Mr. Moody, who sat there in silence, with his face covered with a handkerchief, as usual, was appealed to, whether he would suffer family prayer to be neglected, because such a person was out of temper. "Will not Mr. Moody be our mouth on this occasion?" Mr. Moody immediately kneeled down, and prayed with great fervency. From this time he caught hold of the idea of being the *mouth* of others in prayer, considering himself simply as the instrument though which the sound came. After this he spent much time in passing around the parish, entering every house, and proposing to be their mouth in prayer. He would make but very little, if any, conversation, but was praying continually. He still wore his handkerchief over his face, and kept himself secluded from the world.

At first, the proprietor of the antiques concern upon Bragdon's property, a woman of early middle age dressed in chinos, cotton blouse, and flaxen sweater vest, wasn't up to giving us a tour of Handkerchief's abode. After all, *who were we?* We sort of *showed up*. Though denied once, we came back later, and her mood, though not cheerful, had improved, and, upon her porch, she apologized for inhospitality, giving two good reasons, namely, *she had just been to receive radiation treatment for cancer,* and, secondly, *her husband, two weeks before, had left. Without a word.* What was history when faced with these troubles? History was a shelf full of moldy clothbound books; history was a callousness, an indifference. Nevertheless, she took us to the second floor, she took us to Handkerchief's bedroom, on the corner, looking south and west, looking directly upon his gravestone, upon the river beyond. The room, with its low ceilings, was fitted out with period furniture, a double bed, a dresser, a pair of wing chairs. It was plusher than when Handkerchief had lived there, yet with a puritanical austerity. While we were in her company, no matter her personal predicament, our host enumerated all the data to support the theory of a pattern of hauntings at this particular address, a haunting by Handkerchief; for example: *This friend stayed for the weekend, and he was making a sandwich one night, and sitting by the fire. He went to get more wood, down the back staircase, and told me later there was a man on the stairs, his words, a man dressed in black, his face shrouded in darkness.* While she had never had a sighting herself, she argued persuasively about the possibility of *a presence, a countenance,* and maybe this was a foregathering of her husband who had run off, or maybe it really *was* Handkerchief, who had, after a fashion, abandoned his family; thus one abandonment was like another; all of the abandonments, regardless of circumstances, having similar effects, and when we left her, we left her to these difficulties, and we got in the preposterous Jaguar and went back to the historical society, where the picture was beginning to emerge, a devastating picture, a picture of the almost total occlusion of life by sorrow and remorse.

His sister died in her childhood; at age nine he killed his best friend, *after which Father Moody made his son sit up all night with the body;* later, in attempting to live up to the reputation of his father, he took the post of minister in York, though he was happy enough as magistrate; he then lost his wife, Lucy, during childbirth, and a child, also named Lucy; thereupon, he had an attack of nerves, or a collapse, or a brain fever, could no longer preach, could no longer minister to the flock, began to wear a handkerchief in most company, unto death. . . .

> The death of Mr. Moody was sudden, and attended with some remarkable circumstances. He had in early life been a great singer, but after his indisposition he laid it whole aside; and although he recovered so far as to pray, and sometimes to talk, and even at times laid aside his handkerchief, and appeared somewhat more cheerful, yet he would not sing. At length, one day, which he spent alone in his chamber, he was heard to break forth into singing, to the great astonishment of the family. Almost the whole afternoon, he was singing, with great animation, the 17th hymn of the 1st book of Watts' Hymns: "Oh for an overcoming faith, To Cheer my dying hours," &c. He did Not come out of his chamber that night, and the next morning was found dead in his bed. Such was the end of a good man.

IF I HAD EVER ONCE BEEN HAPPY,
METHINKS I COULD CONTENTEDLY
BE SHOT TO-DAY . . .

———————————

Melancholy isn't about anything. Melancholy has a style or manner but no subject. Melancholy is a way of thinking, a way of thinking *about thinking,* and it needs to consume the sufferer and thus needs layers and strata and veneers in perpetuity in which to cloak and conceal itself. Melancholy attempts to avoid detection. Melancholy is not a preoccupation with death, nor a recoiling from shop interiors or human fellowship, nor is it a lack of interest in things of the world, though these may be characteristics of melancholy. It's more a particular complexion to thinking, a tightening, a spiraling, a funneling, a drilling, an incising, a helixing, the direction of this cogitation being always *down and in,* as when an oral surgeon begins screwing into your molar during root canal. A preoccupation with death, a recoiling from society, an anhedonia, an obsession with conscience, these follow with melancholy, and they may advertise themselves fleetingly as its true subject, but any transient theme will soon give way to something worse, something darker and meaner, something less lucid, because the goal of melancholy is its direction and force and shape. Continuity of the illness. Any meaning of melancholy is vehicular, decorative, like a viny overgrowth on the gates of the crypt where the sufferer is cast down for his or her imprisonment. *All the world is melancholy,* Burton says, *every member of it.*

Months passed after my *unexplained panic event* of Christmas Day in 1986. I lived as though the *unexplained panic event* had not occurred. I didn't speak of it much, and though I began seeing a *mental health professional* for the first time, I had little faith in his counsel, though I liked his stories; for example, his story about the man who *had a compulsion about giving blow jobs to obese preteens he met on the subway.* This tendency was adversely affecting the marriage of this professional man, the client of the mental health professional. When riding the subway, he would, through some secret series of gestures, communicate with the preteen obese boys whom he met on the Seventh Avenue Line, and they would follow him off the trains, and he would make his proposal to them, and they would quickly find places where a professional man and an obese preteen might get the job done, the important part of the arrangement being, in my own view, that the successful professional client of the mental health professional lavished warmth and care and respect upon boys who were more used to being humiliated by their classmates, *Yo, Tubby!* In a suit, the neat, salt-and-peppered, bespectacled professional guy whispered to the boy, *You're just the most beautiful young man,* and then they were alone at the end of the platform, or in some neglected alley, and the man unhitched the trousers of the fat boy and he exposed the little knob of the fat boy, *God, you are so perfect,* and then he put the knob in his mouth, and the boy was perhaps ecstatic, or maybe weeping, but the man was oblivious, the man felt a tremendous security and contentment, though it was ephemeral, this contentment, because soon he fled down an alley, overcoat concealing him, head down, lest the boy should remember him, lest the boy should recall a particular mole, a style of hair, a slight cant of a nose that was once broken in a hockey game. By the time he was within twenty blocks of his co-op, desperation overcame the smart professional guy, like a case of the vapors. He was *in forfeit from his estate,* and he began to plan what he would say to his wife, if indeed he needed to say anything; he planned to look natural, he planned to act routine, to have a latticework of narratives at the ready. What if he had dropped his wallet in the alley with the obese kid? *Shit!* No, the wallet was still here, upon his hip. What if the kid had seen something? Some paper sticking out of his attaché case?

Another guilty conscience out on the streets of the Upper West Side. Next day at work, with the anxiety of a sales presentation ahead of him, the man felt the itch of it, his compulsion, and over lunch hour he would see a pack of schoolchildren on their way to Radio City, and tarrying at the end of the conglomeration of them would be that inevitable loner, the fat kid. My mental health care professional would intrude in these excellent stories with his analysis: *Once we realized that it was about his boyhood in the Depression, how the fat boys represented an abundance of food unavailable to him during those lean times, you know, he was cured. This boy simply represented a striving for sustenance.*

Beyond stories, my principal interest in these expensive consultations with the mental health professional was not the back and forth of conversation, to which I offered as little as possible, but rather *the drugs,* because, by virtue of the *unexplained panic event,* I had been given a certain prescription, and I carried the vial of it with me wherever I went. I remember it once dropping out of my grip on the bus from Hoboken, to be picked up by another commuter, who looked at the label before handing it back. His pitying glance met mine. The drugs, or perhaps simply the combination of drugs and good fortune, stayed further *panic events* for a while. There were only little puncturing spikes of dread. Winter passed with the sort of good times in which Jen and I planned a dinner party, though Jen, too drunk to participate (she was throwing up in the bathroom as the guests arrived), retired to our bedroom, after which I, having entertained the guests, decided to drive them back through the Lincoln Tunnel in her station wagon, drunk myself (and unlicensed), whereupon I struck a lane divider and did $1,200 worth of damage to the front of her car. The guests found a taxi. I drove the sputtering, grinding vehicle back to the house and woke Jen to tell her the news.

March was the birth month of just about everyone in my family, a whole cloud of Moodys, siblings, parents, deceased grandparents, etc., and so, in the middle of my treatment for the *unexplained panic event,* it was March, and the *black thought* came over me, the thought *shrouded in blackness, ten times black.* What can I say of it, but that it came disguised as a routine perception, and that it simply came over me. Who knows where these things come from? *Are they of the air or of the constellations?* as Burton remarks. Some people are lucky enough to have deaths that trigger melancholies, or disasters on the job, or old age, or loss of goods or friends, or bad diet, or *temperature,* or *bad air,* but my guess is that it is the conjunction of physiognomy and ideas, though any such *theorizing* as to causes is in itself a dangerous aspect of illness. I had no particular thing go wrong in my life. This was just a year in my youth, I was twenty-five, and I woke one day *convinced that I was going to be raped.*

The perception deserves respect and amplification, since everything in my adult life seems to have hinged on this morning, including my need to search for my ancestor Handkerchief Moody, but my heart is faint, as you might suppose, *diverse and confused,* and by writing these things I am afraid of conjuring them, and though I do not believe that melancholy is about anything, I am afraid, and my brain is troubled *by reason of a melancholy juice bred in it,* so I choose merely to give the idea that appeared to serve as the trigger of this disease, *hot and dry or cold and dry or pale and ruddy,* this disease. I was convinced that I was going to be raped, *forcibly, sexually violated by some unnamed male, penetrated, bruised, inseminated,* in that way that really suggests the reality of rape, not some minimal, uncomfortable sexual exchange with a queer friend that was unwanted or unsought, but some complete, total rape that would be remembered for the threat of being murdered, held down, left bleeding, violated, something trickling from me. Some crime would befall me suggesting the monstrous dimension of male power, the implicit power in all male exchanges, the exaggerated core of maleness best illustrated in the leather subculture, or in *Guns and Ammo,* or in military training films. It was unclear where this rape was going to take place, what locale, what apartment, what state, it was unclear who was going to be its perpetrator, it was simply something in the air, the way magnolia blossoms are in the air, and for this reason I suddenly found myself *uncomfortable around most of my male friends.* It was the simplest thing, really, a tiny little notion. A mere sentence. I would be having a conversation about the Mets, who were beginning spring training, and I would wonder if my interlocutor, whoever he was, might be *about to rape me.* Absurd! He was some guy I had known for a while, who probably liked me, and didn't want to rape anyone! My friend was talking about the prospects of the Mets. I was talking about the Mets and thinking about getting raped.

A virus on the breeze? Loosed as in a crowded theater, passed along through the circulation of modern currency, a virus of language overheard in some monologue by a psychotic homeless guy in a public square, or an idea that lodged in me like a filament of asbestos from some time earlier, just now getting played out in the disorder of my head? Or was my head disordered from the beginning of my life and just waiting for the right idea to best occupy it? Was there not a little storage facility of misfiring epistemes that awaited this most repellent thought, so that I might be induced to think about it for some time, for four or five months, say, until I was so devastated, until my mind was so taken up with the repellent thought that I didn't have room for anything else, for love, for family, for work, for writing, for exercise, but only for the *down and in* of melancholy. Perhaps caused by God, as *The Anatomy of Melancholy* also supposes: *He can by His angels, which are His ministers, strike and heal whom He will; He can plague us by His creatures, sun, moon, and stars, whom He useth as His instruments, as a husbandman doth a hatchet: hail, snow, winds, etc.*

It was a beautiful day in late March, and I was at my father's house, on the island where he lived, and I remember that he was cutting the field in front of the house with a tractor, and there were horses in the pasture grazing, and the late-afternoon sun was good after the ordeal of winter, and it was in the weeks before Jen vanished for the rehabilitation center, and we were together, and I had great promise, and so what was the problem? Why no gratitude? Why think this *black thought?* Why not put it aside and be content with circumstances?

Astute psychologists will venture interpretations. *I must have wanted to be raped.* Or perhaps: *There was a childhood trauma, and this was the belated articulation of it, the adult harvesting of some tragedy of long ago.* This was the era of suppressed-memory syndrome, after all, and perhaps I was one of its poster cases. A distant relative, or a babysitter, or a grandparent with a problem, perhaps someone like *the client of the mental health professional* mentioned above, had compromised my morals upon an afternoon and I had forgotten the incident. Or this grandparent or uncle or cousin, or whomever, had crept into my childhood bedchamber and upbraided me until I was powerless to refuse. These are all possible theories, and I gave them a fair amount of time over the years, because when one is prey to *morbid thinking,* one becomes first class at nursing any improbable strand of narrative. Though one would rather do anything else. Theories grew in me like backyard vines, grew to invade the healthy part of me, grew to muscle my own desires and ambitions aside, until I was in an adjacent property, isolated, *a cankered soul macerated with cares and discontents,* while this idea went on to conduct my life without me.

Therefore: the thought that I had managed to come up with, on that day in March, was among the worst of all thoughts. Which was why it adhered to me so profitably. The illness needs fear and disgust and shame and obsession to ensure its continuity. Quickly, because of my gift for theorizing, the thought became not only that *I was going to be raped,* which would have engendered only panic, but *that I deserved to be raped.* The thoughts stacked up exponentially, like truckloads at a landfill, and I couldn't evade them, and instead attempted to tangle through them, except that I couldn't, because all these thoughts were *knots,* all inextricabilities, and to try to think them to their conclusion was to become *entangled.* I went home from the weekend disturbed, but on the surface I looked the same — young, presentable, promising — and would have claimed, if asked, that I felt fine. I didn't tell Jen about it, nor did I tell my family, nor even, at first, did I tell the mental health professional, in whose office I weekly sat. The ferryboat returned us to the mainland. The drive home was the same, the same cassettes on the car stereo. We drank as usual, we ate. We turned down the bedsheets.

Then it was the next morning, or the morning after, and I woke oppressed, hoping I would have slept off *this idea,* but had not, nor the next night, if for no other reason but that I had suddenly become insomniac, and there was this noxious aspect to the bedroom, to my *absurd and interrupted dreams;* every night, without fail, I was awake to see the digits on the clock indicate that it was 4:10, as though 4:10 were the historical moment of some relevant occurrence, which in turn led me again to the notion that perhaps I had been abused and corrupted by some distant relation or one of my loving grandparents or a stranger or a Cub Scout leader or a camp counselor or *somebody* at exactly 4:10, or maybe it had happened on April 10, and there was a confluence of digits, or maybe it happened when I was four years old or ten years old, or maybe when I was fourteen years old, which is the sum of four and ten, there must have been something to 4:10; I woke the next day having had only an hour or two of sleep, or maybe four hours and ten minutes of sleep, during which *theory* was part of my dreams and of the substance of me, theory was a chemical in my skull, and my limbs were heavy, but despite all that had happened, I still had to go to work, because there was nothing specifically wrong with me that I could pinpoint, what sentence could serve to capture it — *I have developed this irrational fear* — I couldn't explain how I had been thinking this thought for three consecutive days, and it had begun to exceed the container that held it, it was as much part of things as the air.

In the weeks that followed, I would collide with people while trying to avoid them, and I would attempt to describe my inertia, and my sense was that the words coming out of my mouth were impossible to understand. To a friend, beside the great upended sculpture at Astor Place in Greenwich Village, I said, *Do you ever get the feeling that the history of your family is somehow written on your body?* He was stumped. Had no idea what I was talking about. Or I was at a luncheon with acquaintances from work, and they had chattered away for twenty minutes, and I had said very little, and then someone at the table asked what was going on with me and I said, *Well, I'm having a little trouble being happy.* . . . After a respectful interval, they went back to chattering. Or I came home from work, convinced that I couldn't take another day of it, and found Jen so debilitatingly drunk that it was possible that she didn't recognize me, and I went and put my head in her lap and put her hands on my head, as if this might persuade her to take me seriously, and I said, *I've never been so upset in my life, and I don't know how to stop it and I don't know what to do about it, and nothing helps. I'm just really, really worried.* She tried to say something, but she had her own difficulties, was hurtling downhill on her own, and the thing that was broken in me was so broken that no embrace or expression of support could overcome it.

I wept in the men's room at work, then washed my face and went back to my desk.

I sat in the bathtub at home with the water cooling and wondered if I should saw open my wrists this day or the next.

I lay on the floor in the bedroom, on the carpet, facedown, mumbling, *Can't live this way, can't live this way.*

I stood at a roof party and thought about jumping, watched my body go over the edge, watched its impact on the homely stoop below.

I began to refuse to go out during the day, unless out of necessity, because I didn't want *to be seen.*

I avoided talking to strangers. I went through elaborate maneuvers to sit by myself on trains or in public. I stopped reading. I stopped writing.

I didn't mention to anyone the complexity of these feelings, until, eventually, I told the mental health professional, who remarked supportively that *all of my patients have suicidal ideation.* The drug he had prescribed for the *unexplained panic event* had a mild antidepressant effect, so he said. He suggested that I continue taking it.

I was shameful, my past was shameful, my future was shameful, any bad end that I might come to was an appropriate bad end, and this was best suffered in silence. *This great power of blackness,* Melville observes, *derives its force from its appeals to that Calvinistic sense of Innate Depravity and Original Sin, from whose visitations, in some shape or other, no deeply thinking mind is always and wholly free.* Pleasure was an abstract principle; comfort seemed like a lie. Every morning, in the shower, I imagined my boss preparing to assault me. My friends were going to assault me. All the men in the Port Authority Bus Terminal were going to assault me, a conspiracy of males, all secretly indicating their conspiratorial relationship to one another, was circling around me, preparing to strip me in public, to offend my person, to leave me for dead. *Not actually dead,* because that would have been too easy, just this side of dead, where I could appreciate and linger over the details of my misfortune for years and years.

At first his mind is troubled, he doth not attend what is
said, if you tell him a tale, he cries at last, "What said

you?" but in the end he mutters to himself, as old women do many times, or old men when they sit alone, upon a sudden they laugh, whoop, halloo, or run away, and swear they see or hear players, devils, hobgoblins, ghosts, strike or strut, etc., grow humorous in the end . . . He will dress himself, and undress, careless at last, grows insensible, stupid, or mad.

I was drinking a lot. The mental health professional asked how much I drank, and I revised downward, said three or four a day, omitting the size of some drinks, and the mental health professional indicated that drinking was *a fine social lubricant.* Good news for me, because I had drunk every day for four or five years, perhaps longer, and usually my plan was to have *a couple of bourbons* while I tried to write after work, *maybe three bourbons,* and then I would have *a couple of glasses of wine* with dinner, although sometimes I didn't really have all that much dinner, maybe just some peanuts and then a peanut-butter-and-jelly sandwich, the wine sort of *was* the dinner, and then after the white wine, I would drink *a few beers;* this was the during-the-week pattern, anyhow, whereas the weekend pattern was a binge of several days; on the weekend I didn't worry about numbers of things, I just drank, whereas during the week I worried about numbers of things because there were several stores that I needed to go to in order to ensure that a proper *supply* was available, especially since Jen was drinking a lot at the same time, before going into rehab, and though she herself tried to ensure that there was enough supply there for her, her own supply as opposed to my supply, sometimes it wasn't clear whose supply belonged to whom, and she would be drinking my supply and I would be drinking hers, which I sometimes hid from her, because otherwise it would be gone, and so it was important to ensure that there was enough supply, and therefore to make the trips to these stores, except that I became embarrassed by the quantities of our supply, and how I would be in the same store almost every night attempting to ensure supply, and so I would go to a different vendor, I would vary the locations of my supply vendors, and since I was *afraid of strangers* and didn't want anyone to pay any attention to me, or talk to me, since I just wanted to slip in and buy the Heaven Hill, the brand of bourbon I liked because it looked nicely dangerous to me, or since I just wanted to buy American beer products, I wanted to get out of there fast, but there were always these *guys* in the liquor stores, threatening *guys,* down-on-their-luck *guys,* unshaven and bitter, and I didn't want to be assaulted by them, or by the *guys* owning the stores, who looked as if they might well assault me and enjoy it, and so I varied the locations, and I got out of them as fast as I could and slunk back to our place in Hoboken to drink, happy that the mental health professional had indicated that it was okay that I should drink, that drinking was a *fine social lubricant,* because I had been drinking for almost half of my short life, since I was fourteen or fifteen years old, and it seemed like a great right and an obligation, and I had looked forward to it before I was of age, and I had drunk in the woods with my friends, and I had stolen drinks, and I had drunk every night while in college in a bar where we referred to the waitstaff as *deaf-mutes,* and I had drunk and taken quaaludes, drunk and taken speed, drunk and snorted cocaine, drunk and snorted heroin, drunk and smoked marijuana, even though marijuana made me afraid that I would stop breathing; drinking was the only thing that abridged my accursed timidity, which I had felt since I could remember feeling anything at all, it enabled me to tell my first-ever joke to a woman, it enabled me to sing in front of friends, to paint my masterpieces, and so the idea that I could drink despite *melancholy* was a comfort and a relief, though, as Solomon observed, *To whom is sorrow, to whom is woe, but to such a one as loves drink.*

I didn't reckon on the effects of this depressant, alcohol, on *melancholy,* probably because I was always, in my heart, gladdened by the first couple of drinks and then just trying to live through those next drinks, the next four or five, the slurred words, the constant propositioning of other people's girlfriends or wives; the first two drinks were the drinks that I wanted to have, and the next four were the ones that I woke up heartsick over, how I could have spent *all that money,* how I could have *said all those horrible things.* I crawled out of the bedroom and into the bathroom to splash water on my face, to pry out dried contact lenses, to cough ominously, to take antacids, to look for scabs. I didn't reckon on how even a drink or two on top of *theorizing,* on top of *morbid thinking,* would be among the worst sensations in the whole family of drug sensations that I had courted throughout this period of chemistry. It was like despair become intravenously strong, *hopelessness* coursing through me as though my blood were given fully over to it, as if the worst of the four winds had carried a gale of *hopelessness* down upon me, and I couldn't have a line of conversation without being dispatched away by this fell wind, *a thick, cloudy, musty, foggy air, or such as come from fens, moorish grounds, lakes, muckhills, draughts, sinks, where any carcasses or carrion lies, or from whence any stinking fulsome smell comes.* I felt worse, with stunning velocity, but my first reaction to the failure of drinking to bring forgetfulness was to begin drinking a little bit earlier and a little bit more freely than I had allowed myself before; suddenly, at first light, that Budweiser in the refrigerator, with the glistening condensation on its amber glass, was almost too much to resist, and the moment when I was finally *allowed* to drink became the important threshold of the day, and I began buying pint bottles of bourbon at the liquor store in Times Square that had the bullet-proof glass between you and the bottles; you handed over your money, and the pint bottle slid through a Plexiglas slot. I went home again, Jen was drunk again, I lectured her again about trying to keep her *shit together until she went off to rehab,* told her *she wasn't even trying.*

Hallucinations, or misapprehensions, or conjurations, began after the commencement of symptoms of my melancholy. They began with a frequent auditory blip in which I heard my name called *all the time,* on the street, at the bus station, out the window, in the night, I would hear someone crying out that blunt Anglo-Saxon syllable, and it would often sound obscene, and I would start, and turn, and there would be *no one there;* or merely passers-by. I was often solitary during this time, but my name seemed to be everywhere. When I became used to this voice, which I imagined was the sinister mass of humankind calling out and asking why I was avoiding them when they *loved me so much,* the misapprehensions got *worse,* and they began to include a sense, whenever I shook hands with someone, that this individual was trying to work his or her way toward me for a *kiss;* if I shook hands with the editors at my company, I would worry that they were going to kiss me, or the woman at the post office was going to kiss me. This misapprehension gave way to another in which, out of the margins of peripheral vision, I began to see assaultive couplings, the most grotesque postures, everywhere around me, in midtown, in the park, in the ticket-holders line at the movie theater, and upon turning to verify the credibility of my glimpses, I would see a woman walking a dog, or a guy dropping his lunch bag into a trash barrel, or a couple exchanging shopping bags, and then I would continue on my way, while across the street or on the next corner more of the same. Rape. Prostitutes were everywhere, the city began to seem crowded with them, garish in their makeup, on deserted corners, the hint of a garter belt from underneath a torn skirt, with rolls of corpulence overspilling waistbands, bruised faces, blackened eyes, even on the most populated corners, in front of Rockefeller Center or at Radio City Music Hall, and then when I looked carefully, it was a delivery guy with a hand truck, or a woman giving away leaflets for a new delicatessen. The worse I felt about these insights, the more they bedeviled me, so that the landscapes of the city that I seemed to inhabit were delirious with ungratified sexual want, with desire for the most desperate and barbarous acts. All of which made me want to avoid the streets; it was like the true solution to the problem of graffiti, which involved the elimination of all possible surfaces on which to inscribe graffiti: my solution to the unquiet of my interactions with my fellowman was to avoid my fellowman, wherever she or he might turn up, a fine ambition when I spent a lot of my time in a city of eight million inhabitants. I severed bonds with many of the people I knew, because I couldn't bear pretending to be well. When spring arrived in earnest, I could tell that spring was not going to be a consolation, that the flowers and the leaves and the first warm days wouldn't register, because with all the space given over by me to *theory* and *conjuration,* to the mental health professional's surmises about the *primal scene,* to the drink that had become my one unstinting love, there wasn't room left for seasons.

Jen packed up for her rehabilitation center, in Armonk, which had a pastoral name. Tired of being henpecked by her aunts, I thought; grief stricken about her mother, desiring of good relations with the remaining women of her tribe. The last weeks before her leaving were such a wreck that I thought, in a spate of intuitive reasoning, that it was *good* to get her out of the house, because she was getting *really bad,* and I didn't want her looking at me in my disgrace, and all we did was sleep and drink, so it was fine. She packed up some practical outfits, got in the car with the rebuilt front end, took off. I misunderstood what a precarious moment it was, as Handkerchief Moody must have felt calling for a midwife on the eve of the birth of his daughter Lucy. Once Jen was out of the house, I slumped further into the cave-dwelling part of my back brain. The lonely villain in a monster movie, a suzerain of reclusion, drinking, loathing myself, going out and feeling afraid, cynical, contemptuous, literally disgusted by *my own shadow,* by everything that had to do with me, by my borders and everything contained within my borders, the trouble I had wrought, everything I'd gotten into, while the streets around me were *full of riots of sexual assault,* women of leisure and men of leisure and men of leisure dressed as women; underneath the punctilious exterior of the society in which I had been raised, libertine cravings, unquenchable urges toward excess of carnal delight, everywhere bawds and adulterers, pedophiles and bestialists, lovers of incest and masochism, all institutions of the civilized America were window dressing for the excursion of sexual power into the ghetto of the powerless, a sequence of rapes, Manifest Destiny as the rationalization of genocide by method of rape, the Republican Party as rationalization of genocide, Fundamentalist Christianity as rationalization of genocide; every kind word uttered to another libertine was the means by which sodomy would be exercised, everyone was plotting, the dry cleaner was plotting, the women at the Laundromat were plotting, the joggers in the park were plotting, the joggers would fling themselves on one another during the third mile, strip off their Lycra gear and their running shoes, the altar boys in the church were fleecing one another of their robes, the police were taking money from whores and pimps, getting serviced in return, firemen were sodomizing welfare mothers, heaving them into the flames; there was an unmistakable violence of desire upon everyone, the loneliness would swell in them and they were powerless before it, they would find and take prisoners, they would leave prisoners destitute and used and swollen with venereal infection, and they would go out upon the streets, sick with further need, with the American itch, the incompleteness, the insufficiency, the omission, the shortage; the city needed something, it needed something bad, it needed a scratch, needed to be touched, needed love, needed merchandise, needed conquest, needed to stretch out toward a new frontier that it might pillage, it needed to find someplace to work its gray, violent rhetoric at the expense of a new underclass, to relieve its woe.

When Jen was gone she immediately became the only good thing that had ever happened to me. *Our parents, tutors, friends, spare no cost to bring us up in our youth in all manner of virtuous education; but when we are left to ourselves, idleness as a tempest drives all virtuous motions out of our minds,* et nihili sumus; *on a sudden, by sloth and such bad ways, we come to naught.*

But that's not *half of it*. Considerably more suffering in the biography of Handkerchief, and therefore more suffering to relate. Back then, *people attended worship with their firearms in their hands,* their matchlocks, their wheel locks, their snaphances, their flintlocks, their fowling guns; it was an era when the minister's duty included chaplain at *the garrison,* at least in the lean years of the Reverend Samuel Moody's vocation. About eight years before Handkerchief's birth, *the place had received a terrible visitation by Indians,* according to one source. *Reverend Mr. Dummer,* whom Samuel Moody replaced, *was shot as he was mounting his horse at his own door, and his wife taken captive. Nearly the whole town was destroyed on the same day, there being fifty persons killed and one hundred taken captive.* The Algonquians, of which the local Abenakis were one tribe, had, according to Charles Banks's *History of York, no settled habitations, removing from one place to another according to the requirements of food supplies.* And proving that he could mimic the dubious prejudices of his forefathers, Banks goes on: *Intellectually they had a negligible culture. Their art was crude and their music barbarous, both vocal and instrumental. . . . Their daily life was either a feast or a famine.* Likewise, here quoting William Wood, in "New England's Prospect":

> They present them with a vollie of shot, asking for sacke
> and strong liquors, which they soe much love since the
> *English* used to trade it with them, that they will scarce

trade for anything else, lashing out into excessive abuse, first taught by the example of some of our English who to uncloathe them of their beaver coates, clad them with the infection of swearing and drinking which was never in fashion with them before, it being contrary to their nature to guzzell downe strong drinke . . . and from over-flowing Cups there had beene a proceeding to revenge, murther, and over-flowing of blood.

Another of Banks's period sources adds, *They dye patiently, both men and women, not knowing of a hell to scare them nor a conscience to terrify them.* And what better word than *conscience* in any discussion of Indian affairs, especially where the colonial interlopers are concerned? King Philip's War had come and gone, and York had suffered *sporadic attacks, with the loss of a few men,* not unlike other villages nearby, *nor was it the home of any English leader conspicuous in military affairs, whom the French or their Indian allies wished to kill or capture as a matter of personal revenge, or in retaliation for anything its inhabitants had done in the past.* Nevertheless, in September 1691, Indians farther down the coast had taken some prisoners, after murdering others, and were told by those imprisoned *that the Bostoners were providing many Snow Shoes & Designed a considerable army out this winter to Disrest them at Some of their headquarters, which made them very uneasy this winter & this Company (which attacked York) has been long out ranging the woods to meet with them or their tracks, which failing they fell upon York.* Namely, on the Feast of the Purification of the Virgin Mary, or Candlemas. So Arthur Bragdon, probably a forebear of the Deacon Bragdon who later housed the shut-in Handkerchief Moody, *had gone out into the woods back of the settlement in the direction of Agamenticus to set his traps. . . . The Indian scouts . . . suddenly surprised the young Bragdon busily engaged in fixing his traps; they seized him and a little later came across two other inhabitants.* Banks quotes a French-Canadian antagonist and Indian ally:

The 150 warriors divided into two bands and one advanced first on a garrison and the other on the English people's houses. It was at noon and the morrow of

the Feast of Purification. They made themselves masters of the garrison and the houses without much resistance as they threw terror into the English inhabitants.
There was one of our people killed in that first attack
in which, and the one that followed, we were victorious. . . . There were three garrisons, and a very large
number of English people's houses. All of these were
burned. . . . An Abenaqui, who was one of the war chiefs
and who related all of this, said there were more than
100 English killed and that he himself had counted
them. They took away 80 prisoners. One could not estimate the slaughter of horses, cattle, sheep and pigs
killed or burned.

The irrepressible Cotton Mather, who eulogized Samuel Moody's
uncle Joshua, and who later became an occasional subject for the
study of Handkerchief in his diaries, also wrote an account of the
York massacre: *This body of Indians, consisting of divers hundreds then
sent in their summons to some of the garrisoned houses and those garrisons
whereof some had no more than two or three men in them, yet being so well
manned as to reply: "that they would spend their blood unto the last drop, ere
they would surrender." These cowardly miscreants had not mettle enough to
meddle with 'em. So they returned into their howling thickets.* Of Samuel
Moody's predecessor the Reverend Dummer, much was made in these
accounts: *As he was fleeing he was brought down by a pistol shot as he was
trying to escape on his horse.* And Mather amplifies: *This good man was
just going to take horse at his own door upon a journey in the service of
God. . . . Those bloodhounds being set on by some Romish missionaries had
long been wishing that they embrue their hands in the blood of some New
England minister and in this action they had their diabolical satisfaction.
They left him dead among the tribe of Abel on the ground.*
Moreover, a tradition persisted in York that the *body of the parson
was stripped of its apparel,* and that *on the next Lord's Day a full welted
savage, purposely to deride the ministerial character of Mr. Dummer, put on
his garments and stalked about in the presence of the distressed captives, some
of whom belonged to his church.* Cotton Mather even wrote a poem about
the Reverend Dummer (I'm excerpting here):

The martyr'd Pelican, who bled
    Rather than leave his charge unfed.
A proper bird of paradise
    Shot, and flown thither in a trice.

Lord, hear the cry of righteous Dummer's wounds,
    Ascending still against the savage hounds
That worry thy dear flocks, and let the cry
    Add force to theirs that at thine altar lye.

The list of the massacred at York includes members of the Preble family too, namely John and Nathaniel Preble, Mrs. Priscilla Preble, Obadiah Preble, probably all kin of he (Ebenezer) who would later be lost in Handkerchief Moody's shooting. Obadiah was, as a captive, removed to Canada by the Indians and *as far as known was never returned*

This is the York to which Samuel Moody relocated (from Newburyport), bringing his wife and two children. Into a heavily fortified encampment. Sporadic Indian attacks continued through the 1690s, during which time the General Court in Massachusetts passed an act *to prevent the deserting of the frontiers,* as follows:

> Nor shall any inhabitant of any such frontier town or plantation having an estate of freehold in lands or tenements remove from thence with intent to sojourn or inhabit elsewhere, without special license first had and obtained (from the Governor and Council) on pain of forfeiting all his estates.

The Third Indian War, as Banks calls it, more of same, persisted well into the first part of the eighteenth century, as in the October 20, 1705, attack: *On Saturday the 20th currant about 20* Indians *appeared at Cape Nidduck and carried away 4 sons of* John Stover, *who were at a little distance from the Garrison. Several others that were out of the Garrison retired to it with all speed; on which the Enemy fired about an hour, then drew up the Children in sight of the Garrison and marched off. At York*

4 or 5 Indians *were also discovered; Major Walton with a Company of men is gone in pursuit.* A further legal injunction, at this concurrence of bad circumstances, enshrined the garrison, the structure in which most residents of York lived, as *the* required habitation for communal safety, *and fines were to be imposed for disobedience of this requirement,* as the men of York were also induced by legislation to bear arms at such time as they might go *to publick worship . . . and when they go abroad to work.* Attacks on both sides continued. In 1710, a Benjamin Preble was slain by Indians, and in 1711, Captain Abraham Preble (father of Ebenezer, and presumably of Benjamin, and kin of all those Prebles above, slain during the massacre) woke to find his fishing sloop *misplaced.* Banks gives an account:

> Preble called for volunteers from the townsmen, and Captain Heath in charge of the garrison detailed a sergeant and eight men to aid in its recapture. . . . The whole party, numbering thirty-two men, went in two sloops to chase. After several hours they descried Preble's boat and, outsailing her, found her manned by a Frenchman and three Indians. They made them prisoners and put back to the harbor where they arrived about ten o'clock that night. A summary court martial was held by Captains Heath and Preble, and [Ensign William] Hilton was ordered to execute the Indians. In accordance with this they were put to death immediately that same night and their bodies thrown into the sea. Hilton took their scalps to Boston to claim bounty.

Ebenezer Preble, the victim of this entire tale, died on August 25, 1708, or in the midst of the ongoing conflict with the natives of the region, during a time in which the scalp of a dead Native American fetched a bounty from the local government. In such cramped quarters, in a garrison, he and Joseph Moody knew each other, and likewise from school, the very school at which Joseph Moody would later teach: *Poor, small, and uncomfortable schoolhouses, scant furnishings, few and uninteresting books, tiresome and indifferent methods of teaching, great severity of discipline, were the accompaniments of school days,* as one historian describes it. In York, the schoolhouse wasn't even erected until later, near the parsonage, and so the schoolmaster and his pupils likely went from house to house.

Subjects of this colonial education were classical: scripture, mathematics, some Latin. As the garrison surrounded and protected the progeny of York physically, the Bible and its Puritanical interpretations garrisoned their *souls,* in school and out: *The usual method at that time of reading the Bible through was in the regular succession of every chapter from beginning to end, not leaving out even Leviticus and Numbers. This naturally detracted from the interest which would have been awakened by a wise selection of parts suited to the liking of children.* Cotton Mather, for example, was apparently keen on education as a theater essential to the prolongation of the Puritan experiment (here remembered by his son Samuel, in a memoir once described as "the most colorless book in the English language"): *He began betimes to entertain {children} with delightful stories, especially Scriptural ones; and he would ever conclude with some lesson of piety bidding them to learn that lesson from the story. Thus every day at the table he used himself to tell some entertaining tale before he rose; and endeavor to make it useful to the olive plants about the table.*

Here's Mather, furthermore, instructing his daughter of four, as described in his own diary:

> I took my little daughter Katy into my Study and then I told my child I am to dye Shortly and shee must, when I am Dead, remember Everything I now said unto her. I sett before her the sinful Condition of her Nature, and I charged her to pray in Secret Places every Day. That God for the sake of Jesus Christ would give her a New Heart. I gave her to understand that when I am taken from her she must look to meet with more humbling Afflictions than she does now she has a Tender Father to provide for her.

However, as nineteenth-century social historian Alice Morse Earle (the source of the quotation) pointed out, Mather didn't die for *thirty years.* Religious dread was heavy upon the Mather family, and the very same weight, of course, was borne by the young Handkerchief Moody:

> *Mon. 28 {November 1720} Cold morn., more mod., cloudy P.M.*
> *Oh if the omnipotent Grace of God would take possession of me!*

Or:

> *Sab. 4 {December 1720}*
> A.M. *Father preached. I well-nigh condemned because I never saw the price of the blood of Christ.*

As the dread of religious conscience was passed down from generation to generation of Mathers, therefore, so does one have the unavoidable sense that Handkerchief's dread issued forth along the paternal line.

Samuel's uncle was the Reverend Joshua Moodey, author, among other tracts, of the bloodthirsty "Souldiery Spiritualized," preached before the Artillery Company of Massachusetts in 1674: The Devil *ha's a quarrel to thee, and* Fight *thee he will, and* Fight *him thou must. The first Cry of the* Newborn Babe of Grace . . . alarms all the Devils in Hell against him; *what then shall he do if he cannot* Fight. *He must not fly, Ö nor must he yield, then he must* Fight. Who was it the soldier was enjoined to fight? The native population of New England, of course.

Born in 1675, son of Caleb, representative in the General Court of Massachusetts, Samuel Moody meanwhile graduated from Harvard, with honors, in 1697. He settled in York in December 1700, with his wife, Hannah Sewall. The children were three, Joseph, Mary, and Lucy, who died in early childhood in 1705. Given a promise of *eccentricities* in all the biographical sources, I had hoped for more — considering that Samuel's son *wore a veil* and that his third daughter died untimely. Nevertheless, most of the anecdotes are merely charming:

> [Samuel Moody requested of a guest one night] to lead the evening household service but was answered by a

request to be excused. "But you will pray with us," exclaimed the old man. "No, Father Moody, I wish to be excused." "But you *must* pray." "No, sir, I *must* be excused." "But I command you to pray." "Mr. Moody!" replied the young man, in a determined voice, "you need not attempt to browbeat me, for I *won't* pray." "Well, well," exclaimed the old gentleman, in a discomfited tone, "I believe you have more brass in your face, than grace in your heart."

Or behold the following, with its premonitions of Hawthorne's "Young Goodman Brown," wherein a local traveler meets the devil himself on a country lane:

Father Moody, when returning from one of his parochial visits, fell in with a stranger. Religious conversation was soon introduced and he, without reluctance, joined in it. He demurred to many of Father Moody's propositions. He denied that many of the doctrines then, as now, considered the very pith and cream of orthodoxy, were true. He declared that the Bible did not teach them, and supported this by a whole array of passages from the Holy Scriptures. Our good minister was amazed and perplexed. He had never before engaged so bold and stiff an antagonist. He could not defeat the man, and with much difficulty escaped being defeated by him. "And who?" thought he, "can this creature be? He cannot be a son of New England, or of Old England, or of any part of Christian Europe; he must be the Evil One himself." Full of this persuasion, he turned home and told Madam Moody that he had been disputing with the devil. "And what," inquired she, "did the old fellow say?" "Why," replied Father M., "he said that the doctrines of original sin, and effectual calling, and an eternal hell, are not contained in the Bible; and he quoted abundance of Scripture to support his blasphemy." "But did the devil quote *Scripture?*"

said Madam, who partook of the common notion that the Evil One could not frame his mouth to utter such sacred words. "Yes, yes," answered the old man, "and enough of it too. But mind you! He quoted it in a *devilish* way."

Notwithstanding this lovable version of the Reverend Samuel Moody, his sermons are punitive, joyless, and unyielding. In an original manuscript in York, my father and I read of his attitude on youth:

> The very Foundation of our Nature is laid in Corruption . . . a Nature not only stained with the Guilt of *Adam's* first sin, who was our Representative, and in whose Loins we then were; but wholly depraved, and full of the Seeds of all manner of Sin: which is discovered by the Actions of Little Children. A Stubborn and Disobedient Heart, must needs be the cause of those cross fits, which are common to Children before they can speak or go alone. And does not the Pride and Malice of their hearts appear, in the words and actions of Sucking Babes?

And his attitude on worldliness:

> In a word, the impenitent, resolute sinner, running on the drawn sword of the divine threatening, wounding his conscience, and heaping guilt . . . & after all refusing the only remedy; he chooses destruction and misery; prepares for his own torment; feeds the worm of conscience, yea, fills it with matter of accusation and everlasting reproach: So Hell with its torments . . . is the self-destroying, and foul-murdering creature's own place.

By the end of a day of reading in Samuel's papers at the York Historical Society, we were tired. My father and I were well prepared for repose in our cliff-side lodgings. *How long can you read this stuff?* How many pages can you read of the very philosophy from which you, contemporary American, emerged, before you yawn and reach for the antithetical comforts, for the remote control, for the beer in its Styrofoam sleeve, for the joint that goes around? How long before you *nuke* a frozen burrito and turn up the radio and sing along with classic rock? How many pages of this sort, with their predictable certainties, their Fundamentalist clatter, can you honestly tolerate before you turn away your gaze? The librarian at the historical society locked up at five, and we had to remove our white gloves and finish up, and there was perhaps some chowder awaiting us in seaside comfort, haddock chowder — and the highway signs indicated lobster everywhere about us, in any direction we drove — and yet Handkerchief had no way to circumnavigate the menace I've cataloged, the menace of the marriage of sin and colonial self-reliance, the slaughter of natives, the legacy of Puritan divination in the person of an overbearing father; it came at him at the setting forth of cutlery and of dinner, likewise during grace, *Let us together, Look Up for a* Blessing *on the Portion of wholesome Food Seasonably set before us.* Whenever the repast was served, the correcting voice sang forth across the table, toward Joseph and his sister Mary, it followed them from the table, it made sure they knelt before the straw mat where they slept, until its voice was their voice, and later the voice of their sons and their sons and their sons. No wonder Joseph wanted to get out of the range of his father and *play* that afternoon in August. No wonder the urchins of the garrison were intent upon games, though games were considered the work of the devil: *Playing cards were fiercely hated, and their sale prohibited in Puritan communities,* as Earle has it, and: *Foot-ball wherein there is nothynge but beastlye furie and exstreme violence, whereof proceedeth hurte; and consequently malice and rancour do remayne with them that be wounded; whereof it is to be putt in perpetuall silence.* Between school and chores and prayers, nevertheless some time was contrived by Joseph and his friend Ebenezer, or they played *Scotch-hoppers,* or they played *chuck-farthing;* or they played at *kite-flying; marbles, hoop and hide, thread the needle; fishing; blindman's bluff; shuttlecock; peg-farthing; knock out and span; hop, skip, and jump; cricket; stool-*

ball; base-ball; trap-ball; tip-cat; train-banding; leap-frog; bird-nesting; hop-hat; shooting. Anything to put off the tirades at home.

Just like we did it at my parents' house in Darien. I was preoccupied with *jigsaw puzzles,* had them all laid out on the floor, out of range of combatants around me, first assembling the edges and then the like colors, always using the box to cheat; especially, I favored a puzzle carved out of the reproduction of a Pieter Brueghel painting, *Children's Games,* one of those incredibly crowded Brueghel paintings in which dozens of Flemish *guttersnipes* cavorted on the street of some village, *giddyheads,* playing at all the games, in their breeches, their codpieces, their dresses, all with the rounded pancake faces of Brueghel's country renderings; I loved this particular puzzle so much because, despite its alien appearance, it was just how we played, how all kids played always, in the same ways, according to the same rules and regulations. *Stone-tag and wood-tag took the place in America of the tag on iron of Elizabeth's day, Squat-tag and cross-tag have their times and seasons, and in Philadelphia tell-tag is also played. . . . Another tag game known as poison, or stone poison, is where the player is tagged if he steps off stones.* The kids across the street from us, the Snyders, they were our contemporaries and we played kick-the-can with them, a game requiring a standard-issue twelve-ounce aluminum can but which otherwise stretched back into the prehistory of European peoples. The Snyders, like the Moodys, had soon-to-be-divorcing parents, as did the Montgomerys, up the block; there were also the Robbs, who amounted to a large gang of *boys.* Who can blame us if at dusk we were disinclined to go back indoors and to sit quietly at the table where we would be again cajoled into *eating wax beans?* Who can blame us if we avoided quarreling adults? I had an all-consuming crush on one of the neighbor girls and had persuaded her to show me the lower half of herself unclothed, as if this would answer the question of how I came to be, and thereby, perhaps, why the melancholy in her and why the same in me, and yet this persuasion did neither, and she became shy afterward, and I went back to the puzzles of children's games, in silence, until my mother would tread past, put in one or two pieces, and remove herself from the room, continue on her rounds, my brother would scatter a few pieces to irritate me, and on it went, night, another day, another dawn, nothing apparently accomplished, except ten more pieces in the impossible months-long task of putting one thousand pieces of *Children's Games* together. Kick-the-can, and hide-and-go-seek, and capture-the-flag, games that expanded to fill the vacant lot beside the Snyders, all overgrown with ailanthus and skunk cabbage, another August, and parents were preparing for a cocktail party up the block, and we kicked skunk cabbage, debated the ability of our fathers to prevail in combat over one another, stood upon the old foundation in the woods on the empty lot. Never did it seem that the company of other children completely kept at bay a dread *end of things,* ends of games, ends of television programs, ends of particular candy bars, ends of vacations. Summer would be over soon. When the puzzle was done, I took it apart, shuffled the pieces, began again.

What did Handkerchief wear outdoors on that day, August 25, 1708? (As I write these lines it is also August 25, two hundred and ninety-one years later, this day is sunny and bright with cumulus clouds, a little bit of humidity, high in the mid-eighties, storm front from the Midwest approaching, and in Maine, where this shooting once took place, it is in the upper seventies, with a light breeze from offshore. Autumn has begun to hint about its inevitability. There is the diminishing cadence of crickets, the tomatoes are ready to be harvested, the sunsets are more dramatic and earlier. The seawater no longer seems to be getting warmer.) Boys in the late seventeenth century wore, until they were six or thereabouts, frocks not unlike those of women of the period, *with the exception of the neck of the body, it is much like the dress of grown women,* and Joseph, if he were no exception to the rule, would have just put off his "coats" for "breeches," which, since this is Puritan country, would have been more austere and less expressive, since Samuel Moody was known to denounce *finery* from the pulpit. Additionally, *in the early settlements of Connecticut, Massachusetts, and Virginia, sumptuary laws were passed to restrain and attempt to prohibit extravagance in dress. The New England magistrates were curiously minute in description of overluxurious attire, and many offenders were tried and fined. But vain daughters and sons "psisted in fflonting," though ministers joined the lawmakers in solemn warnings and reprehensions.* Joseph was becoming a man, though; he wore breeches now, and a waistcoat, and perhaps even, as some would later, a *wig,* though these were more often the style of the wealthy and powerful, and Joseph was neither. But, since he had put off womanly coats, he was becoming a man, and, consistent with his father's wishes, he was old enough to have access to *firearms.* No doubt Samuel had managed to train his son in the correct operation of these. Thus the day arrived in which Joseph and Ebenezer, playacting, but also in a good-natured effort to provide a protein source for the reverend's table, *betook themselves to the hunt.*

Or did they? Banks has an opinion:

> A circumstantial story has been built up on unsupported tradition that the two went hunting deer and other game which might come within the reach of their firearms. They separated in a thicket to beat up the game; Moody heard a crackling in the underbrush and saw a movement which he supposed was a deer. Leveling his gun he fired at the object and, hastening to the spot where the supposed animal had fallen, he found his friend, Ebenezer, mortally wounded and breathing his last. . . . As Moody was two years younger we are expected to believe that a boy of eight, armed with one of the enormous Queen Anne Muskets, was allowed to hunt game in the woods when the Indian menace was so dangerous. The idea seems preposterous and yet it has been solemnly told for many years.

Yet if the story has no basis, why imagine it in the first place? What purpose does it serve? Banks observes, *Such an accident might have occurred through the accidental discharge of a musket, killing the Preble boy, possibly in the presence of young Moody. But if this was the cause, thirty years elapsed before the supposed mental distress of Joseph Moody began to be made manifest.* He goes on to situate Moody's later difficulties, his veiling, in his theology, one inherited from his father and his great-uncle:

He was deeply impressed with the belief that he was unworthy of the confidence and support of his parish; that his life in the ministry was a failure in the sight of God and man and that his voice should no longer be heard nor his face seen in the pulpit. . . . The sacrifice on the altar was now as complete as a troubled mind and an accusing conscience could offer. Repetitions of the traditional details of his eccentric habits and queer sayings are in doubtful taste. . . . It was a tragedy of misplaced talent unwittingly grafted on a heterogenous stock. His Puritan inheritance proved his undoing.

Of the years immediately after the shooting of Ebenezer Preble we know little, whether there was grief involved on Moody's part, remorse, or some early-American version of *posttraumatic stress.* Joseph Moody's teens, like those of his esteemed Jesus of Nazareth, are *lost years,* at least until he left home to attend Harvard. The best record of his education has it that *he graduated with high honors Harvard College,* although Philip McIntire Woodwell has produced a few additional clues: *He was not distracted by sports, for there was no such "pigskin and sheepskin" rivalry as later centuries have brought forth. He was never disciplined for "breaking glass," one of the commoner symptoms of youthful over-exuberance at the Harvard of his day.* His likely course of studies is easy to reconstruct:

Freshman year: Review of classical authors such as Cicero, Socrates, Homer, and Virgil. Greek testament and grammar. In the latter part of the year Students begin Logic and Hebrew grammar. Sophomore year: Greek grammar and poetry, Hebrew grammar and Old Testament, Logic, and Natural Philosophy. Junior Sophister year: Natural Philosophy, Ethics, Metaphysics, Divinity. Senior Sophister year: Metaphysics, Divinity, Geometry, Astronomy, and a general review. All four classes study Rhetoric — the art of writing and speaking gracefully — in classical authors, and they practice it by weekly declamations.

Handkerchief comes alive again, historically, only in his diaries. In his early twenties. And if, as Banks argues, there was no real mental illness in Moody until the year after his wife's death, then why the heavy dread of God in the diaries, why the bitter recriminations against self for the most minor infractions? Why, for example, a premonitory mention of the veil, fifteen years before its assumption, in an exchange with an African servant?

> *Wed. 16 {January 1723} Fair and moderate* A.M., *but cloudy at night. Indeed we have had scarce anything that may be called winter weather.*
> *. . . A small boy, Neb. MacIntire by name, laughed at my uncle during the prayer. After the close of school he asked me again and again for permission to go out. Finally, I was obliged to leave, but he wet himself. Curtis, in Cap. Nowell's vessel, brings news from the East that Bassus Allen has been enrolled there as a soldier. I questioned our Flora to some extent about the customs of her nation. She told me that among her people there were certain old men who were able to bring dark matters into the light. They cover their faces with a disc, bound by a leather thong above; they walk about, repeatedly plunging their hands in water, and clapping with their palms. At length, the bond being loosed, they make clear secret matters.*

Dread is hovering, it seems to me, even in the detail about Neb MacIntire laughing at Joseph's uncle and then later *wetting himself.* But with Flora, the servant, the theme of so much of Joseph's suffering is apparent: *the hovering presence of dark matters,* the necessity, in this ritual, of *covering the face.* The occasional lightness of the diaries, the news about neighbors and their travails, these are all to direct attention away from a roiling beneath, as though lightness could do anything but delay the inevitable reckoning.

And there's further disillusionment in the diaries, having to do with Joseph's *infatuations.* From the very earliest entries, Joseph is apparently taken up with his future wife, Lucy White of Gloucester, Massachusetts:

Sat. 15 {October 1720}
Last night much disturbed in a dream concerning Lucy. About
twelve o'clock I kissed Lucy.

Or:

Tues. 18 {October 1720} Fast at Berwick. . . . York
A great part of this night I spent with Lucy.

At least, that's how it looks, that he's taken up with Lucy White. But his sister, who died when he was five years old, just three years before the shooting death of Ebenezer, was also called Lucy. So which Lucy is it who inhabits the above dream of October 15? And which Lucy did he kiss? Or was it perhaps both Lucys named here, while summoning forth yet another, a premonitory Lucy, his daughter, who would likewise die with her mother during the uncompleted childbirth of 1736? All these Lucys with their sad fates. All called forth in the entry above, as central to the text of the diaries as the forty-two descriptions of masturbation, so that love and mortality appear to be mere obverses of each other in Handkerchief's diary, aspects of the same theology. Small wonder, then, given this conjunction, that in the midst of his amorous suit, when another suitable young woman, Mary Hirst, appears in Joseph's ken, he falls for her instead. As Banks observes, *It is known that as a young man he became deeply smitten with the charms of the beautiful Mary Hirst, a daughter of Grove Hirst of Boston, and paid earnest court for her hand in marriage.* Banks leaves out an imperative detail, however, namely that Mary Hirst was Joseph Moody's *cousin.* Here's the beginning of the story in the hand of its author:

Th. 8 {June 1721} Very Warm. Wind S.W. about. Hazey.
At two o'clock came Bragdon, and with him Mrs. Banks,
Beck Donnell, Mary Hirst . . . I was accompanied as far as
home by Miss Hirst who was not feeling well.

Fry. 9 Some Clouds
I showed the girls, viz., my sister and Hirst, an unbra.

Unbra, meaning probably *umbra,* shadow or shade. But is the shade meant to be taken literally or figuratively? Is the *constituent part of darkness* that Joseph introduces to the girls an actual shadow, or an evocation of himself and the inheritance already visited upon him? Whichever, the romance with Mary Hirst begins to accelerate in the months after this meeting. A month later, we find *Hirst likes me, my sister says.* And then, on the fourteenth of July, *Mother admonished me concerning Hirst. I did not take it well.* There's a chemistry upon the premises, for Hirst was staying with the Moodys, and continued to do so for a solid year. A chemistry, unfortunately, that his mother's discipline does little to impair.

> *Sab. 23 {July 1721} Misty and cool*
> *A great part of the evening I spent with Hirst. I told her what I was thinking about her.*

> *Wed. 2 {August 1721} Some rain. Thick and foggy at night*
> *I fear that I am less cautious than I ought to be in regard to H—t.*

> *Fri. 1 {September 1721} Cool morn. Clear and windy.*
> *I aroused by jealousy (at seeing) Parsons talking with Hirst.*

> *Wed. 20 {September 1721} Cloudy. Rain at n't.*
> *I wrote a confession of faith for Hirst.*

> *Wed. 4 {October 1721}*
> *Hirst is strongly solicitous.*

> *Tues. 10 {October 1721} Very cold wind.*
> *Hirst sees her own ill-doing, but what do I do, most stupid and insensible in my sins?*

> *Wed. 29 {November 1721} Some snow.*
> *The sermon was about the Judgment of the Last Day. I very dull. . . . Hirst visited Clark. I went home with her. I can scarcely keep myself from loving her. I did not pray before going to bed.*

Mon. 4 {December 1721} Pretty cold A.M.
I almost hate Miss Hirst.

In January of the new year, 1722, the Hirst saga rapidly mounts toward its predictable climax, not long after the marriage of Joseph's sister Mary (on December 27) to the Reverend Emerson.

Tues. 9 {January 1722}
I do not love Lucy with conjugal affection.

Thurs. 18 Thawy weather
I discussed with my father last night, and with Hirst today, the question of my giving up Lucy — much too freely. Divine Jesus, thou who has been so before, I beseech thee, be now my guide!

Fri. 19 Warm
I said hardly anything of a religious nature, but a great deal incautiously about marrying my cousin. Father did not approve.

Thu. 1 {February 1722} Warm
This morning Father talked with me for a long time, and Mother cautioned me about Cousin Hirst. I have sinned, I confess, in that I have encouraged her expectations.

Thu 22 . . . mist. Hazey.
Father admonished me again about Hirst. Thanks be to God, who, as I hope has guided me successfully in this matter, however I have erred.

Not long after the eruption of the Reverend Samuel Moody in the Hirst narrative, Mary begins to recede. In the midst of Samuel's paternal chastisement, as the translator of the diaries notes, Joseph makes the decision to go abroad in New England to preach: *On Friday a Joseph Page, bound for Berwick, brought a message from Samuel Moody and Jeremiah Wise of Berwick, then visiting him, that Joseph should go to Berwick with Page, and preach for Wise on the Sabbath. . . . The four days may have helped his composure.* Meanwhile, romance abhorring a vacuum, another young gentleman begins to ply his suit upon Cousin Hirst, a friend of the Moody family called Captain Pepperel. Stray bits of Joseph's agony seesaw in the story with observations of her new situation:

> *Sat. 7 {April 1722}*
> *I told Cousin Hirst that I loved her in some degree.*

> *Sab. 29 {April 1722}*
> *Hirst received a gift of the goldsmiths' from Captain Pepperel.*

> *Fri. 18 {May 1722} Cloudy*
> *This morning I received a letter from Father about leading Cousin Hirst back to the way of modesty.*

> *Tues. 26 {June 1722}*
> *I have not been able to think about Hirst and Pepp. as serenely as I wished.*

> *Wed. 27 {June 1722}*
> *After school Hirst went with me to the beach. Seldom lately have we passed an hour together peacefully. Father has been absent up to now. The lecture, therefore, is postponed.*

And then the last trickle of sentiment:

> *Tues. 3 {July 1722} Rain P. M.*
> *I talked with my mother about getting married this fall. . . . Pepperrell {sic} paid a visit to Hirst, which does not trouble me, blessed be the name of God.*

> *Th. 12 {July 1722}*
> *I spent a great part of the night with my dear one {Lucy White}, my beloved, whom, thanks be to God, I shall, I hope, love from now on.*

Thereafter, Mary Hirst's appearances in the diaries are few and deliberately muted, up to and after her marriage, which Moody mentions only in this way:

> Mon. 11 Cloudy and cold
> I wrote to Cousin Pepperell.

The rest of the diaries constitute the remainder of Joseph Moody's bachelorhood, though one might never know this, notwithstanding the occasional mention of the beloved Lucy (*I spent some hours with my beloved, not altogether placidly*, or, *In the presence of her parents, and to her alone, I kept urging Lucy that she should be willing to be married this winter*), because, after the Hirst pages, the diaries are again taken up with mundanities and outbursts of self-hatred — as well as a brief crush on yet another third party, Molly Nowell. (*I probably think too much about Molly Nowell. I hardly fall short of loving her. Only with difficulty can I say it. Oh God, I beseech thee, amend these matters.*) The last entries of 1724 begin to dribble into mere recitations of names and allusions to appointments not fully elucidated: *Something serious at night more than usual hearing. Rose before day*, or *I did not teach school, and I did not feel well*, or *Sought an horse, but scarce shall obtain.* On November 10, 1724, the entry in its entirety reads as follows:

> Tues. 10
> A fine morning. Met Uncle Sewall and the two Webbers at
> Bale's. I transcribed two or three copies of Capt. Pep. We dined
> at Cotton's. Got to Hampton by Dark, to Graves's by 8 —
> Got over the {word illegible}.

This is the entry for the day *immediately preceding Joseph Moody's wedding to Lucy White.* In its entirety. Not a mention of the preparations therefor, the locale of the wedding, as there is not in the weeks preceding, nor in the entire month preceding, a mention of the alteration of life's expectations in the nuptial event, no mention of the possibility of family thereafter, no mention of the way the sunshine mottles the tree in late autumn on a dirt track in meadows along the water in November as one rides toward one's wedding. The absent Mary Hirst is implied, however, in the mention of her husband. Otherwise the last day of the diary is completely opaque. As my father put it with a brutal economy of words, Joseph married *the second choice.*

In *our* last morning in York, we learned of one last, sad chapter of Handkerchief Moody's life. Involving another murder. Banks's account runs thus:

> An unfortunate Indian woman, named Boston, gave birth to an illegitimate child, of which she alleged one Trott to be the father, and she killed it at birth. She was tried and convicted in June of the above year and sentenced to death by hanging. As usual she underwent "conversion" which is related in a pamphlet by Parson Moody and his son Joseph, and went to her doom on Stage Neck, very cheerfully, according to these witnesses.

The passage in Banks's history succeeds another account of execution, roughly contemporaneous with Joseph's diaries, of one Joseph Quasson, also an Indian, also converted:

> When all was ready for the final act [Quasson] ascended the ladder and made a short address, after which he offered a prayer of some length, and out of this scene Parson [Samuel] Moody has made an instructive picture of the way criminals were executed in his day. In June 1704 Mr. Moody attended the execution of six pirates in Boston, in company of his cousin, Judge Samuel Sewall. He relates that there were in the river carrying spectators about one hundred and fifty boats and canoes. Evidently hangings had a fascination for the parson.

Although Joseph Moody might have been present at Quasson's drama, as a respected member of the community (a magistrate, if not yet a minister himself), he isn't included in its accounts. The case was perhaps less resonant. Quasson had killed multiply and ferociously. Patience Boston was married to an African slave in York, and, according to the law, was thereby enslaved herself, though she was a Native American. Apparently, Patience conceived a child with Boston and announced that the child would be born dead, which it was. Boston sued to have her charged with murder, but she was exonerated, which marked the end of their marriage. Patience was then indentured to a master in Manchester, New Hampshire (and presumably later of York), probably the Trott mentioned in Banks, the son of whom, probably her own, she first beat with a stick, repenting after. The next day she drowned him in a well. Her account (which doesn't jibe with Banks's), if any of it is hers, is merciless:

> I went to the Well and threw the Pole in, that I might have an Excuse to draw the Boy to the Well, which having done, I asked his Help to get up the Pole, that I might push him in, which having done, I took a longer Pole, and thrust him down under the Water, till he was drowned.

Handkerchief Moody, only seven months before his wife's death, apparently took an interest in Patience, where he had not in other judicial proceedings, and was among the six or seven local ministers who visited Boston in her cell to attempt conversion. Perhaps Joseph Moody, as a manslaughterer himself, made this journey with personal insight, or perhaps, since his father was fascinated with hangings, he was induced to attend. Whichever, the Moodys initially visited Patience Boston at the Old Gaol of York, erected in 1653 to serve as the house of correction for the entire province (it served in this capacity until 1860, more than two hundred years), mainly as a warehouse for those convicted of crimes such as lying and blaspheming. Total capacity was seven to nine prisoners. Here the Moodys, Samuel and Joseph, read scripture to persuade the Native American slave Patience Boston to renounce her *heinous abominations* and to convert so that they might say of her, like at any other execution, *The mile's Walk was improved in directing, encouraging & cautioning the Prisoner to Hope.* The punishment was exacted in July of 1735, and the Moodys prayed at the scaffold.

The source for most histories of Patience Boston's ordeal is her "confession," but that confession was written, according to local custom, by the Moodys themselves. *A Fruitful Narrative of the Wicked Life and Remarkable Conversion of Patience Boston* is the only piece of writing published and signed by the Reverend Joseph Moody in his lifetime. Unlike many eighteenth-century criminal narratives, noteworthy for gallons of blood and much murderous glee, Patience's narrative is as dull as a tax guide, since, like Handkerchief Moody's diaries, it is mainly concerned with continual and mostly unresolved machinations of conscience. Back and forth, prideful and meek, Patience goes, excoriating herself:

> I saw plainly that I deserved eternal Misery, and Hell was the only fit place for me. I was angry with the Prison Keeper for restraining me from my self-murdering desires.

Or:

> The whole Night after the three Malefacters were Executed at *Boston,* and all the next Day, and the Night following, till almost Break of Day, I was distressed, not only on the Account of my horrid Guilt, and Liableness to eternal Wrath, for my wicked Life, and bloody actual Sins; but for the Wickedness of my Heart.

Her morbid reflection patently suggests the hand of Joseph Moody, as we recognize it now, but the more direct evidence comes at the climax of the narrative itself, when the story abruptly shifts from the first-person narrative of Patience Boston to the recording voice of one of the editors: *THE Reader will excuse it that the Narrative breaks off so abruptly, and will give us leave to supply the Deficiency with the following Extract from the Diary of a Person that was much Conversant with the Deceased, during her Confinement.* This section is diaristic in a style very similar to Joseph Moody's own journal:

> *Nov. 25. Being sent for I visited the Prisoner, and found her in a great Distress, crying out as before; but left her in a very humble, calm, comfortable Frame of Spirit.*

Moreover, these diary entries appear to describe the elder Moody, to the exclusion of the younger, who would then appear to be their author:

> *Thursday, July 24. . . . After the Lecture preached by Mr. Moody . . . I went up with the Prisoner; She finds it hard to part with her Child. Mr. Moody read to her the Passage of Abraham's offering up his son.*

The date of publication also reflects the pamphlet's authorship. While Patience Boston was executed in July of 1735, with, presumably, her confession taken down in its entirety prior to that day, the mere thirty pages that make up her *fruitful* narrative languished until 1738 to be completed, two years after the death of Joseph Moody's wife, Lucy, or almost exactly coincident *with Joseph Moody's assumption of the veil.* As the editors point out, *The Account was not drawn up in haste, but Things were written down at twenty several Times — One Day Week and Month after another.*

No unembroidered account exists of the moment in 1738, after two years of attempting to minister and to care for his motherless children, that Joseph *appeared before his congregation wearing a white kerchief draped from his forehead and concealing all his features.* And yet there is much in Patience Boston's story of his own dark embellishment, especially the evocations of insupportable grief.

> She smote her Hands together often, and kept continually lamenting and roaring and shrieking, for I think Hours together, with little Intermission. Some of her Expressions, which she repeated with utmost Vehemency, ten or twenty times together, were such as fol-

low — O I have offended a merciful God! a Merciful God! I have offended the God and Father of our Lord Jesus Christ. O Sin, Sin, Sin! &c. O now I find it is an evil and bitter Thing to depart from the Living God! O the Sin of Murther! Murther! Murther! — O the Sin of Lying. — O I used to play a Sabbath Days! — O my putting off my returning to God! — O to die Christless!

What appears to be the story of a Native American forced into slavery, expatriation, and madness, and executed by a merciless state, a state bent on the slaughter of the natives, is really the tale, in metaphor, of a morbidly shy pastor's son who killed his friend and never forgot. *I did last Fall bind my self by a wicked Oath that I would kill that Child, though I seem'd to love him, and he me; which is an Aggravation of my bloody Cruelty to him. Having solemnly sworn that I would be the Death of the Child, I was so far from repenting of it, that I thought I was obliged to fulfill it.* The pastor's son who then had to endure the death of a wife and child. The pastor's son who had in his way been wearing the veil already. *I expected no other, but to be Condemned and Executed.* Hadn't the veil covered him since the age of eight or nine? *I am so troubled that I cannot speak in Prayer, God seems to shut the Door against me; and not to welcome me into his Presence.* Didn't it cover him in his imagination, in the briars of his troubled sleep, *I thought I would have given a World had I a World to give, that I had never sinned as I had done,* so that when it occurred to him actually, that scrap that he had formerly used to wipe the nose of his youngest child and which he now fastened over his fretful visage, there was no novelty in it at all? Patience Boston, the *savage,* might very well have been the source of his dark notion: *After the Rope was about her Neck, I asked her whether she did not believe that Christ, who had helped her along so near her End, could help along the few Steps that remained? She (evidently with a Smile, which several others besides my self took notice of) answered, Yes. After her face was covered, Mr. Moody asked her, whether she remembered what she designed to say? She said, Yes, and added,* Lord Jesus, receive my spirit.

WHAT IS THIS WORLD GOOD FOR
NOW THAT WE CAN NEVER
BE JOLLY ANYMORE . . .

Three days into the *family therapy seminar* at Jen's rehab, the two of us were scheduled to have a conversation in front of the entire cast, consisting of a half dozen other alcoholics, their family members, and a pair of alcoholism counselors from the upstate rehabilitation center with the pastoral name. You were not permitted to drink during the *family therapy seminar,* it was part of the agreement, and so I hadn't drunk anything, concluding my career as a problem drinker the prior weekend with three beers at a friend's house while watching the Red Sox. This was ending with a whimper. I wasn't experiencing *delirium tremens* during this episode of temperance, but neither was I comfortable. I perspired a lot. All the broadcast fare on the television in the motel where I was staying while partaking of the *family therapy seminar* seemed to feature minor character actors raping other cast members. That's how it looked each night, after the sequence of confessions and bad-news bulletins that filled our therapeutic days. I couldn't sleep, in my polyurethane motel interior. I spent much of the night swimming in bedclothes, especially the night before our scheduled *communications workshop.* That afternoon we all had gazed powerlessly as a couple in their sixties, Everett and Lucinda, began bickering and then disagreeing violently. Everett, who was the *recovering alcoholic,* denied charges lodged against him, said his wife had been wrong to bring him to this damned place, his wife was a damned fool, needed to have her head examined, and Lucinda had responded, not long after the conversation, with a heart attack. They were a charming couple; he was an old jazz musician who in his bald-ness and robustness reminded me of my grandfather. They told amazing stories, both of them. And they were miserable.

It wouldn't go well for Jen and me, either. The opening round of our own communications prizefight was about how I had *to move out,* had to pack my things, had to find another place to live, and I was unprepared for this and for the fact that Jen had waited to give me this news in public. *I think what Jen is saying is that she can't live with you while you are drinking,* the counselors chimed in. *But I'm not drink-ing.* And so forth. The conversation didn't go well after this blow; I couldn't get my footing, and so I tried to say inoffensive things as briefly as possible. As I was digesting the fact that I wouldn't have anywhere to go when I left the *rehabilitation center,* one of the referees decided that it was time for Jen and me to say that we *loved* each other. *It might be really nice for all of us here if you two told each other that you loved one another.* And there was Jen, radiantly beautiful after her month of AA meetings, her group therapy, her hours in the gym, her walks in the woods; in the other corner myself, pasty from never going outdoors, overweight, with long unwashed hair, believing that everyone in the room was a secret rapist, having decided nonetheless that I would propose to Jen when she got out, but she had got out, and we'd had a couple days together before returning for this *family therapy seminar,* and I hadn't proposed, and here I was, in this hot seat, in this folding metal chair, in a windowless cell at the *rehabilitation center,* and I couldn't think of a time when I'd said I loved her, if *ever* I'd told her that I loved her, nor had she told me that she loved me, nor had my family much told me they loved me, nor had my family much told anyone else that they loved them, come to think of it, although I had heard much abuse of these words, *I love you,* in television commercials and musicals and Hollywood movies. I had never quite heard them in *real life.* It wasn't my experience that actual people said these words at all. Much of American cul-ture purported to deal with the subject of *love.* The popular song and the world's religions agreed: *All you need is love.* Just a few little words, I thought. *Go ahead and say them.* The mood in the room was expectant, but I had developed a reputation for recalcitrance and skepticism about *the program.* One of the other participants, a married woman in her thirties, told me later that she was *a bit cynical* about my intentions. So I felt as if I were failing an important entrance exam of some kind, even as I did my best, which was not very good: *We never say those sorts of things, but we both understand that we feel this way, that we love each other, but we don't say these sappy things.* The counselors immediately began to lecture us, all of us, on this subject, but mostly they began to lecture *me.* Jen looked detached, impassive, folding her arms while seated in her folding chair. *Didn't these people understand that I had lost my mind?* I thought. It was *big of me* that I had made this trip, in the condition I was in, with nonsense in my skull, ideas about self-slaughter, theories, dark insights. *Are you sure that's what Jen thinks?* the counselor asked, waking me from a reverie. I had no idea what Jen thought, and the ramifications of my uncertainty were clear enough. She had decided to leave me.

I filled out a drug history that afternoon, and when the alcoholism counselors got a look at it, one of them pulled me aside in the hallway. She was in her late thirties, with a red bob. She wore sweaters that were *excessively colorful.* Her smile was easy but, at the last moment, reserved. She definitely had kids that she loved to death, and it seemed impossible that she had once been a person in her twenties who stuck needles in her arm or sold her possessions in order to buy cocaine or who simply totaled cars and left friends in wheelchairs. I didn't trust her. I'd had occasion to weep publicly in some of the afternoon *communications workshops,* and the counselor had therefore come to see me, because there was more progress to be made in my particular case. She said:

—What do you want us to do for you?

I felt an ominousness in the conversation. It was a momentous time, but in what way momentous? I was unclear on other people. I had not thought of them much, really, and Jen had gone spinning away into space, as if sucked through a hole in my plummeting aircraft.

—I don't want you to do anything for me.

—You must want something. You're upset. You're distraught. You look like you might want some help. You *act* like you want some help. So tell us what it is that you want.

The corridor was empty, in recollection, as though no one upstate were getting treatment at this moment, as if I were the only person who needed it.

—I'm tired of living this way, I said hurriedly, furtively. —I'm tired of wasting time, tired of being so unhappy . . .

—Are you saying you'd like treatment?

—No, I'm . . .

—We've looked at your drug history.

It was naive to have failed to see that I was going to look *appetizing* to the employees at the rehabilitation center, especially when my mental health professional back home, in a strangely paranoid outburst, had warned me to be on the alert for this very possibility. *These AA people will try to convert you.* Nevertheless, I was surprised. I began negotiating. I had requirements.

—I can't go anywhere there's not a battery of psychiatrists.

—Well, we might be able to work something out.

—But I have to go to work on Monday. And how am I . . .

—Give me your insurance card. I'll make the calls.

—What about my boss?

—You want me to sit with you while you talk to him?

She undertook these logistical problems, which I believed were insurmountable, and, in the meantime, advised me to go to the final *afternoon workshop,* in which a recording of "It's My Turn," by a popular R&B diva, warbled on a cassette player while we each spoke of our dreams of *overcoming codependency.* My only dream was to get the hell out of the rehabilitation center with the pastoral name as soon as possible, and to go lick these wounds that I thought I probably deserved. However, in the confines of the *family therapy seminar,* I claimed to want to reach my potential as a person. I said what I had to say. I talked some of the talk, on a provisional basis. It was almost impossible for me not to see the argot of recovery and the people of recovery as comic, with their *drink signals* and *isms* and *qualifications,* with their episodes of *stinkin' thinking,* their baby-block slogans, *Keep it simple, stupid,* though I really liked the Lost Generation prose of their founders. But I was perched on the bluff between two lives, one short and gray and having all the characteristics of certain outlaw recordings I'd favored when young. I would be like the guitar player slumped over his instrument, electrocuted; I would be as certain writers disappearing into Middle Eastern countries to smoke *kief* and record tales of *Bedouins;* I would be in the White Horse Tavern when my liver gave out, I would fight off multiple paternity suits, I would lance the boils of the American bourgeoisie from a country house in Sligo. But this life had so far resulted only in indolence. The *other* life that stretched out in languid possibility was quieter and longer and had none of the drama of the guitar players or smokers of *kief* or kids in the East Village shivering in front of squats; this life featured long, dull struggles, constant opportunities for humility, much that was not glamorous, laundry, dishes, male pattern baldness. This other life would involve getting to know people who wore sweaters that were too brightly colored. It would involve stammering, feigning interest in sports and the stock market. It would involve doting on nieces and nephews, dieting, exercise. I was an awkward kid who had not grown up, who had stopped growing up somewhere way back in my teens, and who had paid a price, in that the *morbid thinking* had found a ready target in me, *and bright gildings but fringed my blackness.* Readers of my earliest novel, *Garden State,* of which the first three chapters were drafted, despite my illness, in the early months of 1987, can see the fault line I'm describing, which runs through me in the pages of that book, pages 125–126, and is best symbolized in the activities of the protagonist immediately before and after that break. The blank pages were a lot like me. That afternoon in the rehabilitation center, however, impediments to *the decision* had been taken from me by the woman with the red bob, and only selfishness remained to inhibit this new, unforeseeable life of church basements and apologetic notes. There was no reason why I should *not* have opted for the familiar biography in which I ended up copping in the East Village and writing bitter reviews for the *New York Press* about comic books and fanzines, and yet, I seemed to do exactly the contrary; *I turned my back on that life.* All at once. Without much conviction, though sometimes conviction is irrelevant. And that was how I found myself that evening in a van being driven by a taciturn guy whose job it was to drive junkies and alcoholics to various addresses, and it was raining, and the Mets, whose best pitcher was also about to check himself into a rehabilitation center, were losing a game on the radio, and this taciturn driver, who didn't want to hear any junkie bullshit, was taking me *somewhere,* but didn't really tell me where, or perhaps there was only an address for him, past this dilapidated shopping center, along this stretch of the interstate, to Hollis, Queens, and soon I was sitting in the admitting room, at dusk, on a Sunday, in July, and I was being asked if I knew *who the president of the United States was,* if I was capable of doing the nines table, and what brought me to the hospital. I was worldly enough to know that only schizophrenics replied, *A van brought me to the hospital,* indicating severe deficit in figurative thinking, so I said *hopelessness* had brought me to this borough of Queens. And the admitting psychiatrist, who had attended, I guessed, Williams, or maybe Cornell, and who liked, I imagined, Eric Clapton, said, *I think we might be able to help you with that.*

It was an address in which all the doors locked behind me. There was a door between the admitting doctor and the hallway, and it locked, and then the elevator locked, and then the door onto Three North, the adult ward, locked. These hardware fixtures were to keep me *in.* It was an address with rules, and on the first night the rules were being recited for me while a staff person meanwhile gave me a scar search, so that the hospital would know if I incurred new scars during the period of my residence: *Everyone comes here believing that they don't belong here; all the windows open three inches only; no sharp edges permitted; board games are everywhere for your amusement; television has therapeutic value; no physical contact with others is permitted; you will not experience seasons; everyone smokes; the way out is to cooperate.* While everyone else was lined up getting their medications, I was having my blood pressure taken, having blood drawn, answering questions about allergies and childhood illnesses. In fact, I had my blood pressure taken so many times in Hollis, Queens, that I learned to do it myself, to recognize systole and diastole. And when they were done anatomizing me, on the first night, a nurse took me to the empty room, the double, that was to be my residence for the next month. It was considered *bad form* to have your door closed, unless you were changing clothes, and I learned this right away because of the ruckus across the hall. I was in a place where the girl with anorexia nervosa and bulimia who had tried to close the door so she could put her finger down her throat could not do so in privacy. I was in a place where Stan, the acid casualty who had attempted to stay in bed all day, was at the moment being roused by the orderlies for the ingestion of his antipsychotic medication. I was in a place where I was *lucky* to have a first night alone in the room, except that I was on Eye Contact, according to which, like everyone else on the first night in, every fifteen minutes the night orderly came to see what I was doing, and what I was doing every fifteen minutes was being *waked* by the night orderly, so that I got no sleep at all, after which I was roused for breakfast, a special tray they had prepared for me with raisin bran and prune juice. I was in a place where everyone *always* had prune juice at breakfast, because of the legendary side effects of psychiatric medication, though I didn't know this yet, nor that those trays with their decomposition reek would stop me in my tracks forever after, when I hallucinated their homely contents on the breeze. After breakfast, it was time for me to meet with my consulting psychiatrist, a Spanish guy, don't know why he was in this country instead of in Spain, but he was incredibly gifted, this mental health professional, with compassion and dream interpretation, so much that there was a brief flourishing in me of dreams, including this scrap furnished to my psychiatrist upon request:

> At summer camp, I am again engaged in my lonely, thankless job as woodcutter. This day, tired of the heat, humidity, and monotony of the task, I decide to head off into the woods to rest for a while. I go up the hill, feeling carefree, when I hear something rustling among the leaves and underbrush. It's a wolf, and it wastes no time in attacking. I realize that I have had my red axe with me all along, and I brandish it at the wolf, which backs off and circles around. I brush it off my left side, pivot to cover my back, but still the wolf growls at me. When it leaps at last, I bury the axe, with a full swing, in the right side of its abdomen. The wolf howls,

hobbles a few steps, and then stumbles onto the ground, dead. I am deeply shaken as I head back down the hill to camp, carrying the axe, now covered with blood. There doesn't seem to be anyone around, but as I walk down the road (troubled and confused about the wolf), I see the wife of one of the elderly camp directors sitting on a suitcase by the side of the road. I try to hide my axe.

The day I arrived, the hospital had also admitted a Haitian woman called Cecilie, and she was apparently catatonic, so while I was waiting for my *status one current events workshop* to begin, I was sitting in the dayroom, where there was a talk show on (Phil Donahue), watching Cecilie, who was sitting across the room motionless, silent, pretending, as much as possible, to resemble the grass-cloth wallpaper that covered all the walls in the adult ward. Also among us was Diana, a woman in her later fifties who had lived her life with her mother until her mother had died, after which, according to legend, she had shut herself in the house and refused to go out for weeks, didn't eat much or bathe or look after anything in the house, until some friends or neighbors came in and found her. She was the closest thing I had ever seen to an actual ghost. She had the anguished expression of ghosts and wore a translucent nightgown day in and day out, under which her enormous, pendulous breasts clearly rested against her belly, and from which her swollen, arthritic ankles protruded. There was also Holly, a schizophrenic girl with an incredibly belligerent personality and a homely, chubby appearance. Nobody liked her, but she had one bright spot. She drew the best portraits I had ever seen. She drew, in minutes, incredibly perfect likenesses in pen and pencil. She had made a little out of this talent, for magazines and other publications, but she was so difficult that the work never lasted. And Monica, a secretary at NBC who suffered from *bipolar disorder,* and who had checked herself into the hospital after Mickey Mouse told her that she should drag all of her furniture out onto the lawn in Astoria, where she lived, at which point she was ordered to strip down to her lingerie and perform calisthenics for the parade of

Walt Disney characters coming up her street. On good days, she knew this was a hoax and was embarrassed; on bad days, she ventured tangled hypotheses about Einstein and relativity and the RCA corporation. Noel, a junkie who drove limousines for Michael Jackson and other celebrities; Joey, an alcoholic doorman from Manhattan who had such horrible blackouts that he had lost weeks at a time and found himself in distant cities and countries. Stan, the abovementioned *mook* who took seventy hits of acid in one day and was banished by his parents to a mobile home on a distant corner of their property; Bob, a development guy for one of the really adventurous indie production companies and a cocaine addict who as a child had been sexually abused by his brother; Jack, a drunk with brain damage; and so forth. It was easy to be an observer of my neighbors in that environment, it was easy to lose myself in the contrasts between myself and those around me, but that didn't mean I felt any better. It just meant there was a lot to look at.

Meanwhile, the girl across the hall with anorexia nervosa and bulimia carried her copy of *The Power of Positive Thinking* into the dayroom with her. She couldn't sit still. She would watch a minute of Phil Donahue, make some grave prognostications to herself, march out of the room, and then come back a few minutes later and repeat the whole business. She was nineteen or thereabouts, luminously beautiful, if horribly thin, with blond hair and unearthly blue eyes and freckles. Her wrists were crosshatched with scars. When it was time for *status one current events workshop,* they summoned her and me and Cecilie down to the dining room. The residents, the ones doing the summoning, were kids only a couple of years older than I. On rotation, perhaps. I would have known them back when I was in boarding school, they were good at field hockey or lacrosse, they were active in student government, and now they were seeing me on the other side of the table in the psychiatric hospital, beside a catatonic Haitian woman and an Irish bulimic. One of these Ivy League residents was now attempting to get us to read that morning's paper, as follows: *Okay, Kate, Cecilie, will you listen up for a second? The idea of this exercise is just to get you interested in what's going on outside the walls of the hospital. So what I'd like you to do is to take this newspaper and just read a little bit of one of the stories on the front page, and then I'd like you to tell me what's going on in the story. Just summarize it for me. Kate? You're going to have to put down your book, if you don't mind. Just put it on the table there for a second, yes, please. Thanks. Okay, Cecilie? Cecilie? Do you think maybe you could read just a little bit of this? Would that be possible for you?* In a compelling example of how novel writing infects your life, I can no longer remember what was *in* that newspaper, because the actual story that I read aloud to the resident has been overwritten by a headline, *Mob Boss Beats Rap,* that I imagined when I retold this story in my first novel. But I can remember the agitation of Kate the bulimic, who couldn't stop mumbling to me, to herself, and to the resident about things that had happened months ago or years ago or yesterday, in a stream of monology that knotted up all the divergent tributaries of time, and because of which she couldn't concentrate on the newspaper article, though the resident offered to cut her a deal. *Okay, Kate, just read the headline for me, okay? Just the headline would be great.* Kate, the afflicted Irish beauty, attempted to read the headline but couldn't even get through that. Not even half of it. Later, I found out that *current events workshop* was intended as a sort of evaluation: if you could read the newspaper, even a little bit, your *reality testing* was good enough to get you off of status one, meaning that you were allowed to leave the ward (supervised), to go upstairs to the AA meetings, and to go to the gymnasium. All you had to do was to read a headline from *Newsday* about Iran-Contra. And the truth was that Kate, whose gin-blossomed Irish father would arrive the next day to ferry her away to Creedmore, the state facility, the mere name of which struck terror in the hearts of recidivists on the ward, had just spent a month in the private hospital at Hollis, Queens, without ever getting promoted to status two. She'd never once made headway with a newspaper article for the resident. They'd force-fed her, they'd used an IV on her, they'd medicated her, tried cognitive therapy, behavior modification, and she still didn't give a shit about current events. Now her month was up, and it was off to Creedmore. Cecilie, while this adjacent drama took place, never said a word, never lifted the newspaper into her lap, never responded in any way.

I passed the *current events* test, however. And I felt a sort of dim pride about it.

After lunch, which I tried to eat by myself, only to be interrupted by the nurses who would plunk down in chairs next to me and invite over other patients on the ward, *there was some real fun in the dayroom.* A Dominican woman called Conchita was having a visit from her husband, a Hispanic guy, when something went dreadfully wrong. He proffered accusations about neglecting their son, or worse, and then there was some weeping, and then Conchita began *to seize.* I came in at the end. Conchita had flung herself onto the floor, had gone rigid, screaming, and then silent. Her eyes rolled up into her head. Immediately the nurses and orderlies circled around her. Patients rushed nervously in and out of the room, unable to look, unable to look away. *What's going on?* The orderlies tried to get everyone cleared out of the dayroom, but I watched terrified as the head nurse unsheathed a hypodermic needle, swabbed Conchita's arm, and perforated it. Then they hoisted that rag-doll girl up and dragged her, with limp extremities, out into the hall, to her room. The door closed swiftly behind them, and there we were, in the hall, like antimatter particles scattered in some brilliant interstellar event, each with our hypothesis: *Oh, she's upset,* or her husband did it, or it's a reaction to her meds. The husband vanished from the premises, and then, in the dayroom, a golf tournament resumed on the television. Conchita didn't get out of her bed for two days.

Soon it was our national holiday, Fourth of July 1987, the 183rd anniversary of the birth of Nathaniel Hawthorne, and Jen called from home to say that my father had actually *yelled at her,* demanding to know where I was, and she had refused to tell him. I hadn't called my parents yet. Hadn't told anyone anything. In the meantime, I had been promoted to status two, and thus on this national holiday I was permitted to go to the corner store down on Hillside Avenue by the last stop on the F train, with the rest of our eligible ward members, and there I could buy a soft drink and a candy bar. The day was appallingly humid, and when we hit the front door of the hospital, emerged into the imperfect shade of some oaks, the tremendous privilege of being allowed *out* of the hospital seemed instead like a curse.

I wondered what the other residents of tree-lined Hollis, Queens, thought when they saw the parade of *loonies* from the *flight deck* ambling down the block. Did they imagine only tabloid versions of deinstitutionalized schizophrenics with violent pasts? When I was a kid, sneaking onto the property of the drying-out joint next to our house in New Canaan, I never expected to be in a *parade* like this, going down to the corner next to a woman who had spontaneously lost the ability to speak, next to a Jungian analyst who had tried to kill herself, just behind a bodybuilder who was also a compulsive masturbator, etc., all of us trudging down the hill, wondering if things could get any worse. When I was a kid, I thought the difficulties that brought you to the psychiatric hospital were *communicable.* I felt sure that this was the case, that I would catch what those people had, that I shouldn't have any truck with them lest they pass on to me their germs, their viruses. This was true even of my mother's mother, who lay in her massive bed in Pelham, with her liver giving out, when I was very small. My mother said to us, *Come on in and say hello to your grandmother.* But I didn't want to catch what she had. And I did.

The bodega interior was moist. Linoleum heaved under our feet. There was lemonade and the more obvious candies, Kit Kats, M&M's, and I bought candy because I had heard it was important to abuse sugar when you first quit drinking. The proprietors looked at us like our money was good enough, though they knew from which address we had come. From up the street. We trudged back up the hill in the same self-conscious formation. Because it was a holiday and the hospital was short staffed, the nurses decided to allow us some exercise time on the lawn. Some Frisbees and a soccer ball materialized. The younger inmates ran crazily in circles on the lawn, like the mosquitoes of July that fed on our institutionalized flesh. A Frisbee bonked one depressed guy on the head. He paid no attention. And I sat in the shade of a fire escape with a nurse called Linda. Linda, I surmised, had found dead bodies on the ward, had broken the news to the rest of the inmates, had seen people go off to the state hospital, never to be released, had looked after patients who couldn't even attend to their own hygiene or feed themselves, had known teenagers bent on taking out a few friends with submachine guns, had escorted boys to the quiet room, had presided over the electroshock apparatus and helped the convulsed back to their beds. Linda was enormous, almost obese. She looked like a melancholy extra from a Bergman film, one who had prayed to a vengeful God. Her slate-colored eyes were perpetually bloodshot. She scowled a lot. She was possibly the most discerning listener I had ever met in my life. There was a transistor radio playing on the lawn, and the selection was the original version of Elton John's "Candle in the Wind," from the album called *Goodbye Yellow Brick Road.* The sun oppressed me. Summer in New York City oppressed me, but even that doesn't describe my desire to flee entirely *from the visible,* from being perceived, from the tendency of New York City roads to be lined with trash, from rage upon the streets, smoldering racism. The drunken doorman with the convulsive blackouts had called me a *homophobic slur;* the noise in my head hadn't been stilled by the hospital — it was revolving in my skull. I was myself a transistor radio that couldn't be tuned properly; the signal kept fading in and out; I couldn't hold up my end of the contract of my birth; *I was going to be raped.* Nothing ahead of me but numberless days exactly like the one I was having, in which a bunch of mentally ill people couldn't get a game of Frisbee organized, because they couldn't concentrate.

Every kid who grew up in the seventies knew by heart all the songs on *Goodbye Yellow Brick Road,* the magnum opus of the young Elton John. Every American confused its barrelhouse piano and triplets with the double yellow lines on the highway of his life, with the cafeteria food of public schools; every kid had applied its awkward poetics to his life, had done so with Elton John as far back in memory as memory went, in the way that I could remember "Your Song" from particular stretches of the Merritt Parkway when I was being driven back and forth from one parent to another on weekends, with the AM car radio playing and New York deejays with too much reverb wisecracking over the compressed fade-outs of the Top 40, as when we used to sit around on the jungle gym trying to figure out what the hell Elton was *saying* on "Crocodile Rock," what were the words, exactly. And there was the allusive "Levon," and my mother explaining it to me on the way to dancing school on Tuesday nights, some plenitude of loss was summoned by Elton in that tune, as it swept back to *the war* and forward into the distant future, and so my lonely, unmarried mother bought the album, in this way exposing me to that terrifying title track about the character in the mental hospital, "Madman Across the Water." Who was it in *that place?* And why? "Rocket Man" had a line about raising kids on Mars, which upset me because I knew *cold as hell* implied something about the potential for loneliness in all interactions, whether failed or successful. But it wasn't until *Goodbye Yellow Brick Road* that Elton seemed to understand every possible emotion that afflicted a kid in the Connecticut suburbs. A spooky dirge opened the record, when you first put it on your record player; sounds ridiculous now, that bell tolling synthetically in the background, the simulated cry of an owl. But at the time, this dirge summoned the ponderous, sober tones of grief, before giving way to a rave-up about a failed romance. This track was followed soon by "Bennie and the Jets," another song that everybody in my junior high school attempted to decipher: what exactly was a *fatted calf* and what was a *mohair suit,* and why was Elton's garbled pronunciation so appalling, and what was it with the fake audience applauding in the background? Also important in this initiation into the mystery of puberty was "Jamaica Jerk-Off," whose fake reggae was meaningless to me since I'd heard almost none of the genuine form as played by Rastafarians, but whose celebration of self-abuse and sensuality hinted at a possible universe where people got to do things that I would never understand and would never get to do. I spent a sleepover with a friend on Ponus Ridge in New Canaan discussing "Jamaica Jerk-Off," discussing what *jerking off* was, what did it mean, what were the physiognomic particulars; likewise "Sweet Painted Lady," about prostitutes, *whores,* who didn't know what they were supposed to do; or "All the Girls Love Alice," a song about what girls could do to the exclusion of boys, would girls kiss one another *without* boys, and why exactly would they want to exclude boys? There was a forest behind our house, Elton was our subject there; there was a park where I played intramural soccer, Elton was our subject there; "Philadelphia Freedom" was playing in the department store the only time I ever shoplifted (stole a hockey puck); "Don't Let the Sun Go Down On Me" was playing when we moved out of New Canaan and relocated our ragtag household to Westchester County; "Sorry Seems to Be the Hardest Word," during the late stages of Watergate, when my mother's father gave up the ghost. Elton was *always* playing somewhere, saving someone's life; his plane was always touching down; the bitch was always back, at least in that first period of his career, before the portly, drunken, balding, disco-loving Liberace imitator; until then, Elton was the voice of suburban youth.

Have I forgotten "Saturday Night's Alright for Fighting"? What better evocation of the time? The electric guitar, the nasty snare drum at the beginning, not a piano in the joint, not at the outset, the first time that Elton ever sang lead vocals in the studio without sitting at the piano, the sister in braces and boots, grease in her hair, the guitar baldly imitating the style of Keith Richards, tattoos, underage drinking, mischief, breaking things, inattentive parents, guzzling of all sorts, everything my childhood was and was not, no matter that they used it at dancing school along with "Your Mama Don't Dance" by Loggins and Messina, proving that its conviction was partial at best. We weren't smart enough to know that yet, and the record company probably knew we weren't smart enough to know that Elton was a multimillionaire bisexual who owned a soccer team and anyhow that wasn't even his real name.

Buried in the first side of the album was that song about Marilyn Monroe. A song not about stardom but about being nobody. *Would have liked to have known you, but I was just a kid,* that's the powerless using binoculars to watch the spectacle of power; when I heard it first I *was* just a kid, and everybody that went past my bus stop was like the Norma Jean of the original lyric, accomplished, responsible, competent, worldly, in sedans of foreign make, and I was the kid with no shadow, *and that's the song* that was playing on the transistor radio out on the lawn in Hollis, Queens, in 1987, in this bad patch, at which juncture Norma Jean's mixture of pills and booze didn't seem so bad, seemed like a pretty reasonable strategy, in fact. I had managed to land precisely where the storm drains and sewer lines emptied, where the most troubled people landed, at least the ones with insurance. I had experienced the perfection of yearning that comes with childhood, fast cars and mountaintops, a creek out in the woods, the open sea, the perfection of harmony, the shouts of beer salesmen in baseball parks, rock and roll, and all yearning was gone, and even the recollection of how to yearn was gone, the desire for desire was gone, and I was a mediocre adult with bad luck, sitting next to a Hasidic woman wearing rags, opposite Linda, the expert listener, on the front lawn of a psychiatric hospital in Queens. I had never been in Queens before, that I knew of. *I wept.*

Linda accompanied me inside. Took me to my empty room, where I had only three days of clothes that I had brought with me to the *family therapy seminar* at the upstate rehab. And a toothbrush. And a copy of *Laughable Loves,* by Milan Kundera. Linda didn't bother with any preliminaries. She was not the kind of person to waste time on politeness. She looked me in the eye.

—What's going on?

I couldn't believe what had happened to me.

I HAVE SUFFERED WOEFULLY
FROM LOW SPIRITS
FOR SOME TIME PAST . . .

Conventional wisdom has it that *acceptance* of the addictive condition is the initial step on the road to the cure, and conventional wisdom also has it that the addictive condition *conceals itself from the sufferer;* therefore, conventional wisdom would advise that the sufferer should accept what he doesn't know or believe to be true about himself, the thing concealed, the thing veiled within. When we were allowed to fraternize with the junkies and cocaine addicts on the ward upstairs, it was pretty obvious that there was truth in this formulation. The amount of bunk that came out of the mouths of these addicts was inspired. There was, for example, a cocaine addict from out on Long Island. Presentable young guy, the sort you would see these days wearing *complete outfits from Old Navy,* carrying a beeper. Probably had his own powerboat and convertible. He regaled us with plans: *I'm going to get a sponsor, and I'm going to get started working the steps right away, and I'm going to find a home group, and I'm going to go to aftercare, I'm going to reach out a hand to the addict who still suffers.* Talking so fast, it was as if he was still wired, as if a coca supply was stored in him somewhere and weeks later this supply was leaking into his blood-stream on an as-needed basis. I didn't believe a word of his rap. The same was true of my roommate, who arrived three or four days after I did, an African-American guy of great dignity called Ron, who had been a marine in Vietnam and who, in the years after the southeast Asian conflict, had become a narcotics dealer for the Colombian mob. No one was sure why Ron was on the adult ward instead of upstairs on the addiction ward with the other hard-core addict types.

His first night in, Ron told me he had been clean for several days before arriving at the hospital in Hollis, Queens. Then, a week or so later, when a camaraderie began to develop, Ron confessed that he had been high the night before arriving. Later still, he admitted that he had gotten high on the way to the hospital, and, near upon his release, he told me that he'd actually done a bump *in the parking lot* outside the hospital before coming through the door. The tendency at the hospital was to cover over the truth wherever possible. Delusion was the atmosphere in the hospital. It was the very air. It was what you inhaled and exhaled, and the staff conducted doomed raids against delusion and its companion deceit, and they were occasionally successful. In the end, however, this effort was about as useful as saying, *We've got to get all the air out of this room.* My roommate, despite an earnest desire to reach beneath his own layers of delusion, boasted amazingly, *I know how to talk to the white man, make him feel okay about himself,* or, *In the war, I didn't bother to make any friends, they'd just be dead the next day,* or, *Rick, you wouldn't believe what the women out there will do for a drug dealer.*

The residents designed stories to make themselves look as if they would never be in a psychiatric hospital in Queens. Even the schizophrenics did it, even the manic-depressives. Everyone. I was as bad as the rest, trying to use noble birth, expensive education, and a capacity for large words to make myself more impressive, as when I was assigned, by my therapeutic group, a paper on *the meaning of self-esteem.* Here's an excerpt from the first draft:

> What is valuable is necessarily shifting during periods of doubt. Value and esteem (the latter coming from or distantly related to *estimate* and thus, likely, partly about the ability to *count* what is good or just), these depend on certainty since they are ideals. From different vantage points, different tallies will emerge as to what produces the sense of dignity in a life, the ideal sense of dignity. Similarly, if there is little certainty, then doubt permeates the ability to make ideals have clarity. Environment plays a role in definition of esteem or value, also. A capitalist country may rely more often

on the languages of commerce or accountancy, while the result may vary significantly in, say, communist China. As well, the historical environment of a single individual life — social, familial, or educational — also helps formulate these definitions. So the meaning of ideals, often held to be immobile, may sometimes shift.

Meaning what? That self-esteem doesn't exist? Meaning that everything is relative? Meaning, I think, that I was contemptuous of the assignment and could run rings around the doormen and chauffeurs and secretaries of my therapeutic group. So I thought. As you can imagine, these waves of condescension didn't go over well with my neighbors on the ward. Still, while I wore the borrowed robes of deceit, I was also afraid of how horrible I felt, and if doing something about melancholy and its attendant distortions meant cooperating with the programs available to us in Hollis, Queens, then, with few other options, I decided to cooperate. And I saved all records of my cooperation, the records of my character in that month, all the paperwork, all of the fragments:

Q: How have you lost your self-respect due to your chemical usage?
A: Getting too drunk in public and saying or doing ridiculous things. Getting sick from drinking. Also, I found that I was thinking about alcohol much more than I wanted to.

An *Award of Merit* from while I was in the hospital:

This certificate is awarded to Mr. Rick Moody for excellence in Creative Therapeutic Activities, July 28, 1987. Signed Creative Therapeutic Activities Department.

My collages of construction paper, my psychiatric-ward poems produced when they asked us to write things, all preserved, like this little rhapsody on the subject of Hoboken:

Sunday around noon, and the crisp air makes the skyline across the Hudson seem no more than a few yards away. Manhattan looks like an awesome but artificial diorama set on the edge of Hoboken. As I make my way up Newark Street toward the river, the city is empty and silent, except for the occasional old car that limps across the intersection before me. The day feels wondrous.

Or an elegy that I wrote about Diana, who looked like a ghost:

> An escutcheon for her
> Solitary, slippered, limping,
> Badly garbed, grieving, silent soul
> Is her ample bearding. I saw
> Her tug the whiskers until she
> Bled. Once, I startled her at this.

I showed my mother a construction-paper collage from art therapy class. After I got out of the hospital. It resembled something that I'd have done in kindergarten, at the Ox Ridge School of Darien. She was struck dumb by the primitiveness of my art, by the childishness of my efforts, and by the fact that *I was sort of happy about having made my collage.* It had never occurred to me that I might again be happy cutting up construction paper, gluing it down. But it was good to be happy about anything.

Some of us responded to treatment, some of us didn't. Diana, the ghost, became more and more voluble as the weeks wore on, and a concealed aspect of her character surged to the fore: she was a rabid Yankees fan. She had listened to countless Yankee radio broadcasts over the years, even as a child, and knew the earned-run averages and on-base percentages of every player on the team. She would *scream,* if the game was on the television set, when it turned suddenly to Yankee advantage. Was it behavior modification group that effected the change in her?

Our goal in this exercise is to increase our awareness of personal symptoms of anxiety. If we can learn to take inventory, i.e., to recognize our mental and physical symptoms, we are in a better position to decrease these before they are beyond our control.

Or maybe it was our cognitive therapy group, and its list of "Irrational Ideas":

1. It is a dire necessity for you to be loved or approved by almost everyone for almost everything you do.
2. You must be thoroughly competent, adequate, and achieving in all possible respects.
3. Certain people are bad, wicked, or villainous, and they should be severely blamed or punished for their sins.
4. It is terrible, horrible, and catastrophic when things are not going the way you would like them to go.
5. Human unhappiness is externally caused and you have little or no ability to control your sorrows or rid yourselves of your negative feelings.

And so forth. Everything was therapeutic. No opportunity was lost. We even had calisthenics before breakfast in the meeting room at the end of the hall. Calisthenics were therapeutic. The woman who led calisthenics would try to get Stan, the acidhead, to touch his toes. She would try to get Diana to perform a sit-up. She was a young woman in leg warmers with a steely, skeptical demeanor. Nonparticipation in calisthenics was grounds for bitter reproach. And one morning, exasperated, she delivered her theory of correction to all of us: *I'm making you work so hard because I want to get you out of here. I don't want to have to see you come through those doors again. I want you to be the people who don't come back.*

Some of us got worse. For example, every night we played Scrabble. Monica, the bipolar secretary; Bob, the development guy; Nancy, the schoolteacher who had once lost the ability to speak; me. We felt we were the healthiest ones, but sometimes Monica didn't make sense at all, and Bob relapsed immediately upon release, and Nancy, who seemed to be kind of cheerful for a while, soon tried to cut her wrists with a shattered piece of ceramic ashtray. By the time I left, she was sequestered in her room. (She'd been the only one to beat me at Scrabble too, because Bob couldn't concentrate, and Monica would get transfixed by three-letter words like *dog, ant,* and *bed.*) Neil, a sweet, quiet construction guy who had been a Xanax addict, tapered off Valium while on our ward (to detoxify him from Xanax, they addicted him to Valium), at which point he went into a violent panic attack of a sort I recognized from my own travails. His lasted *several days.* The first night, sobbing and sweating, he found me in the day-room. *Rick, my heart has stopped!* He dragged me, beseechingly, to his room and lay down on the bed. *Feel my pulse! Feel my pulse!* He kept probing for it. He had no pulse at all, because he couldn't find the spot, because the certainty of cardiological emergency could occupy his obsessive mind for days. He went pale with fear. I found his pulse right away, of course. It was up over a hundred, probably closer to a hundred and twenty, and you could actually *see it,* thundering in his wrist. *Neil,* I said, *your heart sounds pretty good to me.* He didn't believe me. Later, he bribed a night orderly to release him from the hospital. The orderly took him down the elevator and ushered him out the front door. They had an acronym for this kind of departure: A.M.A., or *against medical advice.*

The patient you could never evaluate, since psychiatric condi-tions disguised themselves from the sufferers, was yourself. Even if I started to talk to the others on the ward, even if I went to career counseling and art therapy and drama therapy, all of which were incredibly embarrassing, even if I went to the gym and lifted weights and shot baskets, I still felt that therapy was for *naught,* that I had made up my symptoms, that my trouble was *weakness,* personal weakness, moral weakness, lack of courage, lack of fortitude, lack of American values, bad child rearing, excess *sensitivity,* for which crimes I would be *raped.* Since I couldn't accept the diagnosis, or my *idea* of the diagnosis (I never could get anyone to tell me the diagno-sis), it was impossible to see the cure.

Fear of light had been a theme in my *unexplained panic event,* as I described it to my Spanish mental health professional, and so the staff at the hospital decided to give me an E.E.G., to see if I had epilepsy, of which *fear of light* was, I was told, occasionally a symptom. In fact, they prescribed a *sleep-deprived* E.E.G. and scheduled it alongside two other such tests they were going to perform on two other residents, so that a group of us could stay up together, so that the night nurse could keep an eye on our activities. The other participants: Conchita, because of her recent seizure, and Cecilie, the Haitian catatonic girl, who was apparently no longer catatonic. A couple nights before, I'd seen Cecilie playing cards with Stan, the acidhead, except that Cecilie wasn't playing at all. She was sitting at the card table completely motionless and silent, as usual, while Stan tried to play both sides of a hand of gin rummy. He was riffing, with nearly perfect alliteration and rhyme and prosody, about the way the game worked: *This is a face card, but it's not an actual face, it's a two-dimensional representation of a face, and an ace isn't a face, and a face isn't from space, and the game isn't a race, and I'm going to be the one to deal, because I got a feel for the deal, the real deal, it isn't a steal, and it isn't a base, which rhymes with a face,* and he would lay the cards out in front of Cecilie, and lay the cards out in front of himself, and nothing would happen, and then he'd pick the cards up, shuffle, deal again: *I'm dealing again, because I'm your friend, your friend with a face, dealing fast, just in case, but not from the free space of the false space, or the arms race.* Then someone from across the dining room would tell Stan to *shut up,* that Cecilie wasn't going to say anything. It was my hypothesis that Stan loved Cecilie, because she seemed both vulnerable and mischievous, even if silent, and Stan didn't have any idea how to talk to her about the fact that he loved her, and she wouldn't have answered anyhow. Worst of all, Stan seemed to understand completely what he had done to himself, that because of taking seventy hits of acid he would never again fit into the straight world of jobs and families. This was why he wouldn't get out of bed some mornings, because Stan *knew* that he had violently excised himself from the straight world, had coated himself in some impermeable plastic, that Cecilie would never know he loved her, and he would never do anything to persuade her of it, and that was that.

Yet not long after the card game Cecilie seemed to be talking. She began saying a few things here and there, and soon became, apparently, charming and pushy all at the same time. She was good at smiling and asking if you would get her a soda from the machine down the hall, and could she have your pudding, and so forth. It was possible that she had stopped talking simply because she was incredibly bored by everyone. There must have been a case study in the literature in which a girl found that she had already said all there was to say.

Conchita's story had also come to light. Besides her Hispanic husband, it turned out she had an Anglo boyfriend, a sort of *Aryan youth,* with blond hair and blue eyes, handsome and winning. Maybe it was he who had helped Conchita get the blue contact lenses. It took me a while to realize that the color of her baby blues was ungenuine. One of my therapeutic goals, see, was to learn how to look people in the eye, which, evidently, I never had done at all. Linda the nurse took me outside and insisted that I look her in the eyes for an entire minute without saying a word. Her bloodshot eyes. It was an uncomfortable challenge that I managed to surmount. And in the course of furthering this skill, back on the ward, I'd noticed: Conchita suddenly had *brown* eyes. I asked her about it on the way to the bodega, and she was pretty open about the whole mess: *I had this uncle, a Dominican uncle, and he raped me when I was a girl, he raped me for a lot of years, for a really long time, while I was living with my parents, and so now I can't stand Dominican men, don't want to have anything to do with them, they are all* no good, *and so I don't want to have brown eyes, because my uncle had brown eyes, and I don't want to have anything to do with him, I don't want to have, like, any of his qualities, you know, and another thing, that's why I don't like to sleep with my husband anymore, because he has brown eyes, like my uncle had brown eyes, because my husband reminds me of my uncle, and that's why there's the other boy, the white boy.* There was a corollary problem too, in the fact that her son, whom her husband believed to be *his* son, was blond, like the Aryan boyfriend. Sometimes, the husband brought the toddler to see Conchita in the hospital, and we'd all be in the dayroom, one big happy family, and sometimes the husband *and* the Aryan boyfriend would be there, and the kid would be crawling around, offering toys to Diana and Monica and Bob and Noel, crawling into the laps of schizophrenics and manic-depressives and junkies. Even though I had come to love my friends on the ward, I still didn't think I would want *my kid* in the dayroom with the new psychotic guy, who would rave, to imaginary friends, *about the dangers of smoking.*

No wonder, then, that Conchita was having seizures, no wonder she and Cecilie were camped in the dayroom with me, long after midnight, waiting for neurological exams. We had just watched, on videotape, *One Flew Over the Cuckoo's Nest* (it's true), had moved on to the inferior *Down and Out in Beverly Hills,* and the night nurse had gone to sleep at the console where they kept the meds locked, and even the orderly who was supposed to be watching Nancy — on Eye Contact because of the ceramic ashtray — was dozing. The ward belonged to us, we were the three fates of Hollis, Queens, and if we wanted we could go from room to room, supervising the dreams of the mentally ill.

Most tales of the psychiatric hospital feature beleaguered romance, but one thing that vanished from my life before and during my hospital residence was *sexual feeling.* I had none, and I'd even purchased women's magazines featuring swimsuit models in the worst of my despair, in an attempt to see if they could kindle any feeling for the allure of the human body. They didn't. Cecilie and Conchita had no such symptoms, though. In the dayroom, lying on the floor, with *Down and Out in Beverly Hills* blathering, they arranged a blanket over the three of us and they launched the reconnaissance vehicles of their flirtation. It was nothing really provocative, and it didn't seem to have much to do with me, and since neither of them was older than twenty-one and each had a *troubled past,* they weren't very good at flirting anyway. They had picked the worst possible target, since my libido had been wiped as clean as a laboratory countertop. There was no danger from me at all. Whatever the case, this was the thing that kept us awake for a portion of the evening: *Who on the ward would you kiss? Who on the ward would you never kiss? Would you kiss one of us? Would you kiss both of us?* The longing was for longing, for the place and time when longing would again be a part of life, for the burgeoning and flourishing of longing. And while I came to love Conchita, after a fashion, as did most guys on the ward (Ron confessed to it, so did Joey the doorman), the scars that she had on account of the Dominican uncle, which made her hate, among other things, her skin, amounted to a complexity for which I, for one, was no solution. She needed *respect.* She needed languorous mornings and evenings, breakfasts in bed, sunsets, reverence, time. So I didn't lay a finger on her, nor on Cecilie, and neither did they lay a finger on me, though these possibilities had pulsed in the room. Soon, as sun broke through trees, romantic skirmishing was over, if it had taken place at all, if it was not simply the remnants of some old habit, and I saw that Cecilie was asleep and had been for a while. A morning orderly came into the room. *This one's asleep. She's going to have to do the night over.* Then he took Conchita and me down the hall through the mysterious adolescent ward, where, I imagined, there were dozens of kids with nose rings and tattoos and brain damage, all *sleeping and breathing,* as they said in the hospital logbooks, and then we went down in the elevator, into the bowels of the building, to the basement of the hospital. Where they connected us to machines.

Sleep, the German technician said to me, after affixing rubber cups to my skull, and I can remember the sound of pens scratching on rolls of paper, taking dictation from my repertoire of night images: *There is a carnival, empty except for myself, and all the rides, the Round-Up, the Ferris wheel, the roller coaster, are constructed of red and white axes. They circle around without audience or attendants.* The voice of the German technician came from inside my head, *You have very nice brain waves.* I murmured some thanks, though it was unclear whether one should thank a technician for being complimentary on the subject of brain waves. *Why are you in the hospital?* Didn't know exactly. I'd given it a lot of thought, and although I knew I needed to be there, I was still in the dark about my illness, *of what did it consist exactly,* since whenever I seemed to locate it, it vanished. And *no one,* not the Spanish mental health professional, nor Linda the nurse, nor my fellows in group therapy, seemed to want to discuss *its name,* as though naming a problem were a dangerous thing; my illness was concealed from me, therefore, except that at certain moments of night I could feel its drift, I knew it, felt it, intuited it, but didn't know its name. To the German technician, I said, *Well, I guess I drink too much.* And the German technician said, *No, no, no, don't do that.*

Did I have a disease of guilty conscience, then? A disease of hopelessness? A seizure disorder, in which the very *light* was offensive to me? A disease of compulsion, by which I attempted to avoid all these things? A sinister history? A lack of faith? A distrust of my nation? A distrust of all people?

The German technician wiped the conductant from my brow and helped me to my feet.

Nobody wanted to *stay* at the psychiatric hospital in Hollis, Queens, but nobody was ready to leave either. Time halted while you undertook therapies, and yet you could also feel the timer proceeding toward its alarm. When people left, we didn't organize lachrymose farewells. The residents just sort of left, and someone met them at the locking doors on the first floor and helped them carry their bags, and they went away to live their lives. Terror, which had been such a part of getting *locked in,* was now associated with getting *locked out.* There was a scripted process of conversations that preceded this solemnity, according to hospital policy, and I went through these conversations toward the end of July. My parents, in sequence, came to see me in the hospital and to see my social worker, both of them upset by the entire business. My mother was anguished by this conversation, denying that I was a melancholy child, denying that the pregnancy that brought me forth was unusual in any way, the bounty of her worry evident everywhere in her. My predicament, of course, called forth her past, in which her mother's alcoholism troubled the land, etc. The disappointment and anxiety of all *those* trips to the hospital come to haunt the present. She was at once impervious and on the verge of tears. My father, in his own visit, was combative, concerned, irritated that I hadn't told anyone about my difficulties *before checking in,* making life hard for the social workers. Friends came, sent notes: *I want to let you know that I was so happy to hear what you have done,* or, *So I just wanted you to know I'm thinking of you, and that I know you're going to be okay.* I was going to have *intercourse with the world,* as Hawthorne put it. I was going to get out.

What had I learned? I had learned that my past didn't exist except in *interpretations of the past;* I had learned there was no videotape, nor audio recording, nor sequence of eyewitnesses who could say, with perfect claim to accuracy, why I had come to be where I was. There were only hypotheses. I had learned that there was therefore no history without *interpretation,* no fact, only the stories of storytellers, and when all the interpreting was done, *it was simply time to go,* and I packed up, loaded my few belongings into my one duffel bag, and got into my mother's car. They signed a book for me, the gang from *inside,* they signed a *self-help book,* of course, and here's a conglomeration of unattributed lines from those inscriptions, from that time long ago:

> It's really been a pleasure knowing you. From my heart I can only wish the very best. I'm sure you will be successful in all your endeavors.

> You've really been an inspiration to me since you have been here. I couldn't believe for some reason that you used so much. I thought you were only in for depression! Take it easy out there in that jungle.

> If you have to, call me. If you don't have to, call anyway.

> Wishing you the best in your future endeavors. Don't forget to use the tools you have learned during your stay.

> I've never met a more sensitive person. Please, I beg you, become desensitized to drugs. Your future is golden and so are you.

> I hope you have a great sober life. Thanks so much for the advice and for making me feel like I had a friend.

> I haven't known you long, but you seem like a goodhearted person and have a good head on your shoulders, stay with that positive attitude, great wishes to you.

> You are such a sensitive person. You really deserve all the best. I sincerely hope you find it.

All the world's a stage, & your name is RICK! That's it, that's all, and that is the most important thing of all. It's been such a great feeling sharing the last couple of weeks with you. Having you here & listening to your life has made me aware of myself more, & I'll tell you, I'm starting to like me. The both of us spent years trying to complete a tragic novel with no ending. I think my friend that the real story is yet to come — You've come a long way in my eyes, & I know you'll find your voice that's inside your heart, & thru your veins flows blood with enriched flavor. There are joys out there, beyond our wildest dreams. The truest form of expression is yours, right from the heart! I love you, man, & thanks!

At the top of one leaf, without any elaboration:

Good luck. — Diana.

Excepting two or three conversations in the weeks immediately after my release, I never again talked to these citizens of my ward. I didn't call them, and they didn't call me, and I thought I knew why. Because when I saw the faces of people at work, the faces of my family upon welcoming me home, I saw an uncertainty that made me want to put Hollis, Queens, far behind me. My family and friends didn't want to talk about it, and I didn't want to talk about it, and it didn't do any good, trying to explain that it was just another address you visited, as when you visited the podiatrist, the gynecologist, the certified public accountant. I was released now, and if I still had *distorted thinking,* of the kind I'd had on the way in, I thought of it the way my brother thought of his tinnitus. It was *part of life,* to be ignored while I tried to deal more actively with job, writing, friends, psychiatrists, laundry. Dark episodes make for good dramas, and more contented times vanish away from our retrospective accounts. Narrators abridge the happy parts at the ends of fairy tales. Here was I, rolling down the window in my mother's Volkswagen, coming into the city on the Grand Central Parkway, here was I, bumper to bumper through the Midtown Tunnel, here was I, getting out of the car, closing the door behind me, carrying my suitcase, here was I, selecting my own channel on the television, or going out to see a movie, afflicted by history, maybe, as well as by my chemistry, and wandering out on Eighth Avenue in NYC, here was I going to get my *prescription* filled at the pharmacy, my medication, without anywhere to go particularly except for the prescription, nor anyone to see, here was I thinking about the guy with the veil, here I am almost fifteen years ago thinking about the guy with the veil, in the Hawthorne story, *I should write something about the Hawthorne story, sometime,* because I was like the guy in the veil, or he was like me, or at least the idea of the veil connected that time back in the early history of the nation to me getting out of the hospital and driving home with my mother; I saw that all these things were connected by invisible lines, fundamental forces, particles of a mystical variety, as I also knew that I would never again be the person I'd been just a couple of months before.

I could tell you tales, I could use words like *recovery, rehabilitation,* I could speak of church interiors, of therapies, I could speak of the way in which the word *rape* gradually began to diminish in frequency in the interior of my skull. No longer did bus rides and record albums and movies and dinners out seem to have the word *rape* attached to them, no longer did passersby on the street have malevolent aspects, no longer was every male of my acquaintance a *rapist,* in the months and years after I got out of the hospital. I could tell you of days, three and four years later, when I realized that, in fact, I was no longer certain that I would die before my time, or that my life would be a sequence of well-intentioned failures, and these increasingly robust certainties are the backdrop for all the later chapters here; I could tell you of an evening out in the country when I won a sequence of games of Ping-Pong with paddles whose rubber was all peeling off, after which I did something completely out of character — went *skinny-dipping* — stealing into a pool, stripping off my clothes, leaving them on the mottled concrete, in the dark, after midnight, *back when there were still diving boards,* from which I could still execute a mediocre flip, plunging in and feeling that there were certain liberties that would never again in my life be curtailed; *I was better, I was better,* I could tell you all of this, but one story above others reflects the time after being *inside:*

Conchita, just before I left, slipped me the following note: *I can't tell you in person because I don't know if I can handle the rejection. I guess I could take it in letter form. The big question is can you put me up in your apt for any amount of time. Please answer me in written form and don't worry I will understand if you can't.* I don't remember if I wrote back. Since I didn't really have an *apt* while in the hospital, having been asked by Jen to move out of mine, I'm sure I tried to refuse Conchita's request in some gentle but supportive way. Some time passed. I took up residence in the *converted gas station* apartment that was my address for the rest of summer. My father helped me move a half dozen worn-out suitcases from Jen's apartment into the *bad side* of Hoboken. We shooed strays off the front step. It was a sublet. It cost a hundred dollars a month, which was what I could afford, since, after the insurance payout, I owed the hospital a couple thousand dollars that I didn't have. When you opened the taps in my *apt,* there was the perfumery of regular unleaded. The ceiling in the bathroom leaked. There were three kinds of wood paneling there, as if the place had once been a paneling showroom. There was a gas pump out front. It was a studio, four hundred square feet, and I had a single futon, on the floor, a couple of sheets, a blanket. A table on which to put my Smith-Corona typewriter. My father and stepmother were horrified at my circumstances, stunned into mute surrender to the swiftness with which I suddenly seemed to *have nothing.* They helped me unpack and then disappeared. I wasn't sleeping; I wasn't writing. The mostly useless antidepressant medication made my skin crawl. I hadn't been on my own in a few years and I wasn't good at *meeting people.* I spent weekends wandering around in the East Village, a neighborhood that I associated with my bars of choice during graduate school, but my attempts to make the neighborhood fit my new circumstances were in vain. The white noise and revolution of the East Village had abruptly become quaint and foolish to me, the lockstep of youthful counterculture.

One Sunday, I'd run out of things to do in town and had come home early. I didn't have a television. I figured I'd read for the rest of the night. Then I was interrupted by the telephone. It was one of those bargain telephone handsets from early deregulation. Plastic, cheap, disposable. In its buzzing earpiece, I could make out Conchita's voice. Crisis has an ambient sound, you know. You can hear it over the telephone line sometimes well before the bearer of the ill news has parted with her burdens. There's a music to bad news, but it's so faint and so repetitive as to be like background radiation. You have to be listening carefully. I'd heard a lot of bad news in the month before this call, so when I realized it was Conchita's nasal soprano, congested with weeping, I was not surprised. You turn aside one messenger of crisis, another climbs your step.

Conchita reiterated her request. *I'm in a lot of trouble,* she said, or something like that. *My husband went crazy and he, um, he beat me up, and I can't stay here, but I don't have anywhere else to go.* She lived out in Queens, and coming to Hoboken would take the rest of the evening, and I didn't believe she didn't have family to take her in, but I felt that it was the right thing for me to do, to invite her to stay with me, that morality was invented for moments such as this, and so I spent a while explaining the intricate maneuvers that would be required for her to reach my block, though I should have just gone and met her. I waited nervously for some time in the gas station apartment, in the light of a fluorescent bulb over the sink.

She had the traditional black eye favored by the wife beater. She had a fat lip that had been bleeding quite a bit, and a couple of related bruises about her face and neck. Have I described her well enough? She was five foot three, maybe even shorter, with cascading brown ringlets; she was as thin as she could get and not look sick; her skin was the color prized by tanning enthusiasts; she had no breasts or hips at all. She wore jeans and halter tops. She looked as if she could have been an exotic model for industrial showrooms. She was smart, brilliant even, on a public high school education, but I don't think she'd done anything but work at franchise restaurants. Her eyes were brown or blue, depending. She smiled a lot, in spite of everything.

Conchita couldn't sit still. In my *gas station apartment.* She tried to make nervous conversation, and I tried to steer it toward practicalities. She cried, tried to stop crying. She wanted to seem tough, but she was anything but tough. It was summer, and the kids from the projects nearby drove up Monroe Street late into the night. The best thing to do was to try to go to sleep. I let her sleep on the futon, and I tried to sleep on some pillows on the matted green hunk of wall-to-wall carpeting that resembled a miniature-golf green. Conchita woke early and made coffee. We were never allowed that life-support beverage back in the psychiatric hospital in Queens, because it was *a drug,* something that would complicate *medication.* We drank a coffee substitute in the hospital. So coffee, if nothing else, was an indication that Conchita and I were now free to make decisions for ourselves.

It was Monday morning, and I had no choice but to go to work. I'd just had a month off for medical reasons, and I couldn't be absent so soon. I asked Conchita what she was going to do. I'd been asking her what she was going to do since she'd arrived at my *apt,* and now I suggested that she go to the *battered-women's shelter,* which was a difficult suggestion to make, because she was a person, a friend, not a city welfare statistic. She wouldn't go to stay with her family, or so she said, and she wouldn't go to stay with her Anglo boyfriend, who had caused the husband to become upset in the first place by demanding that she *leave* the husband, while the husband was meanwhile demanding she leave the boyfriend. This after two months in the psychiatric hospital. If the husband wanted to argue a custody case, where the welfare of the kid was concerned, he would have the courts on his side. She had seizures, she became so depressed she couldn't show up for her job *flipping burgers.* Still, I said she should go to a *battered-women's shelter,* because hanging around in the *gas station apartment* with an emasculated artist guy, tossed out by his girlfriend, so demoralized that he had nonsense thoughts and delusions, heard voices calling in the street, believed he was going to be raped, *this guy wasn't a remedy.* But you can't tell anyone anything.

I worked, and I called her from work, and she made calls on

the cheap plastic handset in the *gas station apartment,* and then I caught the bus home from Port Authority, and in the hallucinatory swelter of early August, I met my Dominican goddess of mental-hospital survival, who had spent the day cleaning up my apartment for me. She had folded some towels and taken some items to the Laundromat. She'd bought some food at the grocery store. She had bought Hamburger Helper, which I wasn't sure I'd eaten since back when my mother was dating, in the early seventies. Conchita's eye was still black-and-blue, but she was smiling, as though she had given me a gift, which she had. A gift I didn't know how to accept. I ate the Hamburger Helper, which tasted about how I remembered it.

Next morning, Conchita went back to the batterer.

This was a disaster, and a disaster that I felt I had caused, by not being comfortable enough with her in my house, in my *gas station apartment,* by not being persuasive enough about government agencies. She had come from two months of getting help, but that help had been insufficient, because the first thing she had done had been to get beaten up by her husband, and now my help was insufficient too. I didn't know what to do, whether to call her husband, whether to call the hospital, whether to try to find her parents; well, there was no going back to the hospital — *the insurance money had run out.* It would have been the human thing to hold her, to attempt to comfort her with just being there, which was probably *why she had chosen me,* because I was no threat, I was white America in the gentlest, most unimposing form, I was the oppressor history of America confined to the mental hospital, you could have blown hard on me and I would have toppled; I couldn't make eye contact, but I couldn't hold her either. Although I welcomed her in, I couldn't solve the problem, couldn't eradicate her memory, nor my own, and so this story has a blunt ending and a complexity of motives funneling around its principals, her motives and my motives, self-destruction and self-preservation mutually indistinguishable; I tried to help; I helped for a couple of days, but I kept telling her she should do something, she should do something, and I didn't do anything myself. She didn't want the resources available to her, so next morning she was suddenly calling me at work, from Queens, saying, *I'm back here at home, and I just want to thank you.* It was the last thing I heard from her, though there were traces of her in the strange order of my apartment afterward. A towel straightened just so. Why such a guilty conscience? I survived.

EVERY WORK, BY AN ARTIST OF CELEBRITY, IS HIDDEN BEHIND A VEIL . . .

The veil turns up in every one of Nathaniel Hawthorne's major works. Sometimes indirectly, but most often without concealment of any kind. It's in his letters (*When applying for office . . . the business is to establish yourself, somehow and anywhere. . . . A subtile boldness, with a veil of modesty over it, is what is needed*), as it is in his very first published short story (*When Robin had freed his eyes from those fiery ones, the musicians were passing before him, and the torches were close at hand; but the unsteady brightness of the latter formed a veil which could not penetrate*), as it is elsewhere in the early stories ("Roger Malvin's Burial," e.g.: *His first impulse was to cover his face;* or "The Gentle Boy": *She hid her face on Ilbrahim's head, and her long, raven hair, discolored with the ashes of her mourning, fell down about him like a veil*), as it is in the preface to a volume containing some of the later tales, *Mosses from an Old Manse* (*In its near retirement, and accessible seclusion, it was the very spot for the residence of a clergyman; a man not estranged from human life, yet enveloped, in the midst of it, with a veil woven of intermingled gloom and brightness*), which includes a passage amounting to Hawthorne's most forthright explication of the idea (after lengthy description of this parsonage, where he and his wife lived in the early years of their marriage):

> Has the reader gone wandering, hand in hand with me, through the inner passages of my being, and have we groped together into all its chambers and examined

their treasures or their rubbish? Not so. We have been standing on the green sward, but just within the cavern's mouth, where the common sunshine is free to penetrate, and where every footstep is therefore free to come. I have appealed to no sentiment or sensibilities, save such as are diffused among us all. So far as I am a man of really individual attributes, I veil my face; nor am I, nor have been, one of those supremely hospitable people, who serve up their own hearts delicately fried, with brain-sauce, as a tidbit for their beloved public.

Ten years after "The Minister's Black Veil," yet Hawthorne has not finished wrestling with the image. In fact, the Old Manse referred to in the book's title provides one of the tantalizing clues about an origin of the veil, in that the land that anchored the house was the historical plantation of Ralph Waldo Emerson's family, going all the way back to when the acreage belonged to the Pawtuckets. That is, the parsonage belonged to Emerson's grandfather William, for whom it was built not very long before he was among the first in Concord to respond to alarms about the British regulars. (Minutemen skirmished no more than two hundred yards from his home.) William served for two months under Washington in the Revolutionary Army, until he died of dysentery, after which his widow married Ezra Ripley, also a member of the clergy, who occupied the Old Manse till 1841. Ripley's son Samuel rented it to the Hawthornes (for $100 a year), and they took up residence there until they were evicted for several infractions: nonpayment of rent, defacement of property (Nathaniel and Sophia scratched their signatures in the windows of the Old Manse, signatures that are still visible), and disagreeable redecorating, including *trompe l'oeil* wallpaper from Europe. Henry David Thoreau planted a garden for the Hawthornes while they dwelt in the Old Manse, and the transcendentalist Alcotts lived right up the street.

The veiled part of this story comes in the fact that Emerson's great-grandmother, of whom Hawthorne may have heard while renting from the Emerson / Ripley clan, was none other than Joseph "Handkerchief" Moody's sister Mary Moody. And that isn't all, in terms of *thematic interpenetration*. Mary and Joseph Moody's own great-grandmother Mary Bradbury was tried as a witch by Hawthorne's great-grandfather John Hathorne. (Mary Bradbury, it bears mentioning, was *convicted of witchcraft* too, though she escaped from jail and hid out until the hysteria of the witch trials came to an end.) Emerson's spinster aunt and childhood tutor, Mary Moody Emerson, was still living in the Concord area when the Hawthornes lived at the Old Manse, and her relation to the Moodys of York was far closer than her name, since *at least from the time she was fifty,* according to Emerson's biography, *death had seemed to Mary a welcome state:*

> "I pray to die," she wrote in July 1826. In preparation for her own death she made a flannel funeral shroud. But when death did not come for her she decided that it was "a pity to let it lie idle." She began wearing it, then, an extraordinary sight — on horseback, riding sidesaddle to the Manse, clad in her white shroud, a scarlet shawl draping her shoulders. She wore out "a great many" shrouds, Emerson believed, before she got to the one that served as her grave clothes. "I wish you joy of the worm!" her friends had called to her gaily when they saw she was breaking in a new shroud. . . . Mary met these jests without perturbation. A woman with a trousseau of shrouds, who sleeps in a bed made to resemble a coffin, is not easily jarred.

Thus, relations between Hawthorne and the veil-obsessed Moody family go back quite a ways, and it's clearly possible that Emerson opined on the subject while the two were acquainted. Though Hawthorne wrote "The Minister's Black Veil" in his days in the *castle dismal* of bachelorhood, and therefore before he knew Emerson well, the entwining of his family with the Moodys, and later with the Emersons, can't have diminished the hold of the veil upon him. Thus the preface to *Mosses from an Old Manse* deals extensively with the

Emersons and also with the veil, as did the next Hawthorne work, his masterpiece *The Scarlet Letter,* which first mentions the veil image in its celebrated autobiographical preface, "The Custom-House":

> But, as thoughts are frozen and utterance benumbed, unless the speaker stand in some true relation with his audience, it may be pardonable to imagine that a friend, a kind and apprehensive, though not the closest friend, is listening to our talk; and then, a native reserve being thawed by this genial consciousness, we may prate of the circumstances that lie around us, and even of ourself, but still keep the inmost Me behind its veil. To this extent, and within these limits, an author, methinks, may be autobiographical, without violating either the reader's rights or his own.

An awful lot of protesting about autobiography in these last two Hawthorne excerpts, in which the author is manifestly writing autobiographically — and revealingly. The insistence in the prefaces that something yet remains veiled, though the first person is so forthright, is a complicated tease that cannot but remind a reader of Hooper's own description of the feeling of wearing the veil, as described to his fiancée, Elizabeth: *O! you know not how lonely I am, and how frightened, to be alone behind my black veil.* The gesture in these autobiographical prefaces, as in Hooper's own tale, is dense and contradictory (If the veil is so uncomfortable, just take it off!), and therefore it's no surprise that the veil is undepleted and persists into the text of *The Scarlet Letter,* as when Dimmesdale, late in the novel, walks past Hester without acknowledging her: *So — with a mightier struggle than he had yet sustained — he held his Geneva cloak before his face, and hurried onward, making no sign of recognition, and leaving the young sister to digest his rudeness as she might.*

Mild allusion continues in the novel that followed in Hawthorne's output, *The House of the Seven Gables:* when Clifford Pyncheon arrives like a ghost to visit with his cousin Hepzibah, *He was probably accustomed to a sad monotony of life, not so much flowing in a* *stream, however sluggish, as stagnating in a pool around his feet. A slu* *ous veil diffused itself over his countenance, and had an effect, morally sp* *ing, on its naturally delicate and elegant outline, like that which a brood* *mist, with no sunshine in it, throws over the features of a landscape.* A fu* ther description of Clifford (who describes himself, anagrammati- cally, as an *evil genius*), makes use of the identical metaphor: *Was he always thus? Had this veil been over him from birth? — this veil, under which far more of his spirit was hidden than revealed, and through which he so imperfectly discerned the actual world — or was its gray texture woven of some dark calamity? Phoebe loved no riddles and would have been glad to escape the perplexity of this one.*

Horace, scribe of antiquity, remarked in his *Ars Poetica* that things repeated are pleasing, and Hawthorne must have been keenly observant of the strategy, since in the examples above, he found himself unable to avoid reprising the same tangle of ambiguities that lingers around his principal garment from the "The Minister's Black Veil." In the examples I've given from *Seven Gables,* the veil is apparently eternal (since *from birth*), is associated with melancholy (since conjoined with *brooding*), divides one person from another (*we may prate of the circumstances that lie around us, and even of ourself, but still keep the inmost Me behind its veil*), and induces in all who would read or interpret it the difficulties associated with riddles and conun- drums.

And, since insoluble, the image, like a pox, forces itself even more dramatically to the surface in *The Blithedale Romance,* for in the very first chapter of that novel, entitled "Old Moodie," we have the fol- lowing: *The evening before my departure for Blithedale, I was returning to my bachelor-apartments, after attending the wonderful exhibition of the Veiled Lady, when an elderly man of rather shabby appearance met me in an obscure part of the street.* Here the veil is manifestly opposed to the veil in "The Minister's Black Veil" — or so it seems immediately, for the Veiled Lady, *a phenomenon in the mesmeric line,* wore a veil that was white, *with somewhat of a subdued silver sheen, like the sunny side of a cloud; and falling over the wearer from head to foot, was supposed to insulate her from the material world, from time and space, and to endow her with many of the privileges of a disembodied spirit.* Perhaps the precursor for

heatrical seer is found in Thomas More's 1817 epic poem, "Lalla
kh," which among its other Chauceresque narratives retells the
a of the Veiled Prophet of Khorasan, founder of an eighth-century
rabian sect, who passed himself off as a god so that, by taking up
the veil, he could hide scars of battle: *O'er his features hung / The Veil,
the Silver Veil, which he had flung / In mercy there, to hide from mortal
sight / His dazzling brow, till man could bear its light.* It's a work that
Hawthorne would likely have read, perhaps during his frequent visits to the lending library of Salem.

As befits a Hawthorne prophet, the Veiled Lady's pronouncements, in *The Blithedale Romance,* are almost impossible to interpret
(unlike those of the Veiled Prophet of Khorasan in More's poem), as
Coverdale, the narrator, learns on first attempting to put a question
to her. *The response . . . was of the true Sibylline stamp, nonsensical in its
first aspect, yet on closer study, unfolding a variety of interpretations.* Thus,
despite a change in fabric and color, the veil retains its celebrated
ambiguity. This remains the case later, as a story-within-the-story
demonstrates:

> Some upheld, that the veil covered the most beautiful
> countenance in the world; others — and certainly with
> more reason, considering the sex of the Veiled Lady —
> that the face was the most hideous and horrible, and
> that this was her sole motive for hiding it. It was the
> face of a corpse; it was the head of a skeleton; it was a
> monstrous visage, with snaky locks, like Medusa's, and
> one great red eye in the centre of the forehead. Again, it
> was affirmed that there was no single and unchangeable
> set of features, beneath the veil, but that whosoever
> should be bold enough to lift it would behold the fea-
> tures of that person, in all the world, who was destined
> to be his fate.

I'm more interested in Old Moodie, though, and in the conjunction of the Veiled Lady with a character of that name, whom
Hawthorne describes in terms that no one acquainted with Down

East sociology can mistake. *He was a very shy personage, this Mr. Moodie,* a point reiterated by Moodie himself: *I am a man of few words.* And Hawthorne's inevitable indebtedness here to a certain agonized resident of York, Maine, becomes even more transparent in his later description of Moodie: *His existence looked so colorless and torpid . . . that I was half afraid lest he should altogether disappear, even while my eyes were fixed full upon his figure. He was certainly the wretchedest old ghost in the world, with his crazy hat, the dingy handkerchief about his throat, his suit of threadbare gray, and especially the patch over his right eye, behind which he always seemed to be hiding himself.* Note the odd combination of the *dingy handkerchief* about Moodie's throat and *the patch over his right eye, behind which he always seemed to be hiding himself,* which accessories prefigure Old Moodie's outfit some chapters later, after the tragedy at the novel's apex: *Nearest the dead walked an old man in deep mourning, his face mostly concealed in a white handkerchief.*

The Marble Faun, Hawthorne's last major work (after it, he finished no other novel, nor any new short stories, though there are uncompleted manuscripts), doesn't develop the veil at any great length, except in one repeated motif, the *veiled masterpiece.* In that novel of Roman landscape and antiquity, suffused with vivid descriptions of the old masters, there is a constant veiling: *Every work, by an artist of celebrity, is hidden behind a veil, and seldom revealed except to Protestants, who scorn it as an object of devotion, and value it only for its artistic merit.* And so forth. There are many such passages. Two further examples that do not take up the matter of concealing masterpieces have instead to do with the oppression of conscience. In the first of these, a character involved in a murder goes to the Church of Rome to unburden herself: *Close at hand, within the veil of the confessional, was the relief;* in the second instance, the veil is directly conjoined to the expression of remorse: *It occurred to him that there is a sanctity . . . which prohibits the recognition of persons who choose to walk under the veil of penitence.*

To complete my archaeology, I ought now to offer a brief inquiry into the word itself, an etymology, noting that it comes from the Middle English, *veile,* which comes from the Old North French, *veilie,* which comes, perhaps, from the Old French, *voile,* which comes from the Latin, *vela,* plural of *vellum,* curtain or sail, diminutive of *vexillum,* denoting *flag,* while the *OED* gives some variant forms, with lovely spellings and usages: *veyll, weyll, vale, vayle, vaill,* such as, *Thir maydens come before the autere, And toke thaire uayles,* or, *But til in to this day, whanne Moyses is radd, the veyl is putt upon her hertis,* or, *The vaile of darckness of the vsurped power . . . of the see and bishoppes of Rome;* we might find some distant Indo-European predecessor, if only there were a written literature of our Indo-European forebears, and this predecessor would also begin with the *v* of modern usage and would somehow lead us back to the first warring huntergatherers on the African continent, who had cause to conceal, to cover themselves, to dissemble, to deceive their neighbors, their mates, who had cause to be ashamed, to have guilty consciences, to steal out across the Kalahari, the *veldt,* to slay, to plunder, to rape, and after to cover themselves with like raiment, and to affix upon themselves therefore the word, *the mortal vaile, man's carkas or body,* supplying ample opportunity for the origin of this concept at the very origin of the species, and perhaps this is why in Hawthorne there is also the obsession with lineage, with genealogy and catalog and iterations of family. Nevertheless, the word seems to spin off into *a veil of stars* in the beyond, the word as refracted in Hawthorne, into the diaphanous beyond, and readers will want to struggle with him, will want to remonstrate with Hawthorne for all his ciphering, to say that the reason his work falls off so drastically after *The House of the Seven Gables* is that he doesn't know when to *stop* concealing, doesn't know what to allow into the record, what to give. I can feel his desperation in the lacerating parentheticals of the unfinished *Septimius* manuscripts, in *The Dolliver Romance,* as he struggles with the narratives, *The virtues of plants &c &c &c,* or, *He should write a poem, or other great work,* or, *Remarks on the fate of young virgins in War-Time,* and it all seems to summon the word *veil,* its denying and embracing, the word just out of reach, almost to be entrapped with each new usage, as though by trying again from a different point of view, *believing nothing, although a thin veil of reverence had kept him from questioning these things,* he might finally catch the jewel, the difference between the word and the sensation, coming morosely to the unsettling realization that each time he has failed again, has failed to get the idea across, Hawthorne the diaphanous, writer of sentimental love letters and dweller in the *castle dismal,* struggling with the Puritanical veil, the guilty veil, the sorrowful veil, the veil of sin, the veil of mortality, the veil of prophecy, the veil of privacy, the veil of the Divine, the veil of the masterpiece, what is the thing that shows forth under the veil, a *dazzling brow* or a disfigurement? Are the two somehow the same thing?

HAD HER EYES PROVOKED,

OR ASSENTED TO THIS DEED?

SHE HAD NOT KNOWN IT. BUT, ALAS!

It must have been the alliteration that did it, that caused the chaos, that lit the light, that flipped the switch, that made Kip Kinkel kill; that ugly sequence of *k*'s, like the stutter of *c*'s in *crack cocaine* or in the second *coming of Christ,* the *k* of Khmer Rouge, krazy as in Krazy Kat, creepy as in *Kaposi's* or *carcinoma;* Kip, short for Kipland, kamikaze, kabuki, Kip with Glock or Ruger or maybe Colt or AK-47, Kip and his keynote address, craven, careless, callous, cold-blooded, calculating, cagey, Kip Kinkel, *a kid who kills,* under the kliegs, for good.

Alliteration, at least, is as good as any other theory. As good as any of the numberless theories that circulate around all schoolyard massacres, around the carnage of Kip Kinkel and his kind. Admittedly, Kristin Kinkel, his sis, lived with alliteration without having to open fire on the cool of her school. Kristin was a cheerleader. A college student in Hawaii. Still, there's a language to this massacre stuff, a tongue, there's catechism, call and response, and at the margins of this language hovers the community, distracted in its lamentations.

The facts, of course, are not in dispute. Eight A.M., and Kipland allegedly appears in the dining hall at high school (one magazine refers to it, alliteratively, as a *crowded cafeteria*) wearing a long trench coat, as if a trench coat is a necessity for a massacre (the Littleton massacre, of course, featured its Trench Coat Mafia), having stolen his parents' Jeep (though he's unlicensed) to make his journey. He's suspended from school, for weapons possession, and yet he has had all night alone to cogitate — having murdered his parents the day before — to think about his entrance. The technicalities, the intricacies of legal language, the laws of the land, are not going to impede him, and so he enters the *crowded cafeteria,* allegedly, right after the honors ceremony for the gifted kids (Kip is a C-average student, according to one newspaper). He slips in through a side door, removes a rifle from under the trench coat, climbs up onto a table, and with his .22-caliber Ruger semiautomatic, begins firing. Three or four single shots, at first, into the gyrating crowd, and then, as if finding his rhythm, he begins to spray the room, until, allegedly, having expended fifty rounds, the clip comes to its end.

After which there is that most modern of intervals, the reloading pause. What vulnerability in that moment. All of Kip's *impulse control difficulties,* which in DSM IV terms would certainly be a reasonable starting point for any etiology of his condition, are arrayed against the reloading pause, against that *entr'acte* wherein the force of the community will be used against him. The reloading pause is the soft, porous core of the guy who means to get even. Because of it, or in spite of it, Kip manages, allegedly, to fire off one last round, from a pistol — his father's pistol — after which the inevitable *student hero,* a wrestler, restores the order of things. The wrestler takes a shot in the gut but still tackles young Kipland, who, immobilized in full nelson or headlock or other wrestling hold, allegedly begs the wrestler and his muscular pals to *Just shoot me now! Shoot me now!*

The facts. After which, language, alert to an opportunity, floods the inexplicable interior of Oregon. *Shy and slight,* one writer opines, *a popular kid,* says another, *a kid next door,* says a third, *weirder and weirder,* says one friend. He tortured animals, he threw rocks at cars, he spoke of blowing up a cow, setting a cat on fire, putting a firecracker in a cat's mouth. *The picture of the accused murderer remains essentially one of contradictions,* says a Seattle paper, *depending on who you talk to and which Kip Kinkel they're talking about.* He was *a cute little kid in middle school,* says one acquaintance. Others point to his disturbing tendency to *dress all in black.* (The same charge is later applied to the Columbine shooters.) He played linebacker on the football team (*didn't see much action*); he hid bombs in the crawl space in his house, including two that were complicated enough to merit, at the direction of an investigative bomb squad, the evacuation of the neighborhood. *This was not a weird kid,* says one neighbor. *This was a trustworthy, Boy Scout type of kid.* Who kept a knife taped to his leg *with which to lunge at the arresting officer* once in custody. He had to be subdued with pepper spray.

The attribution of explanation, in the spectra of calamity, is an important part of the American experience: *why O. J. did it, why O. J. didn't, why JonBenet? Did Marv really bite her?* Even among those who know better. The sitting president of these United States, Bill Clinton, had a theory: *The glorification of violence in popular culture, easy access to firearms, and lax parental supervision have left a river of blood from Mississippi to Oregon.* And yet not only was Kip Kinkel's access to firearms not entirely easy, his parents were not at all lax (his parents refused his interest in weaponry for years, and when they finally relented, in an attempt to find some *common ground,* they kept his guns under lock and key). His parents were successful and esteemed teachers in the local school system. They were devoted to their children. They were involved, committed parents.

Another guy with a theory on the subject of *kids and guns* was the alliterative Jeff Jacoby, formerly of the *Boston Globe,* who easily bested the president in any fatuity sweepstakes: *Kids — the worst kids — become homeroom hit men when they are bombarded with messages telling them: Do what you like. No one will judge you. No one cares. . . . Modern educational theories are built up around the notions that wrong answers are as good as right answers, that grades are oppressive, that truth is a relative concept.* Not that such liberal pedagogy was a factor in Kinkel's education. (And if this was the teaching style in small-town Oregon, why had it apparently affected none of his peers?)

It's the wordlessness of the school-yard massacre that is so startling. Kids with weapons let weapons do the articulating. The triggermen themselves are notorious for their inability to explain their motives. Or notorious for their unwillingness to do so. They have found the one rhetorical strategy that crowds out all others, that makes the chatter of parents and newspapers and television commentators dumb, that replies to all questions and all controversies with a final, incontrovertible splatter. They stand on the table in the cafeteria, or lie in wait in a ditch out in front of school, having pulled the fire alarm, in silence, perfect in the knowledge that they are about to venture the last word, the last of all words. So it seems. In the elongation of time that takes place during their apotheosis, all other attempts at communication are laughable. But then comes the inevitable reloading pause, or else vengeance seems suddenly, curiously fulfilled, or else they suffer with that modulation of ethics, the wave of ethics flooding back over them all at once, and they find they are standing among *bodies,* not dead themselves as they expected to be, their language having failed.

Into this space we lurch with tongues wagging.

Linguistically speaking, though, you have to admit, when you compare Kip Kinkel, say, to his alphabetical predecessor Jeff Jacoby of the *Boston Globe,* that Kip does have the longer-lasting sentiment. His remark will be around for years to come. And that's why there's a list. The list gets bandied about a lot: Scott Pennington kills his English teacher — what better initial victim — with a bullet in the head, in 1993, and gets twenty-five to life; Barry Loukaitis takes out the algebra class in junior high, 1996; Evan Ramsey murders his principal and a fellow student in Alaska, February 1997; Luke Woodham, at sixteen, stabs his mother to death and, next day, goes to school to murder his ex-girlfriend, injuring nine, killing two, October 1997; in December, Michael Carneal fires into a prayer circle at his school in Kentucky; in March of 1998 an eleven-year-old, Andrew Golden, and his friend pull the fire alarm and fire into the crowd as it empties from the school; in April of 1999, Dylan Klebold and Eric Harris enter their cafeteria, begin firing. And so forth. The list itself, the catalog, as a journalistic gesture, generates further lists. In fact, the list itself becomes a frequent compositional trope of murderers, as in the following, from a Web site devoted to unusual news stories:

> Among the chilling incidents recorded within a week before or after the Jonesboro, Ark., shootings, according to

police: Covington, LA (boy, 12, and others, planting bombs in school); Cleveland, OH (boy, 4, brought loaded gun to day-care); Daly City, CA (boy, 13, fired a shot at the principal); Queens, NY (boy, 8, took loaded gun to school); Indianapolis (2 boys, each 8, took loaded guns to school); Kennewick, WA (boy, 12, *had a hit list* of teachers and students to kill); Millersville, MD (3 boys left 3 unrelated bomb threats, and a fourth was arrested for plotting to kill a classmate); West Lafayette, OH (boy, 15, *had a hit list* of teachers and students to kill); Fond du Lac, WI (boy, 14, shot up a school door because of a bad report card). Also, when the Jonesboro Two were jailed, their neighbor was a 13-year-old boy accused of shooting a classmate in the face [italics mine].

All of these kids unable to explain. When asked why a certain victim, why a certain strategy for their bloodbath, they are helpless and reticent. Or they have lawyers speaking for them, or lawyers are intervening to ensure their silence. And that's why I have often found myself oddly interested in Luke Woodham, of Pearl, Mississippi. Unlike young Kipland, who was *impassive* during his arraignment, Luke Woodham speaks, can't seem to shut up, and therefore his human face is uppermost. He's a sobbing, weeping mess, during his confession, in the courtroom, when confronted by reporters. He testifies, against advice of counsel, that it was *heartbreak over losing his girlfriend* that led to his murderous spree: *"I'm so sorry — I'm so sorry," the teenager, Luke Woodham, sobbed,* according to the *Times.* He also alludes to an interest in Satanism, claiming to have *seen demons and even sent them to plague others.* Most important, in his videotaped confession, he admits, *I knew what I was doing.*

Luke, allegedly, was part of a loose fraternity of disenfranchised kids in Pearl who called themselves the Kroth, and who believed *that murder was a viable means of accomplishing the purposes and goals of {a} shared belief system.* In their plan for school-yard mayhem, the Kroth believed that Woodham would be an ideal shooter. As one member said: *Luke was a social recluse all his life. I thought he would be easy to con-*

trol and easy to manipulate. Besides his membership in the Kroth, Luke worked as a cook for Domino's: *Other than school and the job . . . Woodham rarely left his home.* His mother, recently divorced at the time, didn't have much good to say about her boy. She employed, allegedly, any number of nicknames from the *fat, stupid, lazy* class of epithets, and apparently suggested that Luke *was the reason his father left.* When asked, in his confession, about killing his mother, his logic is surprisingly cogent (and chilling). Luke admits simply that *she never loved me.* It's an honest moment in a public affair characterized mainly by linguistic inflation and prevarication.

The events of October 1, 1997, in Pearl, Mississippi, are eerily premonitory of the Kip Kinkel case. Luke kills his mother (multiple stab wounds, a rare instance of primitive violence in this compendium of automatic-weapons slaughter), as Kip killed his parents, and then dons the obligatory trench coat, stealing his mother's car, as Kip stole the Jeep; he enters *the large commons area just inside the front door* of the school, whereas Kip performed in the dining hall; he locates a young girl who has broken up with him, takes her life, and then begins firing at random. As with Kipland, Luke is described as *expressionless* during the shooting, though one is challenged to imagine what the appropriate expression is for mass murder.

Only difference with Luke is that he talks. Before, and after. Here he is in a handwritten note given to a friend less than a minute before the shooting: *Throughout my life I was ridiculed. Always beaten, always hated.* After the crime, his reasoning is consistent: *My whole life . . . I just felt outcasted, alone. Finally, I found some people who wanted to be my friends. I was just trying to find hope in a hopeless world, man.*

The most poignant of all Luke's comments, for me, was buried one night in the flotsam of evening news. In the midst of his old-fashioned *perp promenade,* Luke was captured on tape. On his way from police car to courthouse. He wore a bullet-proof vest of navy blue over a white dress shirt, and with his newly combed hair he looked most like a religious ascetic, like a Mormon on his teenage mission, like an ecstatic preacher. The reporters shouted to him as he trudged along, *Luke, has God forgiven you?* Luke answered this question in the affirmative, without eye contact. *And have you forgiven yourself?* continued one network reporter. *No,* said Luke, passing close now. *How could I?*

If the scariest thing about a school-yard murder is how it is committed in silence, the scariest thing about a murderer's infrequent remarks is how much he or she sounds *just like us.* The murderer who talks with the voice of a child submits the dangerous proposal that we are all capable. That childhood and adolescence are often murderous and often fatal. That only good luck distinguishes the guilty from the innocent. For example, according to one hypothesis: Joseph Moody went out hunting with his pal Ebenezer Preble, age twelve. Joseph Moody was nine. Looking for game in the fields behind the parish in York, Maine, for the wild things of the colonial forest. Fox or squirrel or grouse or quail. The northeastern white-tailed deer. The doe, the fawn, the antlered buck. Perhaps it was down toward the river, the York River, along the Indian Trail that abuts Mill Pond and Barrell Mill Road. Through the underbrush, looking. They were young and short of attention, so when some three quarters of an hour had passed, they began to become impatient, notwithstanding lectures on the devilishness of impatience; *Hell is for fickle hearts.* They had sat through sermons hours long, but here they were excitable with firearms, and perhaps there were clouds that day, and they wanted to have something to show their fathers. Joseph, at least, felt this way, impatient, circling around, as Ebenezer set off on his tramp. Then he heard a rustling in the thicket. Grand and monstrous, this quarry. A bear, perhaps, a mountain lion. He might impress the town fathers with his prowess. He raised his musket, though he could barely lift it. He fired. And struck Ebenezer through the temple. *Hastening in triumph to the spot where he expected to find his game, there lay his friend Preble weltering in his blood, and in the agonies of death.*

A contrary hypothesis has it thus:

> When Joseph was eight years old, an event occurred which may have gone far to darken any spontaneous feeling of light-heartedness through the rest of his early boyhood. . . . Joseph and a playmate, Ebenezer Preble, two years older than he, had found a loaded pistol within

reach. They were, perhaps, toying with it in eight-year-old unconcern, when the pistol, in Joseph's hand, went off, killing Ebenezer Preble instantly. Of the aftermath of this unhappy accident involving, as it did, two families, there is no written record.

And yet, if accidental, why an *incurable* sickness in the heart? Or is this incurable sickness simply part of an inheritance that, as offspring of a Puritan divine, Joseph came into without effort at all? Nowhere in all the pages devoted to Handkerchief Moody does it suggest that Joseph may have *intended* to shoot Ebenezer for any reason. But questions as to motive must have circulated around Joseph as he stood watching the soul ebb from his companion. Adults, having heard the shot, or perhaps having heard the cries that issued from Joseph, came running, according to my own conjecture. *Did I not clean the gun properly?* The burden was heavy. Right away. And when at last, that day, his father, Samuel, came upon the action, or perhaps found Ebenezer's mother (Ebenezer's father, being a sea captain, was perhaps off at sea), his son was already formulating a deceit, or so I imagine: *The Indians have killed Ebenezer. The savages came this way and with their muskets set upon Ebenezer giving the reason that we had trespassed upon their land.*

Joseph formulated an alibi.

What does it *feel like* to be a juvenile murderer, outside of the bluster of public theories about it, outside of spurious public debate, outside of the slick, empty, alliterative headlines of tabloids? It feels as if you are entrapped in Samuel Moody's *inferno*, with all its brimstone and molten rock, as in *Vain Youth Summoned to Appear at Christ's Bar: The way of Lying, for sport, or to excuse their faults, . . . the way of Pride, in ambitious, self-conceited thoughts, boasting expressions, and inordinate imitations of the newest fashion. . . . There are ways of Swearing, Sabbath-breaking, Disobediance to Parents, Drinking and Stealing, that are very pleasing in the Eyes of Vain Youth.* Such a crime as Joseph Moody committed brought down upon him, in colonial America, the paralysis and hopelessness of *hell*. It feels like you're an animal, like you're a dog, like you've been treated like a dog. *Impieties, Impurities, and Vile*

Idolatries, to them you have succumbed. You're the worst that God has fashioned in his likeness.

There was a writer who slew his own wife, in obscure circumstances. Afterward, he spoke of it. This was Mexico, in 1951. The writer had fled there to avoid criminal charges in New Orleans. He took Joan Vollmer Adams, his common-law wife, with him, as he had taken her to Texas and New Orleans before that. They had two children: a boy, Billy, and Joan's daughter by a prior marriage, Julie Adams. The writer was using narcotics occasionally, drinking quite a bit, in Mexico, as in Texas, Louisiana, New York City. Joan had been an amphetamine addict in New York, where she was hospitalized for it — *I was not much surprised to hear of your hospitalization,* she writes to her friend Allen Ginsberg, *as I've been claiming for three years (today being the 3rd anniversary of my departure from Bellevue) that anyone who doesn't blow his top once is no damn good.* But she found that her Benzedrine inhalers were hard, if not impossible, to find south of the border. She began drinking heavily (*Evil people here sell tequila for 40 cents {U.S.} a quart, and with Smith, Kline and French gone back on me I tend to hit the lush rather hard*), *from early in the morning on.* Her husband, meanwhile, was sleeping with young boys, also inexpensive. Joan's patience, she claimed, was infinite. After a time, in Mexico, William S. Burroughs fell in love with a young heterosexual academic called Eugene Allerton, with whom he embarked into South America in search of a mythic Indian drug called *yage.* The story is hyperbolic but true and is to be found in both his novel *Queer* and in *The Yage Letters.* (I'm following closely the account suggested by biographer Ted Morgan.) One can imagine, because of all this, that there was a fair amount of strain between Burroughs and his wife. (As in Burroughs's letter to Ginsberg on the subject:

Now this business about Joan and myself is downright insane. I never made any pretensions of permanent heterosexual orientation. What lie are you talking about? Like I say I never promised or even *implied* anything. How could I promise something that is not in my power to give? I am *not* responsible for Joan's sexual life, never was, never pretended to be. Nor are we in any particular mess. There is, of course, as there was from the beginning, an impasse and cross purposes that are, in all likelihood, not amenable to any solution.)

Burroughs was depressed upon his return from South America, and it's not hard to fathom why. His wife drank around the clock, had *open sores* on her body; he was infatuated with a straight friend who didn't return the honor; he was a drug addict; his children were troubled; he had jumped bail in Louisiana. During a particular afternoon, Burroughs went to get a knife sharpened, and on the way, he felt a heavy sadness upon himself: *Because I remember on the day in which this occurred, I was walking down the street and suddenly I found tears streaming down my face, "What in the hell is the matter with you?" And then I took a knife to be sharpened which I had bought in Ecuador and I went back to this apartment. Because I felt so terrible, I began throwing down one drink after the other. And then this thing occurred.*

Morgan quotes Burroughs himself about the accident:

Let's see, Joan was sitting in a chair, I was sitting in another chair across the room about six feet away, there was a table, there was a sofa. The gun [that Burroughs had brought, intending to sell] was in a suitcase and I took it out, and it was loaded, and I was aiming it. I said to Joan, "I guess it's about time for our William Tell act." She took her highball glass and balanced it on top of her head. Why I did it, I don't know, something took over. It was an utterly and completely insane thing to do. Suppose I had succeeded in shooting the glass off her head, there was a danger of glass splinters flying out and hitting the other people there. I fired one shot, aiming at the glass.

Besides Burroughs, his friend Eugene Allerton, and Joan, the fourth party in the room was Allerton's childhood friend Eddie Woods, and this is his account:

I started to reach for the gun, but then I thought, "You better not, 'cause if it goes off and hits her . . ." And then bang, that was the first impression, the noise. . . . The next thing I knew the glass was on the floor, and I noticed the glass was intact, it was rolling around in concentric circles, this six-ounce water glass. And then I looked at her and her head had fallen to one side. Well, I thought, she's kidding. Then I heard Allerton say, "Bill, I think you hit her." Then he cried, "No!" and started toward her, and then I saw the hole in her temple. Burroughs kept crying, "Joan, Joan, Joan!" Allerton went to get a doctor, and I went to Juanita's place, leaving Burroughs there kneeling in tears at her side, saying, "Talk to me, talk to me." And as I left, I could hear her death rattle — *haaarrrrhhhh.*

How absent Joan is from these accounts. As if her death is read backward against her life, as if Burroughs had somehow killed her *before killing her,* so that only her afterimage remains to be effaced in Eddie Woods's rented room. Joan the ghost can't venture a word, except, in Woods's account, a prophetic recognition of her impending death. What of this last word of hers? So sad in Woods's version, *haaarrrrhhhh,* so destitute. A genuine message from the hereafter, a register of the severity of the moment, of the hardship of her last months. (She was twenty-seven years old when she died.) I can't think of Woods's description — *death rattle* — without thinking that it's a perverse *laugh* on the part of Joan's shade, on the part of the Joan Vollmer lost *long before,* though perhaps the men around her, the witnesses of her puffy, lame body, had failed to notice. Murder always does a wicked effacement, and the greatest justice, perhaps the only justice, is in *memory:* when I began to chase down the facts of the Burroughs murder, it was Joan who sang across the decades to me, who began to materialize, in the space where I was working on Handkerchief Moody and poor Ebenezer Preble. First, there was the photo of her that Ginsberg took, one of only three that I know of, Joan on the Upper West Side, a trampled snowfall behind her, slightly drifting, a dark Upper West Side tenement, her curly dark hair blown over to one side, her smile faint, her eyes downcast, almost closed, as if with a variety of sleepwalking; she clutches a paper bag across her chest, her gloved hands concealed in the photograph, a purse over the left shoulder, a winter light, the artificially high shoulders of her winter coat; she's beautiful and imperious and vulnerable all at the same time — like the women of Morningside Heights when I was in graduate school there — so much so that the accounts that speak of her reading in the tub all day don't seem outlandish; one is tempted to try to reconstruct the titles of the works, Proust in the original, crime fiction, German philosophy. But the next photo of her, *the only known picture of her after living with William,* as one critic puts it, is notable for the differences, how much more haggard she looks, how the curly hair from before looks matted, even if the curl persists at the ends; she has grown sallow, a little distended. Only the eyes, concealed in Ginsberg's photo, are noteworthy, bright and fierce. Then the third photo that is never reproduced but which is nonetheless passed hand from hand, *Joan's morgue photo,* how painful it was to look at it, how painful to acknowledge having had it. I lost the copy on the first day it was in my possession. I looked at it, and then I lost it. Joan laid out in the Mexican morgue with the sheet pulled up but looking, in the conventional parlance, *peaceful,* as if, at least, a portion of the struggle of living with Bill Burroughs was over.

Ginsberg writes:

> I dreamed this during a drunken night in my house . . . :
> I was visiting the big city, and there saw Joan Bur-
> roughs, who has been dead now five years — she sat in
> a chair in a garden with the smile on her face: restored
> to its former beauty, the sweetness of intelligence
> which I eternalized in my imagination, that had been
> lost thru years of Tequila in Mexico City, for Tequila
> had ruined her face & beauty before the bullet in her
> brow. . . . Then I realized this was a dream: and said
> "Joan," as she smiled and talked again as would a trav-
> eler resting on return . . . "Do the dead have memory,

232 • RICK MOODY

still love their mortal acquaintances, & do they still remember us," but she faded before there was a reply and in the place where her ghost was I saw her small rain-stained tombstone, scarred, engraved with a Mexican epitaph in an unknown cemetery.

In 1952, in a letter to Ginsberg, Burroughs begins the process of talking about the murder: *P.S. I am sick lately, no energy and no appetite. (I do get hungry but can't bring myself to sit down alone in a restaurant and eat through a meal, so break two eggs in milk and that is dinner.) How I miss Joan!* The pathos of that exclamation mark. And this from a man who in the same era boasted of killing cats. (*I picked the animal up and held it on my lap, petting it. When it tried to jump down I tightened my hold. The cat began to mew, looking for a way to escape.*) Conscience, like an upsurge of lava, such that one can only feel compassion for the author, even though, by 1965, on the occasion of a *Paris Review* interview, his tone is markedly different, even mildly deceitful:

> And I had that terrible accident with Joan Vollmer, my wife. I had a revolver that I was planning to sell to a friend. I was checking it over and it went off — killed her. A rumor started that I was trying to shoot a glass of champagne from her head William Tell–style. Absurd and false.

In the seventies, as Burroughs's prose style is giving way to the difficulty and incomprehensibility of his cutups, or collages, his thinking about the murder, at least publicly, becomes even less clear, until by 1974 it is a bit incoherent:

> That was an accident. That is to say, if everyone is to be made responsible for everything they do, you must extend responsibility beyond the level of conscious intention. I was aiming for the very tip of the glass. This gun was a very inaccurate gun, however. . . . It's very complicated to tell you. It was obviously a situa-

tion precipitated by some part of myself over which I had, or perhaps have, no control.

That the accident *was an accident* is repeated restlessly, the shame of it like the runoff of a heavy winter's snowpack, as if the repetition will soothe the part of the subject no longer so sure; issues of culpability and the logic of culpability rise to the surface and then dwindle away again; elsewhere, in a different interview, in an effort to lay aside the recollection of things too painful to recollect, Burroughs observes that *love is a virus. I think love is a con put down by the female sex. I don't think it's a solution to anything;* or, later, quoting Conrad, *"Women are a perfect curse." I think they were a basic mistake, and the whole dualistic universe evolved from this error.* As if the repression of sexual difference will preempt the moment in which Burroughs's wife is killed by his own hand. In the later seventies, Burroughs seems to refuse to speak about the incident at all, and a silence on the subject ensues in the public record, at least until the publication of Burroughs's suppressed second novel, *Queer.* In 1985, when that book is finally released, the author appends an introduction about the period in which it was composed: *When I started to write this companion text to* Queer, *I was paralyzed with a heavy reluctance. . . . The reason for this reluctance becomes clearer as I force myself to look: the book is motivated and formed by an event which is never mentioned, in fact is carefully avoided: the accidental shooting death of my wife, Joan, in September 1951.* He goes on:

> I am forced to the appalling conclusion that I would never have become a writer but for Joan's death, and to a realization of the extent to which this event has motivated and formulated my writing. . . . So the death of Joan brought me in contact with the invader, the Ugly Spirit, and maneuvered me into a lifelong struggle, in which I have had no choice except to write my way out.

It's moving to find the accidental murderer, in his seventies, thirty-four years later, still struggling with his crime. And his tone markedly resembles the tone that critic Newton Arvin attributes to Nathaniel

234 • RICK MOODY

Hawthorne: *If {like the Puritans}, he brooded on the black fatalities of human error and vice, it was the result not of any Calvinist theology, but of his somber consciousness of separation from the ways of his fellow men — a consciousness in which the sense of guilt luxuriates like noisome growths in a swamp.* Perhaps the predisposition to conscience is one that *goes with language;* shame goes with language, shame goes with consciousness, shame goes with writing.

I think of Joan Burroughs a lot, as I think of all *dead girls* expunged by philosophies and theologies of the masculine. Many nights, when I was younger, I was in a certain bar on the Upper West Side, and I believed I *saw* Joan, or aspects of Joan's character; she believed that Mayan priests must have experienced some sort of telepathic method of control, she conducted conversations in the bathtub, she received telecommunications from her husband, she wrote marginal criticism in her copy of Marx's *Capital;* once I drove to her hometown, in a rental car, one winter. Loudonville, edge of Albany. Down through the sprawl north of the city, an eruption of old farmlands and houses with grand yards, as in the suburbs of my own childhood. Why should I feel I knew her, when I wasn't born until ten years after her shooting? Why should I feel I was her acquaintance or the acquaintance of others who had her promise and like her were unlucky enough to receive, for their trouble, a bullet in the head? I spent nights in the bars with them. Outside, the streets populated only with panhandlers and religious zealots with their interpretations of law and prophecy. I was willing to listen to the *dead girl* until all hours, to her complaints, her conspiracy theories, to her reflexive poesy, I was willing to go again and buy her cigarettes, even if I no longer smoked, I was willing to overlook her drunkenness, the disarray of her clothes, I wanted nothing from her, except that she should *live,* and deprive those of us who had given over too much time in grieving for our lost friends; she should restore us to a conception of the future that didn't have loss in it. Bring back the *dead girl,* restore her to her environs, in which she lugged around her books, in which she scribbled her ambitions on coffee-stained legal pads. Let us struggle with how to *live with her,* instead of struggling with how to live *after her.* Don't make this last moment be the one in which she looks demurely to the side as her husband raises the pistol; *I can't stand the sight of blood.*

Thus ever back to embellishments of that instant, as in this account from a book of New England ghost stories:

> Dreading the blame of his townsmen, the anguish of the dead youth's parents, and the scorn of his betrothed, the minister concealed his guilt. The town believed that the killing was a murder, the act of some roving Indian. But for years the face of his dead friend rose accusingly before him. In desperation, and determined to pay a penalty for concealing his sin, Joseph finally resolved that never again would he look his fellowmen openly in the face. "Then it was," he whispered on his deathbed, "that I put a veil between myself and the world." As he had requested, "Handkerchief Moody's" black crepe hid his face in the coffin. But the clergyman who had raised it for a moment to compose his features found there a serenity and a beauty that were majestic.

A VEIL MAY SOMETIMES BE NEEDFUL, BUT NEVER A MASQUE . . .

For the purposes of instructing myself about Handkerchief Moody and his crime, for the purposes of understanding Hawthorne's preoccupation with the image of the veil, it became obvious that I needed myself to wear the veil for some unspecified period. It's probably important to observe that this wasn't a *decision,* this assumption of the veil, but a reflex, *the receptor causing action in the effector,* etc., not a journalistic plan, something that I could publish somewhere glossy, next to a photo of a woman in a bra, but an *action of the body,* something that while not identical in degree with respect to my ancestral Moodys was identical in kind, in intention, one with their disgrace and shame. If they were burdened then I should burdened, and so forth. I had planned to don the veil, therefore, since capable of plans, and perhaps even before, in my muscles and tendons and glands and viscera. I didn't do it lightly. The prospect was a lonely one, in ways that I couldn't have known at first, so it was something that required labor and philosophy, but it also had a lot of practical issues associated with it, and so like a lot of sad things, it was also *funny.* Would I, for example, wear the veil to lunch with the guys I usually met at noontime at the Star Burger Deli on Forty-sixth Street? I imagined their reactions in the event that I showed up for lunch wearing a veil, though otherwise turned out in jeans and corduroy shirt. The superintendent at my building, named Carlos, a good guy, a reliable guy; replastered my bathroom ceiling once, never complained about collecting my mail when I traveled out of town. What would Carlos think of the veil? Would he and the rest of the building staff whisper about me, as the citizenry of "The Minister's Black Veil" whispered about the reverend? (*The next day, the whole village of Milford talked of little else than Parson Hooper's black veil.*) And if I needed to visit my dentist wearing a veil? How would my dentist react? He had been gracious about my professional life in the past, as I lay on the chaise longue of dental torture. But would he accept any explanation that I offered? Would he simply fold back the veil and scale off the plaque on my uppers and lowers without discussion? And what about at the gym? Would I wear shorts, T-shirt, running shoes, and *a veil?* How would I fit my portable cassette recorder over my veil? The subway, I figured, would be routine, since every variety of madness and sorrow has already been displayed on the subway. On the Two and the Three trains, during the evening rush, no problem. I would not be out of place.

Then there was the issue of veil procurement. Were there veils neglected on the upper shelves of secondhand clothing stores waiting to be worn by mourners such as myself? What sort of a veil should I wear? Were there various styles of veils? Amy, *my paramour,* suggested affixing my veil to the visor of a cap. I couldn't, however, accept the notion of walking around the city with, say, the baseball cap that a friend had brought me from Cleveland (*Rock and roll!*), a piece of black satin fluttering from its visor. How about a Middle Eastern veil? From nearby Atlantic Avenue, where Middle Eastern culture throve upon these shores. Should I wear the *hijab?*

Around a dinner table upstate, where I had gone to mull over these and other issues respecting *the assumption of the veil,* I worried aloud. A writer friend suggested the professional headgear of fly fishermen. It sometimes had a veil on it, this friend said, by which an angler avoided mosquitoes and other pests. Or there was the uniform of the beekeeper. Beekeepers wore protective netting over their faces, pale beige mesh of extra durability. But in both these cases the veils were appendages designed to *keep things out,* rather than to inhibit the perception of facial niceties *within.* At dinner, a friend named Mona Jimenez suggested purchasing fabric. *This is the way that widows do it,* Mona observed. *They wear some fabric over their faces. It's simple.* The model here, the perfect model of late-twentieth-century grief, was Jackie O., in the funeral cortege after the president's assassination. Jackie in black pillbox hat with transparent veil that merely suggested its status as accessory of mourning. You could see her loss plainly, on television, in newspaper photographs, the sheer veil as indicator of the severity of her tragedy.

To demonstrate her theory of the veil, Mona Jimenez lifted up her napkin and draped it over the crown of her head (much in the way that Buster Keaton wore a handkerchief in Beckett's *Film*). Soon a writer named Jenny was also wearing her napkin, and then a poet in attendance, until most of the guests at the dinner table were wearing napkins over their heads, corners of perfect white drapery effacing their eyes and noses, each advancing possible methods for affixing the veil while laughing self-consciously: *You need a larger piece than this, anyway, you need a long piece to cut down a little bit, it should be a heavy fabric, it should be a lightweight synthetic, it should cover your whole face,* etc. There were suggestions offered about Orchard Street, on the Lower East Side, that epicenter of fabric stores. A playwright and performance artist called Fiona observed that Diamond's, the best of these emporia, was noteworthy for its *silence,* because the bolts of cloth, all arrayed along the walls, were impediments to sound. So hushed whispers dominated when urban buyers of cloth made their proposals and when negotiation ensued.

And I thought: *Here's Handkerchief Moody,* as an adult, in York, his majesty's colonial Maine, in the middle of the eighteenth century, in a haberdasher's at seaside, having already established a reputation as a minister of rather odd and retiring habits, also, according to rumor, *a manslaughterer;* small children scatter out of his path, regardless of the fact that his father is so well-loved, and on this day, on his fell recognizances, Joseph Moody (not yet Handkerchief), ventures into the haberdashery on the waterfront in York, carrying a few English pence, asks the favor of the *proprietress,* who knows him well enough and feels pity for the woe upon him since his wife died, though, on the obverse, *she dislikes him just the same,* because the wretched often implore us to continue to treat them badly, and Handkerchief whispers to the proprietress that he would like a length of that most expensive and rare of black fabrics there, *Is it silken and of the Indies?* Everywhere there are bolts of cloth in a minimal candlelight, and the proprietress, the seamstress, disappears into the rear of the shop with great iron shears, not wanting, for reasons she doesn't quite confess, to measure and wrap up this length of fabric, for it is certainly morbid, in front of the feverish young Father Moody. Nevertheless, she has soon enfolded it in rough brown paper, bound it with heavy twine, and entrusted it to the reverend, *all in silence,* her fabric store garlanded in a solemnity, and soon he stumbles past the next good customer, begging pardon, stepping through the threshold *to the high tinkling of a little bell,* and then Joseph Moody is gone, lost in a forgiving wood, to attempt the donning of his fresh punishment.

Any number of fabric stores up and down the seaboard of the thirteen original colonies, any number of elderly fabric salespeople, any number of silent, secreted shops with their histories of unionized or sweatshopped cross-cultural labor, would have served like purposes for me. But I was upstate. My consultation with the Yellow Pages of Saratoga County led to a number of possible local outlets, but the one mentioned in downtown Saratoga Springs turned out to be a shop for knitters. I would not be the sort of fabric buyer who went into a knitting shop, I decided. What about Kmart or Wal-Mart, where there were enormous fabric departments in the farthest reaches of the store and staff eager for distraction? Next to the houseplants you will find the fabric department, beside the frugal section of the store devoted to *crafts.* Though Wal-Mart obviously exposed me to the possibility of discount fabric, *not top-of-the-line stuff, perhaps fabrics woven by underage believers in strange magic from countries with repressive military dictators.* Wal-Mart implied a veil of homely origins, and yet I was determined to make the journey there, because Wal-Mart was where America shopped, and I wanted my veil to come from an enterprise that merchandised to my nation in its entirety, an enterprise that might fly American flags from its ceilings.

The only requirement was that the veil be black.

Wal-Mart was located in a section of Saratoga Springs scarred by rapacious developers. This was in the foothills of the Adirondacks, that great national forest, but you couldn't tell for the traffic. It was all strip franchises and chain stores. Not one mall to bedeck the edge of this forest, but two. The first of these featured a Department of Labor office, a veterans' affairs office, a flea market, and two churches. All inside. A display of recreational vehicles was mounted here while I was in town, and you could go inside the RVs, if you were serious about buying. There wasn't much foot traffic. And there was a big patch of the parking lot that they didn't plow in winter. But in spite of the beleaguered condition of this mall, a twin was built directly adjacent to it, and this second mall attracted larger tenants, as well as an indoor merry-go-round, a video game parlor, a Spencer Gifts outlet, Waldenbooks. There was a booth where they would perform the traditional on-the-spot piercings for teenagers. There was a Sears department store and a Wholesale Price Club. And around these two malls had sprung up any number of additional high-volume chain businesses, a Kmart, a Staples, and, most recently, out on its own approach ramp at the edge of the Adirondack forest, Wal-Mart.

It was one of the biggest department stores I'd ever been in. More like an airplane hangar than a department store. Wal-Mart, as you passed through its ghostly automatic doors, opened into women's and men's apparel, and as I made my way in — with a brisk stride that yielded almost immediately to the traditional *stunned buyer's shuffle* — I passed through apparel first. Huey Lewis and the News, the easy-listening combo, played discreetly on the Wal-Mart public-address system, followed by Paul Simon's "Loves Me Like a Rock." I was thinking of Timothy Leary, who had recently traveled over to the other side: *Go back down the ladder of genetic memory, find your divinity.* What language was adequate for describing the diminishment of self that one felt immediately upon entering into an American department store? The blunt, joyless compulsion of shopping? The miserliness of all those choices? And what language was adequate for describing, nonetheless, the *relief* felt upon having this capacity for choice overwhelmed? If you accosted a Wal-Mart employee at random and demanded of him or her the location of the soul, how would she or he reply? *I'll see if we have those in stock. They should be over on the third aisle, beside the health-and-beauty aids.* My hesitant step in department store settings reminded me of the unfortunates I knew during my stay in the psychiatric hospital, reminded me of those patients consuming antipsychotic medication. Shopping and recovery from psychosis were, therefore, in my view, related.

After a reptilian promenade, I eventually arrived in the fabric department, as predicted, in the farthest corner of the store. I had to pass through the electronics department and the home furnishings department and the home repair department and the automotive products department and then across the threshold of the crafts section, until, suddenly, all about me, in an expanse mostly neglected by my fellow Wal-Mart shoppers, were *bolts of cloth,* all manner of patterns and pastels and bold single-color styles. There were stripes and prints that you wouldn't be caught dead in, that you would never allow in the vicinity of your sofa or any of your other *furniture accessories* but which someone must have purchased, for here were a hundred yards or more of that malevolent beige. There were lovely subtle shades as well, and a wealth of black styles to choose from. Black fabric in every conceivable warp and stitch. In the front of the department were displayed the bargain materials, nylons and Dacrons, a dollar a square yard, not much more, and I took up each of these cloths and held each to my eyes, to learn of its potential for transparency. I *wore* each of these textiles in turn, briefly. Wrapped myself in them. As I moved into the pricey center of the fabric section, where an employee and her friend were discussing *tragedies of their lives* (the employee, a gray-haired African-American woman bedecked in the regulation apron, was apparently struggling with the terminal illness of her mother), I moved into the more sturdy blends and natural samples, where I hesitated briefly over a black rhinestoned fabric, which I at first considered perfect for my project under the theory that *the uglier the fabric the better.* Next, I arrived at raw silk, imitation silk, cotton bolts, in deepest black, which were of such opacity that there was no way I could wear them and continue to participate fully in life. I would be disguised by my veil, but I didn't need to be *physically challenged,* as the Reverend Hooper was not: it *probably did not intercept his sight, further than to give a darkened aspect to all living and inanimate things.*

I settled finally on something in the middle of the fabric spectrum, a racy silken synthetic that would have made an excellent miniskirt, had I been inclined in that direction, and that draped marvelously without clinging. Then I sought the advice of the Wal-Mart employee whose mother was ill. Her garrulous friend, seeing that business called, made a quick getaway. *I'll pray for you, Eileen.* Suddenly, I was at the *point of purchase,* that moment of reckoning, and I felt myself empowered in the matter of fabric shopping. *Wait just a second,* I remarked. *I need a couple more items.* I was created for Wal-Mart and Wal-Mart was created for me! Wal-Mart was dreamed up by Sam Walton for the provision of ritual garmentry, *made for my sort of romance,* and I was not backing down at this important juncture; I discovered the dozens of spools on which ribbons were stored; I discovered a black spool that was speckled with dust, and I blew upon it, to clear the dust, and asked for a yard of black ribbon, as I had asked for a square yard of the fabric, and then I got my hands on some Velcro sealers, because I revered the whole idea of Velcro as well as the intelligence that gave us Velcro, and *who knew how I was going to affix this powerful black emblem to my head?* But never mind all this, I bantered with the fabric salesperson, I felt suddenly loquacious, I had exercised *freedom of choice,* my step was assured and my posture had improved, and I strode briskly now to the cash registers at the front of the store. *I got my veil and fastening technology, and even a few personal items, for a mere $13.31!*

That night my friend Mona and a sculptor, Randy Polumbo, had *open studios* nearby, and a number of us went around to look at their output. I had thought to ask Mona and Randy to help me with the veil prior to this display of work, such that I could *wear it out,* like a kid on the first day of school with *new fall sneakers,* but the moment didn't seem right. And yet, as part of Randy's studio visit — featuring *solar-powered sculptures,* rubber castings of condoms, footballs with facsimile nipples protruding from them, and other delights — we were offered the opportunity to *shoot* at a number of sculptural castings that, in Polumbo's words, had not passed quality control.

The firearm in question was a BB pistol (also purchased at Wal-Mart). Randy set up the castings on ledges in the snowdrifts outside his studio. We clustered to practice our marksmanship.

I found the target shooting pretty invigorating. Later, I understood why, since the whole issue of *Handkerchief Moody and his abuse of weapons,* the abuse of firearms in which life was lost, was of course central to any search for *the meaning of the veil.* If I had been enterprising, I would have donned my new garment on the spot and with it on I would have taken aim at the plaster of paris *dildoes* that served as targets, thus symbolically calling up a whole lineage of ghosts. Randy had affixed an infrared targeting light to the pistol, in a cruciform shape, and this was appropriate too. We stood in the cold, during the last week of January, firing the pistol at molded penises. One of our number, a Hungarian poet, István, was not at all inclined to take up the American firearm and had to be coaxed into it. Not me. That night, over dinner, in fact, I had recounted a portion of *my history of firearms,* that habit and leisure activity in my family, how some of my earliest memories were of the dairy farm upstate where my father and his friends went to hunt game. The smart snap of a twelve-gauge or a 4.10 were large parts of my childhood. Target shooting with a twenty-two. I liked the smell of empty shotgun cartridges, the way they ejected violently to the right side. I liked to collect empty cartridges and to sniff them; I liked to go out into the skeet field after the carnage and look for clay pigeons that had survived their arc across the blue. I liked clay pigeons at the moment that they were pulverized or fractured, but I especially loved them when they survived, and I would carry them back to the ramshackle frame house on the distant corner of the farm where we camped. It was always cold. *You can always take off a layer, but you can't put another on if you didn't bring one.* My brother was the best shot. The clays would wobble up into the edge of his field of vision and he'd blast them, comically nonchalant as he did so. Shooting expeditions, the mythology of guns: long drives dangling out the back of pickup trucks, tailgates bobbing up and down behind us — we even fell out of the pickup now and then, into the mud canals that served, in autumn, as roads; all of the kids, the Walker girls (neighbors from home), assorted dogs crammed in the back of a pickup, our cheeks crimson from the cold. In the truck with us were canvas backpacks full of dispatched birds that would eventually be nailed up in the garage until ready to pluck. Then our black Lab would emerge from some thicket of briars with another slain bird cradled in her mouth, and we would take the bird, stash it with the others. Best of all: we would chase one another through stands of corn that blanketed that landscape, Indian corn, stalks at the moment before harvest, twice again as tall as we were; we scattered on the least provocation through those avenues of corn, where no one could see us, into that great concealer of children, autumnal corn — it had concealed children going all the way back to when the first *maize* was planted in the counties of New York — full of joy, sometimes in terror, and perhaps *Handkerchief himself had run out into the corn,* having embarked on his life of ulcerated conscience, after the moment when his musket discharged through carelessness (*Don't ever point this weapon at anyone,* as my father said, *and don't ever leave it loaded, and keep the stock broken if you are walking around with it, and always clean it when you are through*), and the weapon fell out of his hands, and he fled to be consumed by fields of corn, fled through the straight lines of it, fled the trouble he had made for himself, until he emerged, *as we did, on a burial ground of village livestock.* Here was the spot where they disposed of the cattle that threatened the herd (brucellosis, anthrax) or were otherwise gone before their time, a grim, melancholy locale where the creek forked away toward somber hills; it was almost sunset, and my sister recognized a protrusion at the top of the burial mound. An upturned hoof, *waving at us,* the unburied vertex of some mostly buried cow, an advertisement for the great beyond of cattle. Were cattle too stupid to rue the loss of their progeny? Did they idle in these fields and low at that one hoof that protruded? Was this where Handkerchief found himself when at last his father learned of his mischief and he stood up straight and offered, dry-eyed, his confession?

We met the kids who lived on the dairy farm, in a rundown house across the county road. We sometimes saw their dad riding a tractor, and he would invite us into the mechanized space where the cattle were fed and where they were milked. He fiddled nervously with the bill of his cap as he spoke to us. Manure everywhere. And his mute kids. They were not from the neighborhoods that had produced us; they knew things we had never seen. One of them was *retarded,* the word we used then; the occasional trickle of drool cascaded down his weak chin. His older brother was a *fat kid,* whose faded sweatshirt did little to cover a protuberant belly, and we had no idea what to make of these children. The interview was quickly over, but we knew that there was something hidden here, some great theatrical of nature played out at the dairy farm, not like in the suburbs, and it was fearsome at night, so lonely in the frame house out on the edge of the woods, who could stay awake alone; the fire behind the screen was all that separated us from the masque of death; this place was its laboratory, its abattoir, and who could stay awake alone to set another perfect cylinder of birch onto the fire, to ensure that the rest of the group, the eight or ten of us slumbering inconsistently in sleeping bags, would stay warm? *I slept.* My father stirred wearily beside me, took over my shift, prodded the flames.

Guns, in the fallen state of adulthood, could never compete with this perfect infancy of weaponry and its rituals. My brother and I used to *shoot at each other,* with BB guns, in our early teens, and I can remember hitting my brother in the ass as he retreated frantically on his bicycle. He did the same to me. There were the later attempts at marksmanship, shooting clays out on the island where my father lived, out over the Atlantic, tidal reek in the air, changeable skies, and submarines in the distance on the high seas, but this shooting as an adult — the spontaneous murder of defenseless Canada geese, the occasional pruning of the local crow or rabbit populations — this shooting, with strolls across the backyards of million-dollar homes, during which we unloaded multiply at birds whose first moment of freedom was to be released into slaughter, it didn't have the *wilderness* of my early expeditions. May I never forget the ephemeral beauty of the pheasant, the male with his crimson neck and his show-offy tail feathers, and how, as a kid, the sound of pheasant reminded me of bicycle horns, a lonely, pastoral warble.

Next day, after target shooting, I asked Randy and Mona if they would consult on the assembly and ritual assumption of *my veil.* It was late afternoon, and Mona brought needle and thread. I tried on the square yard of black cloth in the mirror over my sink. I gathered it around my face, pushed back my unkempt hair. I let the fabric cascade over my shoulders. I was an off-the-rack cultural primitive from a science fiction film. I was an extra in some tale of Marrakech. And the world, through my veil, looked filmy and insubstantial, dark, vaguely threatening, and my feeling, immediately, was of shame and embarrassment. Still, in addition to the problem of proper design for the garment, there was also the problem of *affixing* the veil. Mona, when she arrived at my room, got directly into the business of shearing off hunks of the fabric, trying to make a circular adornment of which one might say, as Hawthorne did, *Swathed about his forehead, and hanging down over his face, so low as to be shaken only by his breath.* She wasn't using the most precise shearing style, but this was a rough outline. My idea was to employ ribbon (with Velcro sealers) around the outside of this drapery to steady the veil on my face. But Mona and Randy both found this too Arabic looking. We decided instead to affix a black band around my head first (sewing the ribbon end to end), to which headband we would anchor the veil itself. I sat in my desk chair. Progress was slow. Mona sewed the veil to the headband while I clutched the rag to my skull to insure stability. After twenty minutes or thereabouts, it was attached in some fashion and Randy fired off a number of photographic portraits of me posing in my ancestral garment. When the novelty of this construction had come to an end, Randy and Mona repaired to their own work and I was left alone with my creation.

I looked like a lighting fixture. Randy had suggested also a *mushroom,* but I felt that I looked most like one of the ornate pink lamps that my grandmother had left unused in her house in Norwalk. I couldn't get comfortable with the way my veil fell across my features. I had warned friends that I would wear the veil out to dinner that night, to expect this eccentricity, but when the dinner hour arrived, I stripped myself of it. What was my resistance? Why was I so uncomfortable with it? Though I had read that Handkerchief Moody had removed the veil from his face at dinner, he dined unaccompanied (*He chose to eat alone, and kept his face always covered with a handkerchief when in com-*

pany). His problem was how to get the food into his mouth without befouling the veil, not the fact of the veil itself. There was something comic and malevolent about the whole idea of wearing it. So I went uncovered to dinner, telling myself that I would screw up courage in succeeding days. *I am bound to wear it ever, both in light and darkness,* according to the Reverend Hooper, *in solitude and before the gaze of multitudes, and as with strangers, so with my familiar friends. No mortal eye will see it withdrawn.* But I could wear mine *only* in solitude, and when some guys came driving up the lane to collect the trash at the estate where I was living, I stashed my veil immediately under a pillow, so that I should not be seen for what I was. An impostor.

Maybe it was the material itself that was wrong, maybe it was my design. Maybe I hadn't done the living yet by which I could arrive spontaneously, through the imperatives of my own circumstances, at the assumption of the veil. I had apparently squandered my first square yard of blackness trying to simulate the identity of a person who, *in the aftermath of murder,* could feel driven so to atone. So I suffered through another trip to Wal-Mart, with friends.

Then, when Amy came upstate to visit, we cut a length of ribbon together and simply folded the appropriate length of fabric over the front of the ribbon. I tested this new headband by itself, attaching the unimpeachable Velcro sealer. It was after dark, and I felt at last something close to awe. Amy asked me if I was being dramatic. In my writing studio, I released a spider trapped in an ashtray, released him into the food chain of my desk and environs, recollecting that in a late Hawthorne story, "Grimshawe," spiders were recurrent, that the protagonist collected the company of spiders, that spiders there were *an emblem for the protagonist himself.* I chased my spider into a corner. I pressed a somber drone into service on my cassette player. The light was low. I asked Amy if she knew what the veil meant, and she replied that she had never liked English classes in which she had been invited merely to decipher meanings. *The scarlet letter was a scarlet letter. The veil's a veil. Books don't mean one thing, they mean a lot of things.* If only I felt this way. I took the ribbon, and its enfolded veil, from her hands, wrapped the experiment around my face.

In the mirror, faceless, expunged, a body without aspect, denied the window of expression, the eyes. How had Handkerchief Moody felt it? Out in the woods, had he brought a scrap of mirror with him, something to serve as looking glass? For there is no veil without eyes to perceive it, no concealment without others who *might once have seen,* as among the blind there are no veils, and so if I veil myself *by myself,* am I really veiling myself at all? Handkerchief, out in the woods, with his friend Ebenezer Preble twenty-five years or more buried and moldering, Handkerchief at the commencement of his ministry, according to his father's urging, Handkerchief having learned his Puritan theology from his father, Handkerchief having read Cotton Mather and his peers: *I sett apart this Day, for the Exercises of a secret Fast in my Study, on such occasions, as were offered, in my own exceeding Sinfulness, Unwatchfulness, and Unfruitfulness: and my want of Divine Assistance for the Discharge of my Ministry: and such likewise, as I saw, in the Condition of my Family, and in the Confusion, either distressing, or threatening of the Land, in the State of the Church abroad . . .* Having read Jonathan Edwards, or like commentators, apologists for an Angry God. Out in the woods, surrounded by spiders, by woodland animals, by witches, or by the memory of witches and agents of devilishness, or so it seemed to me, having worn the veil myself, *with innumerable trunks and thick boughs overhead,* Handkerchief — *he supposed that the guilt of some unforgiven sin lay upon him* — with the scrap of looking glass that, mounting sin upon sin, he had actually *stolen* from the fabric store back at seaside, this glass, because whilst the proprietress was in the rear of the establishment, *he felt he couldn't tell her of the nature of his endeavor,* and so the only just conclusion was to abscond with this small hand mirror that lay on the glass table in the rear of the store, and now in the amber light of dusk, not far from the consecrated plot of Ebenezer Preble, at the village parish in York, he, with twine, fixes this handkerchief to his face, the first feeling one of *gladness.* Such relief as he stumbles out of the woods, pine needles and brambles upon his frock coat that he will not easily see, he can just make his way into the nightfall with this scrap upon his brow, yet such temporary relief that when the furrier who lives at the edge of the wood just beyond the garrison looks up from hind hoof of steed to see him emerging upon a footpath and *starts,* the godforsaken minister won't pay any mind at all. He's in his thrall now, he is Handkerchief — Joseph Moody left far behind, kneeling — and so he will be henceforth, wearing the garment of indignity, impervious to mockery, solitary in his self-inflicted ecstasy.

THERE BEING A HEAVY RAIN YESTERDAY, A NEST OF SWALLOWS WAS WASHED DOWN THE CHIMNEY . . .

Perhaps it would be useful to know what a father and son, on a five-day driving trip (when two or three days should be the limit), *talk about,* when not arguing about which restaurant to patronize or which hotel. To satisfy interest along these lines, I have kept a partial record, which I append here: *how seniors in the old days were the only boarding-school students allowed to walk across the lawns; Latin as a required course of study; strip development, lamentations upon; the proper way to eliminate starlings from an attic; the yen versus the dollar; the collapse of the gold standard; characters of various presidents with particular attention to the fortieth and forty-second presidents; bonds versus securities and real estate in a balanced portfolio; particular lawyers and the undependability of lawyers in general; literature, including especially women writers; blood pressure; mitral valve prolapse; cinema; neighbors, their inevitable tendency to disappoint; contractors, difficulty controlling; routes from various points to various other points, including routes to and in the state of Maine; the American justice system, just can't trust it; Tchaikovsky as minor composer; why Brahms would bother to write variations on a theme by Handel; multiculturalism, pro and con; family trips past; family calamities past; family addresses past; the past; the inevitability of rain;* and so on. This was six months after I had worn the veil. As the days passed, these topics became less friendly and more heated, especially insofar as they had to do with contested political issues, and I began to feel as if we were closer to the source of the family, to *the origin of the veil,* or at least to the origin of the myth of the veil. We were beginning to inhabit the veil's complex range of possibilities. We were exhibiting all the love that is covered over or blemished by that fabric, the cruelty, the obliterating silence of familial Despond, the remorse of Puritan New England, as, e.g., the appendix to Handkerchief Moody's eulogy goes, *His conscience being very tender, his Work lying with uncommon Weight on his Mind.*

Maybe it was just the rain, because as we started up the interstate from York, it grew dark, as it likewise did during Hawthorne's trip to Maine in 1837: *Shower coming on, the rapid running of a little barefooted boy, coming up unheard, and dashing swiftly past us, and showing the soles of his naked feet, as he ran down the path before us, and up the opposite rise.* By the time we elected to stop in Boothbay Harbor, my father's childhood Illyria, it was raining miserably, *foreboding darkly.* The fog was a veil itself. It would linger for the rest of the trip — the trip of my adulthood therefore strongly resembling the earlier trip of my youth. Fittingly, Maine was shrouded in fog as dense as fiberglass, in light drizzle, as it was shrouded in its past, never, in my opinion, having entirely given itself to the present of history, with myriad hurricanes battering its dramatic coast. In fog we got lost (as Hawthorne also complains), planning at first — after leaving York — to take the interstate to Augusta, to head from there south toward the shore, through what had been revealed as ancestral lands, but instead we got trapped on an inland alternate route and then in frustration detoured twenty or thirty miles back to Brunswick, at which point my father fell into a black mood and suggested putting up for the night at his childhood haunt, the Ocean Point Inn of Boothbay Harbor, where he would show me again the old baseball diamond where my grandfather used to pitch softball, where he would again explain why the sport was boring to him, where he would tell anew of his chum Haynes Huzzy, and others. The islands across the harbor shimmered in mist. Ahead was the very island to which my father had taken his motorboat, one summer in a heavy storm, though he could easily have *missed the island* and landed on Portugal three months later. Here, in Ocean Point, my grandmother once found a package of condoms, cigarettes, and a church key. *In my father's things.* The condoms were *wishful thinking.* And this was where that guy used to dive in the harbor for lobsters *without a wet-suit,* would just go over the side of the rowboat, plunge down into the water deep, and come up with a lobster, which he would heave into the bottom of his skiff. Hawthorne's descriptions of his trip to Maine have a similar cast and sprawl, full of affectionately told country recreations: *A ride, yesterday afternoon, to a pond in the vicinity of Augusta, about nine miles off, to fish for white perch. Remarkables — the steering of the boat through the crooked, labyrinthine brook, into the open pond. . . . Myself smoking a most vile American cigar; the pilot, after drinking his brandy, giving a history of our fishing expedition, and how many and how large fish we caught.*

I had worked hard to connect my father and my grandfather and all their stories of Maine to the Maine of Handkerchief Moody, sort of the way C. G. Jung was always trying to connect the gnostics to the alchemists, but the two would not meet, at least not until I started trying to tease out a narrative of *my grandfather's father,* one Hiram Clement Moody, for whom my grandfather was named, for whom my father was named, for whom I am named myself, though I don't much use my real name, and about whom I knew very little until I started digging around, except that Hiram Clement Moody had been a stonemason, that he came from the state of Maine, that he had something to do with the construction of South Station, Boston. This was according to the blarney of my grandfather, anyhow, and since his father had died when my grandfather was still in the single digits, there was no reason to believe him entirely. His stories were inherited too.

It was in 1897, or about a hundred years prior to that very afternoon, when the city of Boston came to see that, with the unwieldy size of its commuter population, it had become necessary, or at least expeditious, to create two new railroad terminals, so as to render obsolete the dozen private terminals then operating in the city. *Attention was directed to the possibility of divorcing the suburban, or short-distance service from the long-distance service; and placing the former at a different level.* Thus was born North and South Stations, which emerged at a time when the metropolises of the northeast were indeed becoming cities, when the agricultural basis of America was giving way to large-scale *corporate enterprise.* The Puritan garrisons and Indian Wars of the northeast were already memories, stuff of books. Their effects dim, mythic. South Station, like Pennsylvania Station, was intended to move people numbered in millions. People who had to *work.*

In order to construct South Station, enormous hurdles had to be negotiated, engineered. There were a number of streets that had to be emptied, for example, and there was a drainage problem at the southern tip of Boston where, during one memorable storm in the second decade of the nineteenth century, the high-water mark of the flood had been far above levels desirable for the station. To put it bluntly, South Station, as proposed, was underwater: *Originally, the entire area was flooded by the tide.* This didn't stop the heroic engineers. The project commenced in 1897. Pilings were driven into the wet, sandy soil, pilings loaded with pig iron. After the pilings, the engineers undertook the science of figuring out which tracks would culminate where. Sheets of paper swabbed with coal-tar pitch waterproofed the walls, etc. And then the contractors began to build the face of the building. They used the local stone, because *in eastern New England, granite is about the only stone which can be obtained in large quantities for building purposes, and granite was used throughout in all foundations and retaining walls.* They used especially good granite for the face of the new South Station. The quarries mined included Deer Isle, Maine, and Stony Creek, Connecticut, as well as quarries in New Hampshire, Massachusetts, and Rhode Island. And when the builders were done with the face of the building, they finished laying the terminal and attached a head house. *The track rail used throughout the terminal is the New York, New Haven and Hartford railroad standard, 100 lb rail, 5½" wide and 6" high with rail head 2¾" wide.*

My grandfather's father shadows this brief history because it was his particular job to work the quarries for projects just such as this. At the time of the South Station project, he was working in Stony Creek, Connecticut, having relocated there, not long before, from Maine. Stony Creek was famous for its pink granite, for a variety of stone not found elsewhere in large quantities, except in Scotland. (One of the most beautiful contemporary buildings in New York

City, the Sony building on Madison Avenue, is faced with Stony Creek pink granite.) Much of this fine granite was used on the front of South Station: *The main entrance to the station is at the intersection of Federal Street, Summer Street, and Atlantic Avenue, and it is here that the main architectural features of the station are found.* Chief among these architectural details, moreover, was ornamental stonework in profusion (the head house alone cost, apparently, $1,565,000, *or 21¢ per cubic foot*), for example, the beautiful old clock that still overlooks the office buildings of the financial district, and likewise, situated over the clock, the most animate of architectural details, *a large granite eagle.* A great stone bird of probably eight or ten feet, probably the *Haliaeetus leucocephalus* preferred by nationalists and scoundrels. Here, the bird looks as though for all time it is about to rise into the sky in search of prey (the bald eagle is actually a *thief,* it is said, *stealing most of its food from the smaller osprey,* and was much maligned by Ben Franklin, who felt that the wild turkey would make a superior national bird), perhaps some cowering example of the rodent family, field mouse, chipmunk, or maybe a tasty morsel of fish. The granite eagle's attitude is frankly carnivorous, and one wonders, in gazing upon it, if the freedom of transit, as typified by South Station, means the liberty to prey upon smaller animals and to consume them.

The story, with all the hyperbole of any Maine fish story, is that my great-grandfather *carved the eagle himself.* The eagle, see, was entrusted to a school of stonemasonry more known for its grand achievements, for historical carvings, namely some *Italian* school of stonemasonry, and this eagle, carved in Firenze, let's say, or in Milano, was shipped to South Station, there to be mounted on the top of the building's entrance, but when the eagle arrived, after transoceanic voyage, it was *chipped or broken,* its beak busted clean off, and though this flaw would be invisible to the future throngs of commuters unless they were in the building adjacent and equipped with a high-powered lens, and though the *busted-off beak* could be easily cemented onto the bird, it apparently offended the high standards of workmanship to which my great-grandfather aspired. Thus, according to the fish story, my great-grandfather decided to copy the

Italian carving himself, in secret, until he finished a perfect likeness. How he came to carve this adroitly, in addition to being good at hewing cubes of granite out of pits in the earth, I don't know, and there are but a few other pieces of ambitious carving in his hand. But let's say this factual absence is owing to my great-grandfather's selflessness, by which reason he didn't want his superiors (the Norcross Brothers of Worcester, Mass., O. W. Norcross, prop.) to know of the damage to the original piece, nor of his skill at plagiary. If my great-grandfather was anything like my grandfather, he undoubtedly embellished the narrative, as I in my turn may have embellished it, so that the truth of the story, again, has everything to do with the desperation of the tellers and their own symbolic inclinations.

Apparently, my great-grandfather, who died in his early sixties of stonemason's disease, was *an artist.* He did some lettering on the Bunker Hill monument, in Charlestown, Massachusetts, I'm told, and also a statue of a sea captain in the Thomaston cemetery, a piece that my cousin the Reverend Jack Moody, a painter, describes as *a bit wooden.* Yet since he likely had no money to pursue this ethereal ambition, since there was no *education in the visual arts* in interior Maine in the 1860s, he must instead have worked the quarries.

Here's what I know about being a stonemason at the turn of the century. From *An Historical Study of the Stony Creek Quarries,* I know that the granite of Connecticut *was formed eons ago, when magma cooled.* (Granite has a number of different minerals in it, viz., feldspar, quartz, biotite, hornblende, and pyroxene.) In Stony Creek, the granite amounts to an *igneous intrusion which extends to great depth.* The first Stony Creek quarry opened in 1858 and operated for fifteen years, and the granite it mined was transported mostly by railroad. It was used for breakwaters up and down the coast. A quarry at Stony Creek mined rock for the pedestal of the Statue of Liberty. The Beattie Quarry, from which came the rock my great-grandfather mined, produced two million tons of stone, and in 1892–93 this quarry worked exclusively on the contract for South Station, *which kept 200–700 men employed for 5 years just cutting and polishing.* During this interval, Stony Creek exhibited its granite at the Paris Exposition, where *it received honorable mention and a diploma.*

There were boarding houses near the mine, owned by the Nor-cross Brothers: *One boarded only "Americans," while the other was for the Swedes.* The character of the laborers at the quarry was *as rough and hard as the stone they worked with.* The best carvers were Italian. Respiratory illness, which felled my great-grandfather, was a con-stant problem: *Silicosis accounted for the early death of a large percent of the stone cutters. According to one quarry worker the average life span of a stone cutter was forty-five years. The very early stone cutters used hand tools and didn't have the dust to contend with, therefore they weren't troubled with silicosis.* The illness progressed as follows: *In the early stage they coughed a great deal, to relieve this they used whiskey while working. Even-tually, as the illness developed they would hemorrhage; the second hemorrhage usually resulted in death.* If drinking relieved the symptoms of their occupational disease, it also served for more general purposes: *At one time there were seven taverns and, as the nearby towns were dry, the saloons were well patronized, especially on Saturday nights. The "floater group," usually the stone-cutters, were a rough group, interested in liquor and fighting.*

H. C. Moody lived beyond the years allotted to his profession. However, the photographs of him that are scattered among my liv-ing relatives show the ravages of a case of stonemason's disease. His wedding photo, in which he sits between his bride, Maria Tate Witham, and her sister, finds him with an almost theatrical mas-culinity, legs crossed casually, large hands dangling as if on display, as if hands were ornamental, his hair half tamed with some lacquer, his face preserved in a malevolent pout, both sensuous and fierce, his languid physique framed, of course, by the women, in their dark, austere dresses. Generations of the fairer sex have swooned for guys like this. But the photo of my great-grandfather nearer to his death, with his next-to-youngest son beside him (my great-uncle, perhaps because my grandfather was an infant at the time of the photograph), portrays a much different man, seated again, legs crossed in the same way, but with an entirely different languor, the languor of weakness. He has lost the greater portion of his body mass, a fact that cannot be concealed by the heavy woolen coat he wears, his hands are crossed in his lap, his cheeks are gaunt, accented by a mustache, which he has let grow bushy and grand. His hair has thinned. And his eyes have lost the fierceness of youth, though traces of it remain amid a mostly undiluted melancholy. Seated now because it is probably demanding to stand, not in the nuptial throne as before. Seated while his young boy stands, the boy he'll leave behind before long, as with a great many other children. Seated, having been *subdued* by the life in the quarries.

That my great-grandfather's family was in Connecticut toward the end of the century was in itself *not a good sign,* since they were *from Maine,* as far back as there was a Maine, even before, and so it can only have been the economics of stonecutting that drove them thence. This is confirmed in a partial diary by my grandfather's brother Harold Wellington Moody, my uncle Hank (the boy in the photograph), who in later life became a middle manager for International Harvester, and then a farm owner in Waldoboro. Hank's diary of several months in Stony Creek, from his twelfth year, is like a more taciturn version of Handkerchief Moody's diary, but even in its stark, minimalist repetitions, there is drama and struggle:

> *Mar. 16, 1900.*
> *There is about two inches of snow on the ground today.*
> *I went to school although it was a hard day, there were only one half of the scholars there, the teacher let us out at noon. My Papa went down with me to school this morning. The strike isn't settled yet. Papa is loafing, he goes down to Stony Creek every morning to the Stone cutter's meeting.*

> *Mar. 17, 1900.*
> *Charles come on the half past eight train.*
> *The committee went to Boston to see Duncan about the strike. I went over to Mrs. Rackliff to sleep with her because her husband went to Boston.*

> *Mar. 26, 1900.*
> *I went to school today.*
> *It is still snowing pretty hard.*

We had a letter from Charles and said Arthur {another of Hank's brothers, in his later teens} was coming home. The strike is settled — .34 for 5 h. that is the stone cutter's price.

Apr. 17, 1900.
It is kind of drowsy today. I went to school to-day. Clinton Julian is Very sick. The strike is on again.

And so forth. Soon Harold Moody tires of diaristic restriction, like so many kids before and after him (myself included), settling into a rhythmical style that is without ornament of any kind:

Apr. 25, 1900.
It was pleasant to-day.
I went to school to-day.
Clinton isn't much better.

Apr. 26, 1900.
It is pleasant today.
I went to school.
I played ball to-day.

Apr. 27, 1900.
I went to school.
It is pleasant.
I played ball and tag.

Apr. 28, 1900.
I got some wood this morning.
We played ball a little while this morning and got wood tonight.

The meager budget on which the Moodys survived is indicated distantly, just beyond the sandlot that is so prominent in Hank's diary, in the specifics of what they ate (dandelion greens, sap from local maples, peach blossoms), and in how they spent what resources they had:

Mar. 25, 1900.
I tapped the trees and I have a great deal of sap. I went to
Sunday School and got a Sunday School book.

Apr. 23, 1900.
I went to school.
It is a good day to-day.
We had dandelions for dinner to-day.

May 2, 1900.
I went to school.
It is pleasant.
Clement come home tonight but isn't going back until morning.
Mamma went greening to-day and got a basket full.
She got some peach blossom.

Meat, centerpiece of the American table, is mentioned as a repast *once* in the ninety days of the diary (and it's only fish), and not coincidentally it is contained in one of the longest entries:

Mar. 31, 1900.
It is pleasant today.
We played ball, the score was ten to ten.
Clement come from Roxbury last night.
We had our first flounder since the strike.
There was a game of men put on today.

Unclear what a *game of men* is, in the context of this tale, unless a game of baseball mounted by the stonecutters for the benefit of their families, but in the midst of Hank's list of quotidian activities, it has a forlorn feel, as does any deviation from his usual catalog: *Pappa tapped my shoes, he went up to Brewer's and got two pounds of butter and paid twenty cents a pound for it; Charles and Iva were to New Haven and brought home a pair of shoes; I been riding Hiram in his cart.* My grandfather, the baby of the family, makes these cameo appearances in the diaries, occasionally as a three-year-old's scrawl — on the verso board at the front of the book, *Hiram,* and on one page where he copies Hank's wording, *very good,* into the margin of the page. The diary ends abruptly here, in fact, on May 31: *It is pleasant. I went to school and played ball and got perfect in number {sic} and the teacher told me my writing was very good.* This is the end, at least, but for one entry from two years later, which is simply a shopping list:

4 lb of corn
3 lb of stew meat
1 lb of raisins
2 lb of pork
1 head of cabbage

Warren July 1, 1902
One month after date, I promise to pay Harold Moody 1 dollar and .50 at 4%, for value received. C. McKeller.

Why such a lengthy silence between these last entries? Kids often fail to keep their diaries for long, because a twelve-year-old boy might spend a late winter hunched over a composition book in candlelight, only to abandon it once the days get longer and other boys are in the meadows boosting raspberries, chasing cats, entrapping fireflies, or standing in the dusty lots of American baseball. Maybe the diary was just a school assignment. More likely, however, the better part of Hank Moody's silence inheres in the fact that in 1901, according to one source, Hiram Clement the stonemason succumbed to the *fit of coughing* that did him in, just as my grandfather, who would have been four at the time of this death, later died himself in paroxysms of coughing brought on by his own emphysema. Seventy-five years later. So the Moodys, who had relocated to Connecticut because *that's where the quarrying was,* returned to Maine and bought a house in Warren, not more than ten or fifteen miles from Thomaston, where the Maine lime quarries were. There they settled, with, apparently, enough money *to buy meat,* at least for a time. If my great-grandfather was not dead yet, he would be soon.

I visited the Stony Creek quarries myself, much later. They still exist, as quarries always do, like barrels of plutonium. I was driving to New York City, down the Connecticut coast, one Monday morning, *during the rush,* and was jammed into the slow part of the interstate, heading into New Haven, when, in a patch of stop-and-go, I saw the sign. *Stony Creek, Leetes Islands.* Finding the quarries would be possible by dead reckoning, I hoped; I'd seen them on the map, and I knew they would turn up the way, in former times, you encountered *strawberries along the brookside* just by having a taste for strawberries, and so I just kept driving off the interstate, toward the water, looking for signs and residual traces. Heading out of town, I found a turn off of the county road that had the correct semblance. The houses nearby were fashioned of rock and mortared up with moss; this avenue resembled northern New England, with its rich past, more than something you would ordinarily find in this paved-over Nutmeg State. Marshes on either side, herons in the shallows, not much in the way of development, bordered by hunks of waste rock, like teeth of the maw of antiquity. A town park was marked off in these woods, but it was mainly a hideout for truants, and in a dusty parking lot at the end of the road, slabs of the local product were everywhere around, tagged with the aerosols of the last thirty years, indicating various couplings and uncouplings here. It was starting to rain, and I parked the car and plunged onto the footpaths that had been cut through the park, didn't matter how long it took, feeling the quarries around me, knowing I was *closer,* feeling the clearing up ahead, long before there was a clearing, where leaves would seem to part for revelation; recklessly I flung myself off the paths, into the woods, as though merely seeing an old quarry in Connecticut would summon up all the mysteries. Who was the interpreter of all this, who was it who had been through the things I had been through, remorse and trouble and melancholy, whereas around me my contemporaries swarmed with their spawn, with their spouses? Meanwhile, I was marauding through the woods in Connecticut, toward a thinning of tree trunks, until I stepped over a spot where a chain-link fence was most permeable, onto a bluff, in a clearing. *Overlooking the pit.*

The stunning feature of a quarry, on first impression, is the wastefulness of it. The landscape seems squandered, unless of course it is one of those quarries in which local indolents have managed to found a swimming hole or a spot to get high. I had seen my share of these over the years. I saw a quarry pond in Vinalhaven, first time I traveled to Maine with my father, and the water was nearly flush against the top edge of the rock. The spot was deserted. The quarries in Dorset, Vermont, where I swam a hundred times while teaching nearby, were otherwise. Improvident, beer-guzzling boys of that town would climb up into the limbs of birches and dive out over the edge of that quarry, narrowly avoiding smacking themselves on the granite ledge on the way down, into the oddly brilliant water that collected there, while nearby the gay men of southern Vermont transacted brusque exchanges of venery. These Vermont quarries were always full. But the Norcross Brothers' quarry in Stony Creek — out of which half a dozen skyscrapers had been blasted, the base of the Statue of Liberty, South Station of Boston — was completely empty, and so I felt the invitation to travel out some ways into the pit, where the walls of scarred rock reached above me, as though I had sequestered myself, in this endeavor, in an archaeological text, which I guess I had.

After a good ten minutes of gazing at the spectacle of the crust of the earth, I blithely decided to walk out of the quarry on the dusty road instead of returning through the woods. This was when I heard the whistle go off. One of those whistles that, in films of labor-organizing or factory life, indicate that the hour of five o'clock has arrived. A piercing squeal. But it wasn't five o'clock. Then, for a brief instant, there was silence. A red-winged blackbird plunged out of a tree. I heard it chitter. A lower echelon of my ridiculous, awkwardly questing self knew the identity of this Stony Creek silence, this silence preliminary to *the blast,* and perhaps it was a genetic knowledge I was experiencing, or a knowledge from the realm of the collective unconscious, since I was a stonemason's great-grandson. So when *the blast* came, I was surprised, *but not surprised at all.* The rain of pebbles and dirt was audible immediately after, and then, again, all settled into silence. I had narrowly missed standing in the middle of a quarry *during blasting.* In fact, if I had come in by the bona fide entrance, I would have seen the sign I now saw: *Danger — Blasting. Turn OFF two-way radios.*

I duplicated this quarry trip with my father, the old man, long after the particulars I'm describing, on a bright humid day in summer. We drove right up to the front gate of the quarry, where an old El Dorado the color of the ocean was parked with all the windows open and the radio blaring. In the car a large disheveled guy of about twenty-two or -three, in T-shirt and jeans, lounged with his feet up on the dash. Security. Encounters with *security* are in the category of things that make me really uncomfortable. I have often believed fervently that I would set off theft alarms in department stores or metal detectors at airports, though I have stolen nothing and am carrying neither guns nor explosives. Thus, I stammered out my request to the security guy in the El Dorado mainly because I was in the driver's seat that day and he was on the left side when we pulled in: *Uh, we were wondering if we could take a look around, because, uh, my great-grandfather worked here at the turn of the century, so we're sort of, uh . . .* Remarks like this always trail off. Amazingly, the *security guy* waved us in skeptically, and my father got out and walked around amid the piles of rubble and pebbles and the scoured walls of the quarry. Because of the *security guy,* because of the threat of alarms going off, because of the possibility of *punishment,* always just outside the margins of vision, I found it difficult to get *comfortable* in the quarry and mostly stayed in the car with the air-conditioning on. When my father got back he said, *What are you doing in there? That guy is probably asleep!*

The same tone as in the frequent remark of my childhood: *What the hell are you doing in the house on a day like this?* And it played just about as well in this venue. *What the hell was I doing inside?* As Kafka says in his letter to his father, *Dearest father, You asked me recently why I maintain that I am afraid of you. As usual, I was unable to think of any answer to your question, partly for the very reason that I am afraid of you, and partly because an explanation of the grounds for this fear would mean going into far more details than I could even approximately keep in mind while talking.* The whole processional of fathers and their histories is a burden, you know, and the sense of failing these fathers is constant and overwhelming, and the failures are visited on the sons, and on their sons, and so forth. It ruins most of the pretty days in August.

Likewise, at the Ocean Point Inn of Boothbay Harbor, where we stayed according to my father's wishes, I labored over the enigma of my great-grandfather and his lineage. I had learned a lot about the Moodys in the eighteenth century, but I had no idea, really, how my great-grandfather landed in Ash Point, Maine. Or later in Stony Creek. A copy of the *Historical Notes Concerning the Moody Family* that was among my grandfather's scant possessions when he died didn't give much away, besides theorizing that our branch of the family dangled improbably from the main trunk of William Moody of Newbury, Massachusetts, which trunk featured Samuel Moody, Joseph "Handkerchief" Moody, etc. So I was trying to find substantiation for this theory, and to this end, the doleful librarians in York had been good enough to point me toward a lengthy treatise, *The Family Tree by Alice Moody Chapin: Seven Hundred Years of Moody Ancestors,* notes from which I was reading late into the night. Seven Hundred Years! What could be better? As I encountered other genealogically obsessed persons, I was always astonished and satisfied by my sense of them as well-meaning, dogged, persistent, and *homebound.* The family tree, that nasty, weedy shrub, is a good hobby for persons with agoraphobia or chronic alcoholism or narcolepsy. Fitting their S.A.S.E.'s into another envelope and shipping this envelope off to other dogged, persistent, homebound agoraphobics between loads of laundry and antiseizure medication and the cashing of S.S.I. checks. This was the genealogist's task. There was a grim, joyless poetics to any list of names, and all genealogical study quickly turned up the mechanical nature of the endeavor. Another user at the library at York had pointed at *The Family Tree* in my possession and whispered, *Lots of mistakes in there.* And the author of the Moody genealogy herself admitted as much, right in the first chapter: *It is possible that there may be some mistakes which could be due to very old information, some of which may be just supposition. But I have been impressed with the hardship this family went through and the courage that it took to do the things that they did.* I didn't care about mistakes. I don't care about them now. *Genealogy is a dream,* as family is, with all the dream language thereof, and the bliss of genealogy comes when the dream turns out to be multiple, tropological; the bliss is when your lineage and mythological origin collide with mine, and we come to agreement on terms: *a colored fountain in Denver, a character witness from Ireland, the carriage that plunged into the lake.* The more baroque and romanticized genealogy becomes the better. I like the campfire-scorched meals of my ancestors, their sewing kits, the kind of chairs they used, the people they killed, because I first learned about family from a car salesman, and it was therefore the fantastic language of the people that was spoken to me. So Alice Moody Chapin's poem about her lineage was anapestic, hexametrical music to my ears:

> I've always been proud of the Moody name.
>   It was short and simple and carried some fame.
> But the background it covered was large just the same.
>   There was Ralph Waldo Emerson's aunt, I think,
> Who carried that name and she learned at his birth
>   Of the talent he used while here on this earth.
> There were ministers, pastors, and preachers galore,
>   Who landed with courage on our rugged shore.

Well, hers was not the sort of poetry that was going to challenge the unimpeachable gift of our one good Moody poet, namely William Vaughan Moody of Kentucky (whose stepmother tried to induce him to work in the family stonecutting business), one of whose poems happens to mention my nickname in passing:

> Eeny, meeny, miney, mo,
> Cracka feeny, finey, fo;
> Omma nooja, oppa tooja,
> Rick, bick, ban, do!
> Eeny, meeny, miney, mo,
> All the children in a row.

Cracka feeny, who is he,
Counting out so solemnly?

Alice Moody Chapin's poetical voice is less confident, sure, and her poem doesn't scan properly, and she is not above *the moon in June* and similar rhymes. But though she is a hideous poet and a rank jingoist (*I think we owe our President {Ronald Reagan} a vote of thanks for trying to clean out of the country and the government those groups that are destroying this special thing that we have*), Alice Moody Chapin is, at least, *willing to go as far back as the Vikings* in search of the Moodys, even if such an endeavor feels faintly like *a racial-purity campaign.* For her vision, at least, we must applaud her:

> After [King] Harald [of Norway] had himself crowned, he went not only to the baths and had his hair cut and combed, but also proposed marriage to the same princess [who earlier refused him] and this time, I am glad to say, was accepted. The man who cut Harald's hair was a trusted Earl of the Court Circle and a great friend of the King's. His name was Earl Rognvald of Molde, Norway, and he appears to have been the first known ancestor of the Moody family. He gave the King a new name, Harald Fine-Hair, and indeed he did have a fine head of hair. All of the history books know him by that name today.

No other source that I could locate confirms Chapin's theory that Earl Rognvald of Molde, who apparently styled this famous *coiffure* about A.D. 900, had anything in common with the present Moodys, beyond certain phonemic resemblances, but that does not stop Chapin from reverie on the subject of Vikings, including quotation from the Poetic Edda, as well as the following: *The Viking Age was a tremendous explosion of supermen on the European scene reaching as far to the East as Russia and the Black Sea, as far to the West as England, Iceland, and the Islands north of Scotland, the Orkneys, the Faroes, and the Shet-*

lands. Finally, finally the conception behind Chapin's mythologizing becomes clear:

> Earl Rognvald came into the King's service from a town in Norway called Molde. After his brother Sigurd settled in the Orkneys, Rognvald migrated there with the Moody name. There were many variations of it before it reached its present spelling of Moody.

Whereupon, Chapin then quotes from another source as to the precise direction of our early English genealogies:

> Moodie, Moody, Mudie, perhaps from Old English, *modig,* Courageous. Johannes Modi served on an inquest made at Peebles in 1262. . . . William Mudy, merchant, had a safe conduct to visit England in 1365 with four companions, and William Mudy, armiger, with two horsemen, in 1367–8. . . . Sorlet, rector of Assend (Assynt) witnessed the charter of Bishop William (Mudy) to his brother-german Gilbert Mudy in 1455. . . . Thome Mwdy and Robert Mwdy appear in Brechin in 1450, the former held land there in 1461, and in 1496 John Mwdy held land there.

Or, as another source exclaims, *This line is one of the most illustrious in Great Britain. A great many others are said to be derived from this line. It cannot be definitely determined from which the American families came but all are supposed to trace back to Harald MacMudah and family.* Soon, the Moodys, having diluted their Norwegian aspect, moved into the region surrounding London, and *in this conducive atmosphere the Moody family served the King for 300 years.* Culminating, of course, in the day when Edmund Mowdye saved the life of Henry VIII:

> The king was in the XVIth year of his reign. The King, following {a trained hawk], lept over a diche beside Hychuyn, with a polle and the polle brake so that if one

Edmund Mowdye, a footman or equerry had not lept
into the water and lift up his head which was fast in the
clay, he had been drowned. But God in His goodness
preserved him.

For which *Edmund Mowdye otherwise Moody of Bury St. Edmunds in the
County of Suffolk* was granted coat of arms and an estate, such that
even the Moodys of York, Maine, had it on their graves, attesting to
their affiliation.

Chapin then diverges about John Moody, one of the other original
Moodys on the North American continent, observing that his line
eventuated in the nineteenth-century evangelist Dwight L. Moody,
of whom more below. This was all of little interest to me or my
father as we spent the night in Ocean Point, with the rain thundering on the roofs outside, and not simply because it was tedious, but
rather because Alice Moody Chapin had a much more interesting
chapter, an entire chapter, on Clement Moody, mentioned some
chapters back, the probable ancestral patriarch of our line: *It is supposed after years of investigation that Clement was a new immigrant from the
Isle of Jersey in England. He settled in Exeter, NH, and was known as a
member of the Jerseyman colony there.*

There were three hundred names in Chapin's list of descendants
of Clement Moody of Exeter, several hundred of whom were probably lost to time, hovering just outside the margins of my history.
Still, it wasn't really the distant figures that made me race through
this passage, nor the comedy of her unyielding political opinions
(*And when a strike developed in the American Woolen Company in Lawrence,
Massachusetts, in the year 1912 the Unions sent up gangs of goons from New
York who created havoc which never had been seen before — like overturning
a street car on the bridge which crossed the Merrimac River. . . . This was my
first introduction to the Union's criminal actions*); actually, what made
Chapin's manuscript galvanizing was the appearance, on page 117,
in a list of eighth-generation descendants of Clement Moody, of one
Hiram Moody, that is, my great-grandfather, the stonemason, beside
the names of his brothers and sisters. I turned the pages with hands
trembling. It was *tantalizing;* this was history by *shadowing forth;* this

was a summoning from the register of events parallel and still out of reach, like a film of your life story in which you are played by an actor who can duplicate your awkwardnesses perfectly but who is *more beautiful than you will ever be* and who then goes on to play a bank robber or superhero. What if the daily self, in the midst of rinsing vegetables, emptying garbage, shoving through a turnstile, is not *the genuine self?* Every mother with a mother before her, every father with a father before him, and the gamboling of our cherished identities, in the face of this past, is a kind of narcissism. I came upon the name of my great-grandfather, and the town of his birth, *Whitefield, Maine,* and a system of conjectures was connected up.

Small wonder, then, that as we left, my father too seemed to slip away into the register of his childhood histories, as he has often done as he has gotten older, so that his movie of the present seems to have another film playing simultaneously over it, something in black-and-white projected over it, as in the nightmares of film projectionists. This other film was of the backyards of Ocean Point, of the gang of kids frolicking there, of loves lost, of fish caught, of sedans driven fast over winding roads, a story of sons rather than of fathers, and on our trip it was occasionally hard for my dad to tell which film we were attending. This kid on the beach with the baseball cap, now, or then? It all became clear at the *self-serve gas pump,* Boothbay Harbor Texaco station, which would not reveal its contemporary secrets to my father and his gold Jaguar. The regular unleaded would not pump, and the pump would not accept the credit card he offered, and he became more and more frustrated, as the attendant's voice sang out over a loudspeaker, *Swipe the card through the reader. Swipe the card.* This didn't help, as he swiped and swiped (a hideously contemporary verb, *to swipe*), and he became enraged, lashing out across the paved lot, *Just turn on the pump! Just turn it on!* Who could blame him, because he had clawed his way out of these summers of World War II, on this coast, when the islands *shut in the prospect of the sea,* and there were no self-serve pumps and no credit cards and a guy in coveralls checked your oil. This was the least dignified of human endeavors, now, fitting the credit card with the hologram on it into the machine that sold regular unleaded or premium before going into the *minimart* to buy some *minidonuts* or maybe some *artificial chocolate drink* and some *fat-free potato chips*. The condition of the present was immaterial. It was watered down and mass-marketed. And yet, just when it seemed my father might meander off into the past and never return, he understood, stopped fighting it. The gas flowed. The receipt was disgorged. Then we were trapped behind a *recreational vehicle* the whole way off the peninsula, in steady rain.

We took the road to Augusta, a road that Hawthorne himself took, in 1837, on his own tour of Maine. "The Minister's Black Veil" was by the time of his journey published, and he was evidently well known for it, since the footman employed by his college friend Horatio Bridge, with whom Hawthorne was staying, discusses the story with him in passing:

> Conversing with [Mr. Schaeffer] in the evening, he affirmed, with evident belief in the truth of what he said, that he would have no objection, except that it would be a very foolish thing, to expose his whole heart — his whole inner man — to the view of the world. Not that there would not much evil be discovered there; but as he was conscious of being in a state of mental and moral improvement, working out his progress onward, he would not shrink from such a scrutiny. This talk was introduced by his mentioning the "Minister's Black Veil," which he said had been translated into French, as an exercise, by a Miss Appleton of Bangor.

Hawthorne and Bridge stayed in the towns of Hallowell and Gardiner on their tramp to and from Bridge's home in Augusta. These towns, by coincidence, are no more than eight or ten miles from

Whitefield, Maine, the town in which my great-grandfather would be whelped before long. My father and I were bent upon Whitefield, therefore, birthplace of my great-grandfather, in possession of recent genealogical information from the Chapin manuscript, which indicated that the Moodys were in Whitefield for the better part of a century and a half, perhaps since an eighteenth-century land grant to my great-grandfather's grandfather.

My experience of Maine was of *certain terror* at the removal of myself from the coast; my experience (in all the trips I had ever made there) was that what community there was in Maine was on the coast. To travel inland from the coast was therefore to venture into that section of the map where all the roads were privately owned by paper companies and obscure governmental agencies who, no doubt, tested biological agents upon the local wildlife; to be in *interior Maine* was to be in Passadumkeag or Oquossoc, where there were blackflies that might clean the flesh from a human skeleton in minutes, where there were guys with no teeth who shot tourists for sport, where moose ravaged cars, and bears gored local residents. This sequence of prejudices, of course, was ironic now that it was revealed, in the Chapin manuscript, as I had long worried, that the Moodys of my strain were *all* interior dwellers, sheep farmers for a number of generations, going back to when this part of Maine was inhabited mainly by the so-called *savages*.

The road from Boothbay north wended between interior towns, between stands of maple and birch and oak. There were villages consisting of no more than a general store and, at the same time, satellite dishes, like sci-fi overgrowths. *The country swells back from the river in hills and ridges, without any interval of level ground,* as Hawthorne put it; *there were frequent woods, filling up the vallies or framing the summits; the land is good, the farms looked neat, and the houses comfortable.* This last observation was not so true in 1998 as in 1837. On our trip, there were mobile homes in profusion and they did not look comfortable. The farms were often run-down, or even abandoned. In no more than a half hour we were standing in front of a dilapidated Congregational church, devoid of ornament, badly in need of a paint job. *Whitefield town center.* A farm equipment business nearby, a couple of ramshackle houses, little else. We got out of the car, in the rain, checked the names on the small wooden plaque memorializing soldiers of the First World War. There was a single Moody on the list.

Part of the job of the amateur genealogist involves, as I have remarked, *work with graveyards,* and this is certainly among the really pleasing responsibilities associated with the task. Since childhood, I've revered graveyards, necropolises, ossuaries. Anyplace having to do with death. Back when I lived next to a *famous psychiatric hospital,* we were also just up the road from several colonial cemeteries, and not only had I a number of my first *stolen* cigarettes in them, but also some of my first kisses. Graveyards were places where collective reservoirs of mythology and fable were more powerful than the image repertoire of television and popular culture. My childhood fantasy had been to make out with a girl from up the street in a graveyard and maybe to have the dead *shouting encouragement* from their resting places. My childhood fantasy was for the faithful departed to stride through the land at night, exerting their influence upon the business of the living. As in York, where my father and I trod upon Handkerchief Moody's grave, I had ascertained that there was a graveyard in Whitefield that had a couple of relevant Moodys in it. My hypothesis was that any concentration of Clements necessarily had something to do with our family. To this end, we spent a while driving uninformed and haphazardly around the sparsely inhabited latitudes of Whitefield, looking for more graveyards, rain like a mere idea of precipitation drizzling fitfully upon us as if to complete and fulfill a theme. There was, according to a compendia of Maine graveyards, the Blackman Cemetery on Hunts Meadow Road, surrounded by an old, sturdy stone wall, and here lay Catherine Moody, daughter of Ezra and Loisa, and Clement, and Clement 2nd, and Huldah Moody, wife of Clement 2nd, all of them dead in the middle part of the nineteenth century, and *Infant,* that bit of human potential never actualized, and Jonathan, and Leweazer Moody, *where the hell did he get that name?* and then there was Kings Mill Road, where there was Jeremiah Moody, and Mary E., and Manville and Mattie, and Cyrus, and Anna Moody. There was even a Preble Cemetery in Whitefield, Preble being, of course, the surname of the boy

accidentally slaughtered by Handkerchief Moody. We drove along
these county roads in the rain, stopping wherever there was a
sequence of mossy stones, and yet we didn't feel that we were close
enough *to the veiled center to which we were bound.* So we drove back
toward the town post office. A lot of dandelions in the yard at the
post office. No one, at the moment, mailing anything. My father
ducked inside and came back out with rumor of the Whitefield Historical Society, *back down to the school,* as the locals would have said it.
We drove a quarter mile or so, on a ridge overlooking acres of feed
corn animated in a light breeze, and we found the historical society
closed. The town hall, however, was *open for business.* There was a
single good-natured government employee therein, and a single customer chatting with him, about insoluble problems relating to a
boat license. While this grizzled customer was waiting for the good-
natured civic employee to rustle up the crucial forms, he began having a further exchange with an older woman who had followed us in,
a sibling or relative of some kind:

—You up to see Mother this weekend?

—On Vinalhaven, trying to repair that truck.

—You weren't up to see Mother, then? Is that what color they got
that form now?

—That's for a boat. . . . I got a new pickup here too; you seen that
out there? It's all rusted up like your bus. You got an auction this
weekend?

—Nah, I'm tryin' to get ready for the fair. You ever hear that saying: those that don't make mistakes don't do nothing, and those that
make too many lose the job?

—Just told me here that I'm not allowed any more vehicles. Only
allowed three. This is the new car over here, seen it? (Points out
window.)

—I seen it.

My father and I sat patiently through this exchange and its attendant silences, which, in its entirety, crept up around ten or fifteen
minutes, and the bureaucratic delay was the only irritating part of
the waiting, since we were being treated to the laconic Maine conversational style that my father associated with his parents and their

native provinciality. It was both winning and heartbreaking at once, reinforcing, for example, the stereotype that *all inlanders of Maine had unrepaired cars on cinder blocks in their yards,* that the town would need to have an upper limit for numbers of such cars that you were allowed to have in your yard. But when the town hall of Whitefield next emptied out, as soon it did, the good-natured proprietor — who also told us that the historical society of Whitefield was only open on Tuesday nights and that the town hall of Whitefield had burned *back a ways* — gave us maps of the sites of all the graveyards, and even a town map as of 1803, marriage records, etc. *It was a Moody bonanza,* showing exactly where the *three* Moody farms had been at the Windsor / Whitefield line, Clement Moody, Scribner Moody, and Jonathan Moody; indicating where contemporary roads ran through this property; pinpointing Moody Pond, its location; enumerating a great number of Moody marriages; and so forth. A whole history of Moodys. The cemeteries were hard to get to, unfortunately, especially the Moody Cemetery, of which it was written, *This is an incredibly rough, grown-up-to-brush plot. . . . Cannot be seen from a distance at any angle. One has to know where it is then charge through the brush until one comes to it.* This was the cemetery that had the greatest number of names from the Chapin genealogy of my ancestors. We settled instead on the Blackman Cemetery, where there were the aforementioned cousins, Deacon Clement; Clement the second; Huldah, wife of Clement the second; Catherine, daughter of Ezra and Loisa; *Infant.*

There was something about the landscape, though, driving along the road where my ancestors had driven their own carts, upon which they had herded their woolly flocks, seeing the mild incline of a hill where they might have exercised themselves, the rain, the crickets, tractors in the distance. The sense of strange, distantly attenuated doubling was not obliterated by, for example, cellular telephones and satellite dishes and Internet service providers that may have made inroads in rural Maine. *The heart* is an invention of the heartsick, *the land* is an invention of nationalists, New England is a slogan of commissions on tourism, and *family* is a commonplace for politicians and religious fundamentalists. Yet, when you are cradled in the lap of these institutions, in the perception of those who came before you, ten or eleven times before you, the length of your earthly insignificance made further insignificant like the heavens hurtling away, you are glutted with sentiment.

Moody, as in *brave, bold, proud, and high-spirited,* in, e.g., Barbour, writing in 1375, *Thretten Castellis with strynth he wan, And ourcom many a mody man;* moody, as in *angry, wrathful,* in, e.g., Bale, *In his modeye madnesse without just profe did he excommunicate him;* or in Dryden, *Angry Jove, the moody sire;* moody, as in *subject to moods of ill-humour, depression, and the like,* in, e.g., Shakespeare, *And moodie Pluto winks while Orpheus playes;* but Partridge's slang dictionary also gives moody (noun), meaning *gentle persuasion, blarney, flattery,* and *lies, deceit, and, in another sense, something that goes wrong,* quoting from the following: *What he said was just a load of moody,* and also moody (verb), denoting *put into good humour by means of ingratiating talk; wheedle, flatter,* these usages being from the early part of the twentieth century; likewise, moody (adjective), meaning, *simulated, faked, as in "a moody ruck" or faked quarrel,* prison slang, evidently, since 1945, in which *two stall-holders pretend to start to get attention, draw crowd.* Thus a word that denoted the best that masculine power could offer, in 1375, courage, boldness, fortitude, came by Elizabethan times, about the time of the Puritan odyssey to the *New World,* to connote instead a sort of preliminary bipolar misery, giving way, in the twentieth century, to blandishments and simulations, to hyperbolic storytelling, almost exactly coincident with my family's own tendency to tell stories in this way, by exaggeration, as though a family named after a word can come to influence the word, until the word instead resembles a family, and thus *moody* now refers to my own family, and I am its example, a storyteller, a purveyor of blarney, a stager of mock quarrels and dramas, in order to direct attention away from myself. In Maine, I experienced the thrall of history as a thrall of language, a thrall of names and narratives in words, so that every chapter of the story of the Moodys sent me hurtling back to chapters of other stories, and thus it wasn't long before I saw that Hawthorne, on his trip from Augusta to Thomaston, *may well have traveled through this very town where I had stood,* and along the very roads that we took from

Whitefield down toward the coast, for Hawthorne talks at some length about the roadside audiences for his travels around Augusta:

> People looking at us from their open doors and windows; the children, perhaps staring from the wayside; the mowers stopping, for a moment, the sway of their sithes; the matron of a family, indistinctly seen some distance within the house, her head and shoulders appearing through the window — perhaps drawing her handkerchief over her bosom, which had been uncovered to give the baby its breakfast; — the said baby, or its immediate predecessor, sitting at the door, turning round to crawl away on all fours.

What if on his travels Hawthorne had to *pass directly alongside the Moody farmland of Whitefield?* It's more than possible, since among the most direct routes from Augusta to Thomaston was one that passed through the north end of town. And what if, in some fashion, his renown, and particularly *the tale of the black veil* itself, were in this way passed on to the Moodys in their inland sequestration? What if an *artist making his way through the countryside* was enough to leave behind a seedling of an idea about the arts as a calling and profession for those who came after? My great-grandfather wasn't born yet when Hawthorne traveled through Whitefield, and thus he could not be the baby in the above passage. (Hawthorne was in Lenox on the very day of Hiram Clement Moody's birth, and he was busy preparing the new edition of *Twice-Told Tales,* the collection that contained "The Minister's Black Veil.") And yet maybe this baby, or one similar, was his *immediate predecessor,* as indicated above, or maybe his father, Scribner, was one of the children lining the side of the road, an upstart in his later teens, who heard about *the veiled parson named Moody* at dinner after the coach went through, about Hawthorne's story concerning the veiled Moody, and thereby passed along the notion of *the man of letters* and, by extension, the life of the artist. Whichever the route, by the time of his majority, when Hiram Clement might have accepted the farm belonging to his father,

Scribner Moody, according to primogeniture, he instead set off for
the quarries south of Whitefield, according to the route that Hawthorne took:

> Left Augusta a week ago this morning, for Thomaston.
> Nothing particular in our ride across the country. Fel-
> low-passenger, a Boston drug-goods dealer, traveling to
> collect bills; at many of the country-stores, he would
> get out and show his unwelcome visage. In the taverns,
> prints from Scripture, varnished and on rollers; such as
> the Judgement of Christ — also, a queer set of colored
> engravings of the story of the Prodigal Son.

About these quarries: the quarries in Thomaston and in Warren,
the quarries where my great-grandfather settled professionally, were
not granite quarries but *lime quarries.* Lime, of course, is as old as civilization itself; the Romans themselves used it. Lime is produced just
about everywhere, in most of the United States and Puerto Rico, is
integral in the manufacture of *paper, steel, sugar, plastics, paint,* is available in *bulk or in bags, and can be shipped by rail, truck, or barge.* (In the
eighteenth century it was shipped by oxen or, in winter, by sled.) In
the modern day, lime is often used *in the treatment of stack gases from
industrial facilities, power plants, medical waste incinerators and hazardous
waste incinerators,* as well as in *potable water softening and to remove impurities from drinking water.* Limestone, the mineral initially being quarried in Thomaston, is *formed from the skeletons of marine invertebrates.*
Chalk, its relative, is composed of *the shells of minute animals called
foraminifera.* In the case of the best-known deposits, *the Cretaceous
chalks* (e.g., the White Cliffs of Dover, England), the source is *coccol-
ith algae.* To put it another way, my great-grandfather left home with
considerable carving skills, left home, maybe, to become an artist,
and wound up digging the fossils of fish.

F. L. Morse's *Thomaston Scrapbook* contains abundant history of
lime quarrying down to the coast. In Thomaston, Warren, Rockland,
and surrounding localities, lime was *the backbone of commercial activity.*
Morse repeats much lore on the earliest lime industry Down East (*I*

have read somewhere that one McIntyre from the Warren Scotch-Irish settlers, *quarried and burned lime in the 1730s*), right up to the present Maine State Prison Quarry, a prison one cannot avoid passing, as we did, along Route One in Thomaston. By 1794, according to Cyrus Eaton's *Annals of Warren,* there were thirty-five lime kilns in the area, burning *Taconic limestone,* of which Morse says, *Taconic limestones are round, with quartz rock,* which also accounts, I suppose, for the ubiquity of marble in those parts. What I like best about F. L. Morse, though, is how he breaks away from generalization about the mines in order to take his time elsewhere, an argument he once heard at the general store, a storm he remembers, etc.:

> One day, a year or two before the first World War, I was
> returning to my Morse's Corner home from the Rock-
> land Post Office, when a wind storm arose, so bad that I
> was actually afraid to drive across the big bridge. I
> drove into the Spear stable and waited until the wind
> died. When I reached home, I found that the Alden
> Austin barn had blown down and its wreckage was in
> the road at least 100 feet from where the barn had been.

This windstorm of Morse's description has nothing to do with the lime business, his ostensible subject in this chapter of the scrapbook, and it's likely exaggerated anyhow. And the windstorm never comes up again. Although other blustery yarns do. This kind of narrative exactly resembles, I think, my grandfather's storytelling style, a Maine storytelling style, in which the mischief of digression is its own reward, in which the telling of the tale is more important than its subject. Yet Morse eventually returns to his subject: how many of the Thomaston lime businesses were bought out by a syndicate located in nearby Rockland, and how, by the end of the nineteenth century, lime was no longer regionally important in the way it once had been. The same result had come to pass in Warren, as Eaton notes of the year 1850: *In the manufacture of lime, there has been of late* *years an apparent decline; partly from the fact that those most extensively* *engaged in it have found it for their advantage to carry on the work at*

Thomaston, where the rock is easily obtained and the lime shipped, and where the many new roads and bridges render it easier than formerly to collect wood and other materials. So: the Moodys who put down root at Ash Point, in South Thomaston, in order that Hiram Clement Moody might work in the lime quarries nearby, arrived in all probability as the business was beginning to decline. Which caused H. C. Moody to *move on.* With wife and children in tow. To dig pink granite.

Hawthorne's last recorded night in the great state of Maine is at Owls Head, which happens to be the next peninsula over from Ash Point, where my great-grandfather would live. He departs by water for Boston, though the ship is immediately lost in fog:

> Fired a brass cannon, rang bell, blew steam like a whale snorting. After one of the reports of the cannon, heard a horn blown at no great distance, the sound coming soon after the report. Doubtful whether it came from the shore or a vessel. Continued our ringing and snorting; and by and bye something was seen to mingle with the fog, that obscured everything beyond fifty yards from us; at first it seemed only like a deeper wreath of fog; deepened still more, till it took the aspect of sails; then the hull of a small schooner beating down toward us.

On just such a day did we attempt, and fail, to locate the Moodys' house at Ash Point, at the mouth of the Penobscot Bay, whose archipelagoes innumerably freckled the waters beyond, *some are large, with portions of forest and portions of cleared land; some are mere rocks, with a little green or none, and inhabited by sea-birds, which fly and flap about and cry hoarsely.* Eventually, a beauty fatigue overcomes you on the Maine coast, or perhaps the remorseless fog of the past is upon you and you can take in no more. That night, after our labors and upon my urging, we therefore repaired to Moody's Motel, of Waldoboro. The companion business of this establishment, Moody's Diner, is well-known to visitors who have traveled down Route One in Maine, since it's among the best-known diners in the northeast by virtue

of location, location, location. The food at Moody's Diner is not *nou-
velle* or *haute cuisine*, it isn't *Pan-Asian* or *Polish-American;* it is diner
food. As the introduction to the official cookbook of Moody's Diner
opines, *The Moodys are a large family. Most of them have worked at the
diner, many of them still do. They run the diner like a restaurant, not a
museum, serving good food; fast, hot and inexpensively.* They roast their
turkeys upside down. Their meat loaf recipe calls for both onion-
soup mix and cornflakes, green pepper optional. In fact, they have
four different meat loaf recipes. Their recipe for Martian Salad consists of
instant pistachio pudding, Cool Whip, mini marshmallows, and
pineapple chunks, with nuts according to taste. Many kinds of pie
are available at Moody's Diner. *Seven pages of pie recipes,* in fact, are
included in their cookbook. Yet there is no recipe for a lobster roll of
any kind. My personal feeling, without wanting to offend my relations, is that, had you a cardiological condition of any chronic sort,
you would want to visit Moody's Diner only now and then. And yet,
since I don't have a cardiological condition, I have in the past and
will continue to devour the pies and breakfasts of Moody's Diner
without hesitation.

Interestingly, I learned while in residence that the lodgings at
Moody's Motel had *preceded* the diner. The story goes as follows,
according to Bertha Moody, in her cookbook of Moody's recipes:

> In 1927 we built three small cabins. Each had one room
> and a screened porch with dry toilets up back. There
> was no running water then; we bought spring water
> from Mack's Bottle Works in town and took a glass jug
> of cold water to guests when they came in. The cabins
> rented for $1.00 per person — that was before the days
> of sales tax. Since we had no eating place we sent people
> downtown to Brown's Restaurant under the old Star
> Theater.

The cabins had not changed much at the time of our visit, although they now had running water and cable television. They were
also more numerous. Pulling into Moody's Cabins in my father's

Jaguar was a challenge. When we gave our names at the office (my father visibly uncomfortable at the entire undertaking), the desk clerk asked laconically, *Moody, huh? Any relation?* After three days in the rain, in each other's company, we just didn't want to get into it. Each of our cabins was large enough to fit a bed and a chair and the all-important cable television set. The interiors were white with teal curtains. The exteriors were white with evergreen trim. You could hear Route One in the distance. The modesty of the cabins was more than enough to suggest the roadside attractions of another era, for example, the sequence of lodgings that accommodated Humbert Humbert and his child sweetheart: *To any other type of tourist accommodation I soon grew to prefer the Functional Motel.*

Down the hill, between the cabins and the diner, was a gift shop that in part specialized in local gimmickry such as napkin holders in the shapes of Maine crabs, but which had a predictable sideline in Moody paraphernalia. Cookbooks, notepads, T-shirts, pens and pencils, shot glasses, and the like, all with my surname upon them. I loaded up on these *souvenirs,* not long after we checked in, and headed for the cash register. A dour-looking woman, in late middle age and with a pursed smudge where her lips ought to have been, preceded me in the line. As she was being rung up, she gave me and my load of useless items the once-over.

—You must be a tourist, she said with the disdain that only a summer resident of Maine could muster.

—No, I said, —I'm a Moody.

I wasn't a tourist, because I had been there for eleven lifetimes *as a possibility to come;* I was an outcome of the Moodys and, in this way, one of the outcomes of the state of Maine, of all colonial settlement, one possible outcome of all possible outcomes. This didn't satisfy the lipless resident of Waldoboro, who just wanted to buy a *Wall Street Journal,* and she muttered to herself pejoratively while I made my purchases, headed back to the cabin up the hill, and fell deeply asleep watching CNN.

Bertha Moody continues:

> In the summer of 1930 we bought a small house by the entrance to the cabins and opened a small restaurant,

serving only breakfast and dinner. Next, we installed gasoline pumps in front of the restaurant. The road in front of the cabins and restaurant was Route 1, now it's 1A. In either 1931 or '32 we put a very small lunch wagon next to the restaurant and sold hot dogs and hamburgers through the day. In August 1934 the present Route 1 was opened. We had to buy land there that adjoined ours and then built a road to connect our business with Route 1. That was where the present Moody's Diner was born.

There was nothing left on our archaeo-anthropological tour, really, but my great-grandfather's gravestone, and his house in Warren, Maine. There might have been more, had we found that evanescent nugget of genealogical gold that connected us to the line of Handkerchief Moody. We had been prepared for that revelation, but the likelihood of it had receded, like the farthest margin of expanding space, before us as we tarried Down East. I had slept in Moody's Motel, which had the dampness, from excessive rain, of summer camp cabins past. I woke feeling afflicted with the trip, with research, with the Moodys, with the abraded self that comes from drifting in some fisherman's net of history, and Warren didn't fail to reinforce the sensation. It had once been large enough to have a trolley that connected it to Thomaston, large enough to have shoe factories and sawmills and lime quarrying. But now the St. George's River of Warren was just a spot to fish, if that, and Warren was an inland town from which one might commute, on county road 90, to Rockland or Camden, and not much else, like so many towns that once were noble in this account, Milford, Danvers, Newbury, Portsmouth. It's a town with a lot of ghosts. I didn't much care about my great-grandfather's house anymore, nor about the priest who lived there most recently; I didn't care whether the grave was kept up, or whether we were mentioned in the *Annals of Warren* (although I loved Cyrus Eaton's eccentric chronology of Warren, which is very close to being an epic poem: *1809, barn of Capt. N Williams struck by lightning, lost with all contents; 1825, many people carried off by influenza; 1835, Halley's comet appeared, visible only a few nights due to fog*). I didn't care because, though I didn't have the exact parameters of my genealogy worked out yet, I had a good idea now of its thrust. Hiram Frederick Moody III (the author of these lines), son of Hiram F. Moody Jr., son of Hiram F. Moody, son of Hiram Clement Moody, son of Scribner Moody, son of Clement G. Moody, son of Scribner, son of Scribner, son of Clement, son of Clement, son of Clement Moody, at which point generations even further removed are hinted at, though ultimately obscure, ultimate begetters obscure, no sign of a William or a Samuel or a Joseph Moody, all of which meant that the Moodys of my line *had no conclusive relation to the Moodys of Handkerchief Moody's line,* unless I was willing to make one up. All of this was reinforced later in the murmuring interior of a library in Boston. Standing in Warren, in the rain, on the avenue of former industries, it seemed that there was no other conclusion. It had been coming to me in the prior few days, when I was sodden in the graveyards of Whitefield, knocking at the doors of government agencies, standing in lines at public libraries, and, like a really good scientific theorem, this notion would stand the test of much further inquiry: Moody family reunions, weeks of riffling genealogical papers and tomes. *We were the no-account Moodys.* The dead wood on the family tree. The dross that made the gold nuggets shine. We were shut-ins of history. We were the leftovers in the repast of American achievement. We didn't marry well, and we didn't get invited to dine with the other Moodys on the holidays. Therefore, my line, for some hundred years or more, had been *liars* about our lineage. Indeed, we were always looking over the fence at those other Moodys, as poorer relations might gaze upon the mansion of the more affluent. Look here, at the glorious grounds laid out around their manse, look at how the horses thunder across the meadows in pursuit of the fox, see the gardens where comely maidens stroll in the afternoon, see the kings and queens and dukes and viscounts whose carriages draw near to the gate; *those* Moodys went to Harvard, *those* Moodys preached from the pulpit of the eminent towns of the colonies, whipping up American pride in the revolutionary hour, *those* Moodys are immortalized in works of literature, in poems and odes and stories and monographs, *those* Moodys cast their progeny wide upon the land *New England,* those Moodys made their vision of God and of man identical with America's vision of same, such that *their name never died out,* such that festivals still honored their name, such that Octobers in Maine featured veil wearers in period dress, *those* Moodys wrestled with the morning of the nation, while *these* Moodys, my Moodys, perhaps once acquainted with the others, back in Exeter, or on the battlefield at Louisburg, had otherwise retired for a century or more to the inland to look after sheep; every dawn they were up with the sheep in the rolling hills watching the moon set over a stand of aspen, every evening too, or pulling at weeds in the vegetable garden out front, with a brood of hungry children, boiling up a soup over the fire, scouring the landscape for dandelions to make a pot of these greens to go with that soup, wondering why *those other Moodys* had what they had not, *great expectations,* the ears of governors and bishops, why God's mysterious intention raised up one family, kept another down, so that this family here had to scratch away at the tundra over a long winter, proving after all that God was a meritocrat, God could tolerate, permit, even bless such hardship and such plenty at the same time. I had thought, since I believed that I was *related* to Handkerchief Moody, that there was a genetic inclination that had been preserved across the centuries, *a vulnerability, an insight, a recoiling, a burden,* a Moody style, the kind of thing that got my father fired from his job in the middle of his life's journey, when he called his boss *an asshole;* or that got my cousin Jack, the minister, removed from Trinity Church on Wall Street in the late sixties so that he could preach instead out in the suburbs (he was a little *too creative* for Wall Street); that induced my grandfather to quit his job at General Motors just as it was about to pay out, so that he could go and buy a minor car dealership in suburban Massachusetts; that urged my great-grandfather off the farm and into the quarries; that sent me for a long Fourth of July in Hollis, Queens. But it was becoming apparent that the more likely and reliable assumption was that the simulated tendencies of families were bits of mythology by which a family constituted itself. Families were, in this view, *nothing in nature, and everything in recitation.* Families were a system of agreements between the generations about what was acceptable mythology and what was not. All lineage, all patrilineal inheritance, which ignores, of course, matrilineal cross-pollination in each and every generation, which ignores, e.g., that I can trace my matrilineal heritage much farther back than in the case of my father's father's fathers (according to researchers at Oxford, and by virtue of a DNA sample I provided on a cotton swab, your author is of the tribe of "Helena," who *was born about 20,000 years ago in the strip of land that joins France and Spain near what is now the town of Perpignan*), all patrimony is just a game, a way to make unity out of disparity. Therefore, my Moodys, *the failures,* at least for a couple centuries, had created the reputation of the other Moodys themselves in order to shape their own ideas of destiny. Those Moodys, in truth, couldn't exist without my Moodys, and vice versa, as each needed the other for the coherence of supposed identity. And the things that made a Moody, when we spun out our tales, a large nose, which seemed, actually, to come from my great-grandmother Maria Tate Witham, the ravages of alcoholism, which actually came from my mother's poor family, a tendency toward rambunctiousness when seriousness was required, or a weighty conscience that came from a distant relative who shot and killed his best friend and who *later wore a veil out of remorse,* these were all embellishments, these were implications suggested by storytellers among the neglected, storytellers *looking over the fence* at what might have been, or what might never have been at all.

Were we like *all the Moodys?* Were we like Dwight Lyman Moody, the founder of the Moody Bible Institute in Chicago, and also of the Mount Hermon Boys' School, and at one time probably the most famous preacher in the English-speaking world? *Let us awake and put on the whole armor of God; let us press into the conflict; it is a glorious privilege.* He began his fatherless adult life, as any good American religious did, as so many Moodys did, *as a salesman,* a shoe salesman, both in Boston and Chicago, which ambition vied in his early life for attention with his spiritual longing:

> For two years he celebrated his pursuit of money in the
> same letters that enthusiastically wrote about things of
> the soul. For example, in early 1857 he bragged to his

brother George about quickly earning 25 percent on a
$100 land investment. He rejoiced that he "lent 100
dollars the other day for 17 per sent [sic] a day. I tell
you hear [sic] is the place to make money." A few sentences after unabashedly revealing his sin of usury, he
urged George to study "the promises in the Bible,"
maintaining, "I find the better I live the more enjoyment I have and the mor [sic] I think of God and his
love the less I think of this worlds [sic] trouble. George
don't let any thing keep you from the full enjoyment of
Gods [sic] love."

Moody had his initial conversion experience soon after but didn't
immediately leave behind the provincial lad within, and notwithstanding the success of his Sunday schools, he was *burdened with a
sense of inadequacy . . . when his mother chastised him for not visiting
Northfield,* where she was attempting to raise a large brood of children on her own. There were other melancholy intervals too: *in my
work I was quite discouraged and I was ready to hang my harp on the window.* And all this *before* the Chicago fire burned down his house and
left him without a site for his Christian meetings, after which he
became a little bit of a tyrant in the administrative confines of his
preaching empire (*For better or worse, D. L. Moody was incapable of let-
ting go and delegating responsibilities for the Chicago Avenue Church that he
no longer felt led to pastor*). And then there's his theology, as in his sermon on being *born again,* wherein it is written that *you may go to
church all the days of your life, and yet not be converted,* likewise, *You don't
see anything in the Scriptures which says, "Except a man read the Bible he
cannot see the kingdom of God."* This emphasis on mystical, personal
experiences of God, well, I don't happen to believe a word of it, have
never been contacted by that divine agency Moody invokes, despite
many years of requests for just such contact, and I suspect mostly
delusion in the Born Again, and anyway, what is the evidence of
this rebirth, if it includes boorishness to one's employees, tolerance
for segregation, a refusal to speak out against anti-Semitism, anti-
intellectual boasts (*An educated rascal is the meanest kind of a rascal*),

premillennialist nonsense, tautologies that teach nothing (*He knows that his eyes have been opened; that he has been born of the Spirit; that he has got another nature, a heart that goes up to God, after he has been born of the Spirit*), and the like? Only when Moody talked about his own failures (*I believe a man may be vile as hell itself one moment and be saved the next*) did he start to sound like Handkerchief Moody (*I go on without repentance, oppressed by the unspeakable burden of the damned*), like the Moodys of my acquaintance, only then did he seem to have the requisite Moody shame: *I have had more trouble with myself than with any man,* or, *It is easier for me to have faith in the Bible than to have faith in D. L. Moody, for Moody has fooled me lots of times.* Okay, maybe we *were* a little like D. L. Moody, or at least I have felt like him, especially at the hour of his death, when he had uttered a number of really inspired last words, such as, *There is no valley here. God is calling me, and I must go.* Well, except that he didn't die. He hung around awhile, bothering everyone. Hours later, he tried again: *This is my triumph; this is my coronation day!* Still no luck. He tried to get out of bed and apologized to his wife for causing her such worry. The doctor moved to give him an injection, and it was then that Dwight Lyman Moody finally pronounced his last mortal words, *It's only keeping the family in anxiety.* Did he mean his hesitation at the hour of death? Or the balderdash of a certain kind of life in Christ? Or the Moody name itself?

Okay, maybe we were like D. L. Moody. But were we like *Rick Moody, the women's basketball coach of the University of Alabama?* He was born in 1954 and grew up in Mobile, Alabama, where he went to high school, until moving to Grove Hill. His college degrees are from Patrick Henry State Junior College, Troy State University, and, for the M.A. in physical education, the University of Alabama. His playing experience was at the junior college level, but his coaching experience is immense: a year coaching ninth-grade basketball in Shalimar, Florida, two years doing junior varsity at Chochtawhatchee High, Fort Walton Beach, Florida, followed by two years coaching the varsity boys' team there, after which he returned to his alma mater, the *Crimson Tide,* to become assistant women's basketball coach; a brief period back among the boys' high school team at Guntersville, Alabama, where the team went 91–48 and made state tournament appearances in 1987 and 1989, from which job he became head coach of the women's team at Alabama. For a total prep career record of 159–80. While head-coaching the *Crimson Tide,* Moody has amassed so far a record of 219–92, the best ever at the university by about 119 wins, including eight consecutive seasons with twenty wins and a Final Four trip in 1994.

The more stylized and predictable the public rhetoric about the *other* Rick Moody gets, the better I like it: *For Moody, the 1994 season contained an endless stream of highs that helped keep him on top and loving what he does for a living.* Or: *Moody is an avid outdoorsman who loves to hunt and fish. He can also be found on the golf course challenging {his son} Ben for family bragging rights.* And yet Moody's cheerful, predictable press package begins soon to veer into the darker material:

> "It all started in September 1992," said Moody, who made history in April 1994 by taking Alabama's first basketball trip to the Final Four. "The 38 years prior to that had been very simple. It seemed as if my marriage, my family, my career had been on a steady course that kept carrying me forward. Rarely do I remember taking any backwards steps or having anything major happen in my life that would quote 'get your attention.'" But in September 1992, Sandra, whom he married in August of 1976, discovered a tumor while she was doing a routine breast self-examination. It was malignant.

Moody falls back on the traditional battlefield metaphor to describe how his wife's struggle against cancer helped him learn to coach women athletes effectively: *Most of the things I learned, I learned from Sandra. She taught me how important it was to have a good attitude. It was her attitude, the way she handled that adversity, that made her successful in winning that battle.* Not long after his wife's illness, he lost his beloved assistant coach and *longtime friend,* Dottie Kelso: *It was a devastating time for all of us. As I thought that I learned all I needed to learn in the previous years, I had not learned as much as I thought I had.* It wasn't long after this gauntlet of troubles that Rick Moody, the women's basketball coach, made it to the Final Four: *Honestly, I expected to be there. That's not a boastful statement. It's just me. I did not expect anything less.* Like Dwight Lyman Moody, Rick Moody has developed a *total faith in God.* One that has enabled him to become a deacon at his church and also a *motivational speaker* of some reputation. Now, even if he struggles with a bad season, as he did in 1999–2000, it can only make the unalloyed success of his early career *more* interesting. Because, in the Moody family universe, *it's not how you play the game that's important, it's how you lose;* it's that you experience the indignity of knowing that victory is hollow and selfish. To experience the humility and regret of loss is far more ennobling, far closer to the spiritual journey of being a Moody in these Americas. In the *Crimson Tide* game I saw on television, Moody stalked the margins of the court in a style that was reminiscent of a small-town *salesman,* anxious, humble, good-natured. And he was wearing a microphone that day, so his euphonious accent, of the thickest Alabamian sort, rendered poetical his exhortations and warnings.

There's a depressing homogeny to athletic or professional success that has nothing to do with the true Moody tradition of ignominy. It wouldn't be good for the other Rick Moody to win perennially, and thus *I'm glad for his losing season,* as I was glad that I didn't get a teaching job in Tuscaloosa when I was there on the same campus with Rick Moody in 1993. Interviewing to teach writing. The English department at the university couldn't agree on whether to hire me or the other candidate. The search was scrapped, and I sold my second novel instead. *If I could pinpoint a moment* when I began to feel better, when I began to feel the floodwaters of my morbid twenties begin to recede, this would perhaps be the time. I was no longer going to be *raped* by my forefathers, seduced by the airtight theology of them, by their claims of inspiration from above. No longer going to be violated by history, by the American heavens and their bloodshed and their morbid rage and hatred, by the faceless skulls of American history making room for some more franchise restaurants on the site of a farm that was itself on the site of an Indian burial ground, before that a pristine wilderness that the likes of me have never seen; maybe I wasn't the end of something, the end of a system of cruelties. Maybe I was the beginning of something.

Hawthorne's final sentences on the state of Maine, from his 1837 trip, are those I have already excerpted, on the local coast, the edge of the continent:

> Penobscot bay is full of islands, close to which the steamboat is continually passing. Some are large, with portions of forest and portions of cleared land; some are mere rocks, with a little green or none. . . . Other islands have one house and barn on them, the sole family being lords and rulers of all the land which the sea girds. The owner of such an island must have a peculiar sense of property and lordship; he must feel more like his own master and own man, than other people can.

This vision of solitariness is delineated even further, with a rendering of the Maine lighthouses of the shore:

> Other islands, perhaps, high precipitous black bluffs, are crowned with white light-houses, whence, as evening comes on, twinkles a star across the melancholy deep; seen from vessels coming on the coast, seen from the mainland, seen from island to island. Darkness descending, and looking down at the broad wake left by the wheels of the steam boat, we may see sparkles of sea-fire.

Can I have been alone in interpreting these lines as allegory for the life of the writer as Hawthorne lived it then? I had a lot of time to think about it on the way home from Maine, since, though I had tried to fly out of Portland the next morning, to avoid the eight-hour drive back down to New York in my father's Jaguar, it was pouring, deluging, and no flights were scheduled. There was no choice but to accept the long, dull ride and to fall into torpor, in which a writer (or a sculptor, or a preacher) seemed to me like a lighthouse on its promontory, like a keeper of the lighthouse. In days past, if he failed to illuminate the lamp, ships foundered and were lost.

Maybe it was all about wakes. Maybe no trip was complete till contemplated according to its wake. Maybe the artist was he or she who looked into the wake of a craft and saw reflections of lighthouse beacons jitterbugging upon the waves.

So far as I am a man
of really individual traits,
I veil my face . . .

When I started this book, I told myself *I would conceal nothing.* All of myself, so far as it was illustrative, would be material. Eccentric habits (an almost total avoidance of telephones, a tendency to eat the same meals over and over), grand mediocrities, malfeasances, failures (I couldn't make it in book publishing, I was turned down at every doctoral program I ever applied to, I was fired from most of my jobs, I was completely inept at Little League, I never became competent in a single musical instrument), all these would be *in bounds,* so far as the rules of this adventure were constructed. The only requirements for admittance to this canon were that tales of my life had to be interesting, relevant, and subjectible to style.

Why this feeling, then, that I have left something out? Some weeks now I've been nauseated with this perception. Going about chores, I have felt it swelling in me, out to dinner I have felt it. Awake at night again. There were things I wasn't getting down. For example, *my work* is left out of these pages, the circumstance of my work, and all that business about a movie that was made of a certain book by me, etc., all of that is left out, the people I have met and the places I've gone, especially insofar as these have to do with *the movie,* all left out, and the contemporary writers I know are left out, various people I kissed over the years, exacting descriptions of their kisses, these things are left out, how I get, spend, and save money, how I spend it stupidly, if this is indeed the case, the financial enterprises that I patronize, the name of my accountant, these are left out, where

I get my groceries, left out, what groceries I purchase, whether I use shampoo, conditioner, or both, the origin of the word *shampoo,* favorite health-and-beauty emporiums, why I will never again eat a cheeseburger, my decision to refrain from eating *our friends in the animal kingdom,* my obsession with species of ducks, entirely left out, my fully grown brother and his wife and their adorable two kids, totally left out, my trouble learning to swim, not apparent, my participation as a tenor in the chorus at boarding school, also in a madrigal group, why bring it up, my stepparents, you wouldn't even know I *have* stepparents, though they are good and reasonable people, a hit-and-run fender bender that I caused once in Providence after drinking late into the night and fighting with a girlfriend, left out for the obvious reasons, anything at all having to do with therapy or therapeutic programs or self-help books, remarks about seratonin reuptake inhibitors, simply *not here,* my father's dog, that cat belonging to Amy Osborn, *my paramour,* the town I live in now, certain disagreements in my family so violent that there are people to whom I am related who in all likelihood will never again appear in my life, etc., all these things unremarked upon, as though they didn't deserve to be in any book that has anything to do with my life. Interesting dabs of color, they would look good splashed across a sunset, but they are not relevant and are not subjectible to grammar, not in any interesting ways, and, in any event, they are *not* the absences that caused me to lie awake late into the night.

Sex is left out. Should I yield up the revelations of *repressed-memory syndrome,* though there is no such memory, though the theory of *repressed-memory syndrome* seems quaint and reductive? Should I include all such sexual activities as might fill out a life, especially when they are conjoined with neurosis and mild examples of mental illness in interesting and vivid ways, as in the case of the fetishist who could not perform unless there were flies copulating in his room? Should I be including *sex* here? Should I speak of bad jags of promiscuity that I have already alluded to, of certain unusual tastes, even if I don't have any? Is this the sine qua non of the hidden and therefore that which must be memorialized? Should I speak of sexual difference, of the politics of gender, of identity and gender in my own life? Is it not a fitting subject, since it's much in evidence in the work of Hawthorne, whose "Minister's Black Veil" is a carnival of repressed sexuality and gender politics? (*The sexton pulls his bell lustily,* etc.) What else is left out of this account? *My mother is left out,* as I've said, though a mother has to be left out of any account of patrimony. Yet there are days when I have suspected that whatever it is that hovers just out of the sight lines of the narrator of these pages, *my mother typifies that thing,* so maybe it is my mother, tiny and white-haired and surrounded by verdant acreage in Virginia, pliable and tender and inscrutable by turns. In the course of wondering whether it was she who was left out, probing the notion the way your tongue stabs at a dental ache, I have returned frequently to one instant that passed between myself and my mother having to do with the day my sister died, a subject that I assured myself would not appear in these pages, *as it has already appeared in too many pages.* It would be preferable if I would reserve my reasoning on this subject here, but that would amount to more concealment when what is needed is more candor: so, against my better judgment, I will now report that it was a November five years ago when, for reasons that I leave to you to sur-mise, *I had begun to get a lot of telephone calls,* and since I will do almost anything to avoid talking on the phone, I had procured a *digital answering machine* that I could turn down so that I would neither hear the phone ringing nor the answering machine picking up, and so that I would not have to listen to the message unfolding, nor feel tempted to answer the phone in cases in which the caller was one of the people in my life to whom I actually *wanted* to talk on the tele-phone, and this arrangement assured that I would work and avoid the phone altogether, except that it resulted in *too many messages* and too many calls to return, and I was therefore often miserable about the arrangement, for which reason I sometimes forgot that the ringer was turned off and the volume turned down *for days at a time,* and the messages really piled up and sometimes they went unreturned, and thus even people who were encouraged to call were turned away from calling; likewise, my building in Brooklyn was wired in such a way that the doorbell rang on the telephone line, so that people who were just stopping by to *say hi* or those who were dropping off packages were frustrated because the phone was turned off and I never got the message. *These are the preliminaries:* I had been out to dinner and a movie with a friend, can't remember the movie, haven't seen the friend since, and I had arrived home late and slept uneasily, an indicator of nothing. When I woke I ambled into the kitchen to make tea, where I happened upon the *digital answering machine* and found that it was blinking with twelve messages, though I could have sworn it had been empty the night before. I put on the kettle, dropped a tea bag into a mug, debated with myself about whether I really wanted to listen to these twelve messages, which were probably someone's fax machine on *autodial* or some misdialed number and therefore nothing that I wanted to hear first thing in the morning, etc. Nevertheless, I decided to listen.

The first call was from my father. The *digital answering machine gremlin* announced the time of the call: very early in the morning, impossibly early, since my father was never awake after nine o'clock. He could only have been calling early in the morning to some bad end. His voice sounded incredibly irritated, *Call me as soon as you get this.* Click. As must be clear to you, the sound of my father *enraged* is a sound to be avoided at all cost, a sound that probably got the best of my mother, a sound that, forty years later, still means corporal punishment to me. Whole tributaries in the river of my life have gone unnavigated simply because they might engender this sound of my father *enraged.* This first message therefore intimated something awful. The second message was placed a half hour later. It was no better, was actually worse, his tone even more irritable with something like desperation creeping around the edge of it, *We'll pick you up in forty-five minutes; meet us downstairs.* This call placed at three or maybe four in the morning. I began to get really worried. But does the word *worried* describe it? Come on. Something in language *hides* these instants. Language obfuscates as much as it reveals. Seconds had passed, mere seconds, in what I've described, and I haven't gotten close to the sensation, so *worried* must stand here for all kinds of somatic effects like hyperventilation and difficulty swallowing, instantaneous somatic effects, and enigmas, like the sense that my apartment had a whole ominous layer beneath its surface. The next

messages were like a torpedo, on radar, approaching the hull of a target, and they culminated in a sequence in which my father was *at the
door of my building,* and he was distraught, *Where are you? We're right
out here.* And probably the worst thing I ever heard from my father's
mouth, in my whole life, *Open up the goddamned door, goddamnit!*
Then: dead air of the receiver summarily replaced. That message
from long before I had awaked, last of twelve. After that message
there was nothing else to say to the *digital answering machine.* Now
they were gone, my father and my stepmother, and the question of
what had happened was unresolved, and I no longer had any appetite
and my heart was like a malfunctioning drum machine. So I called
the person in my family who used to hear *all this stuff,* the person in
the very center of my family, the person able to appeal to all con-
stituencies and all quarrelsome points of view. I called my sister.

While I was driving out to Jersey, an hour later, in a rented car, I
was fixated on the perfect, unexpiable failure of having been unreach-
ably asleep while my sister was seizing, going to the hospital, etc. It
was a burdensome thing, my contempt for myself, and the abject
horror of her boyfriend surprising me on the telephone with the *fact
of her death* was fitting devastation for the likes of me. This is another
thing I have concealed from these pages, this moment, this loathing
for myself, and do you blame me? Is it right that I therefore include
it, that you might know me better, and that, knowing me better, you
might know yourself better, or that guy sitting next to you on the
subway, or at the next table in the library? *Even this confession doesn't do
it, though,* nor does it deal with the issue of my mother, whom I next
saw when I pulled the rented car into the driveway at my sister's *con-
dominium.* My mother got out of her car, and I got out of mine, and
she came at me as if she was *briskly acquainted with loss,* which she
was, since she had lost her parents already and her brother, and therefore she was bent upon the exigencies of comfort, according to which
she *held me,* and perhaps that was what I needed, *to be held,* or that is
what you'd suppose, that it's human *to be held,* and it's explicable that
someone would need to be held upon losing their sister or losing
their daughter, but the problem was that I could not give myself to
the *nakedness of grieving,* couldn't uncover myself for the comfort of

being held, because there was something else unexpressed, beyond this sobbing in my mother's arms, my mother sobbing likewise, my brother, inconsolable, sobbing, the stunned relations around, my sister's children all weeping, this instant often coming back to me now, the look of my mother, as if whispering, *My role is to know everything there is to know about how to remember and yet to survive,* and I have survived and now had many responsibilities for surviving, but even this isn't enough. Even this doesn't say what there is to say.

Maybe it's simply the case that *concealment is essential to identity,* that, notwithstanding the cultural trends toward reality-based programing, notwithstanding talk shows and talk radio and their confessional opportunities, we need a part of us that will never be known, so that the more we reveal, the more we are enveloped in veils, layers that refuse to be known, additional integuments of guilt and concealment, such that *any memoir is a fiction,* an arranged narrative, a *bildungsroman,* just as many fictions are veiled memoirs; the two identities, the two narrative strategies, concealing and revealing, depending upon and excluding each other by turns.

No matter where I concentrate my attention, a tale untold, a veiled tale, a shadowed lineage, a history of history, *no civilization without its opposite,* without the *black conceit* that Melville imputes to Hawthorne, which *derives from its appeals to that Calvinistic sense of Innate Depravity and Original Sin, from whose visitations in some shape or other, no deeply thinking mind is always and wholly free.* The veil captures this annihilating blackness that makes of the domestic and patriotic impulse a farce, so that the idea of marrying or reproducing or running for office seems about as practical as putting up a wind sock to gauge the progress of a hurricane. All life is ebony, or murderous, *everywhere the blackness of the veil,* as poor Elizabeth Short, otherwise known as *the Black Dahlia,* learned, murdered in Los Angeles in 1947, allegedly a friend of Marilyn Monroe's, found with her head separated from the rest of her, naked, in a city park; or, likewise, the *blackness of black holes,* somber objects of enormous density, such that even light lacks the velocity necessary to escape their gravitation, blackness of the *blackbodies of physics* that led Max Planck to quantum theory; *blackness of blackguards,* scoundrels practicing *blackmail,* or the *black of blackouts,* as when alcohol rushes into the bloodstream, delirium of *blackouts;* the *blackness of the New York City blackout,* its looting of shops; the *semisolid, black-capped plug of greasy material blocking the outlet of a sebaceous gland in the skin,* otherwise known to teenagers internationally as the *blackhead;* the *blackness of blackwater fever,* that dangerous form of malaria in which, during the destruction of red blood cells, waste cells travel through the kidneys and into the urine; the incredibly copious *black fauna* of planet earth, such as the *ursus Americanus,* or *black bear,* most familiar of North America, whose cubs live an extremely tenuous existence because of the predation of adult males (*the fathers eat their sons*); likewise, the *black widow spider* of the genus *Latrodectus,* whose neurotoxin is sometimes fatal to children; the Atlantic black dogfish (*squalis cubensis*), found in the deep waters of the Gulf of Mexico; black of the sub-Saharan goshawk; black of the black blowfly maggot; black of the black bullhead; of the black carp; of the black cockatoo; of the black guinea fowl; of the black crappie; *the blackness of the blackbird,* in dead of night, perching bird whose flocks may be quite large, as on the island where I now occasionally live; the blackness of the black Labrador retriever; the black marlin; the black lemur; the black oystercatcher; the black stork; the black tern; the black sea bass; the black rhinoceros; the black rat; the black stag beetle; the black swallowtail butterfly (I used to catch them in New Hampshire, at summer camp); the black swan; the black vine weevil; the black vulture; the black wildebeest; and then, of course, the *hyphenated* black fauna, such as the black-capped gnatcatcher; black-billed magpie; black-bellied hamster; black-backed jackal; black-crowned heron; black-shouldered kite; black-tailed deer; and the black *flora* of our domain, species so numerous that they could be said to be a carpet for this world of slaughter and carelessness and remorse, black alder, black calla, black cosmos, black cottonwood, black gum, black ironwood, black horehound, black-eyed Susan, black bearberry, black huckleberry, black mangrove, black raspberry, black olive, black peppermint, black walnut, black hellebore; topographically, the *blackness of such black places as* the Black Belt of Alabama, known for its fertile soil; the Big Black River of western Mississippi; the Black Canyon on the

Colorado River; the Black Hills of Wyoming, all these places darker and darker, known for tenebrosity, negation, hellishness, until we arrive at the Black Hole of Calcutta, where it is said by some that 146 British prisoners were kept overnight in a fifteen-by-eighteen-foot cell, after which only 21 survived, though these deaths, as in *all civil conflicts,* are disputed, each of these bodies like the bodies laid out around the advancing figures of black-garbed teenagers in their school-yard massacres across our great nation; *the blackness of the Black Friars,* or Dominicans; *the blackness of Black Friday,* otherwise known as September 24, 1869, when two investors, Gould and Fisk, attempted to corner the market in gold, which colorless coinage persists in every market crash thereafter, including the one in 1987, on October 19, Black Monday, occurring one week before my father bought an apartment for me to live in after I got out of the psychiatric hospital; *the blackness of the Black Flags,* the predatory band of Chinese and Vietnamese who infested the waters of Southeast Asia; *the blackness of the black dwarf,* exhausted core of an exhausted star; *blackness as an unknown,* as in the black box of computer design, in which an element's internal structure is unknown but its function clear; *blackness of the black dose of senna,* used as a laxative by Arabs; *blackness of the Black Dragon Society,* the ultranationalist party of Japan in the early twentieth century; *the Black and Tans of Ireland,* who attempted to put down the independence movement; *the blackness of black-and-white movies broadcast on early television,* and though I can't put my finger on it, I feel that people younger than I who didn't grow up on a diet of the monochromatic past, the black and white, are lacking the subtlety that I encountered in *Days of Wine and Roses, The Bank Dick, The Great Dictator, Frankenstein;* which also reminds me of *the blackness of the plague, the Black Death,* which appears to have begun its epidemiological journey in eastern China, following the estimable Silk Road of traders until it arrived in the Mideast, after which, like the rest of civilization, it eventually reached Italy, in 1347, after which, in a mere eighteen months, it devastated most of Europe, killing about half of all those infected, as in a contemporary account by Michael Platiensis: *Those infected felt themselves penetrated by a pain throughout their whole bodies. Then there developed in their thighs or*

*upper arms a boil. . . . This infected the whole body and penetrated it so far
the patient violently vomited blood. This vomiting of blood continued for three
days without intermission and then the patient expired.* The black scar of
Manifest Destiny, the recollection of which should cause aggravated
insomnia in all North American adults, the brutality visited upon
those who preceded us here, as in the case of the great Indian chief
Black Hawk, of the Sac, who, coerced into a deal with the pale hordes
coming over the Mississippi, attempted to renege and was put down,
and who then wrote his autobiography, containing the following:
*But, I considered, as myself and band had no agency in selling our country,
and that, as provision had been made in the treaty for us all to remain on it
as long as it belonged to the United States, that we could not be forced away.
I refused therefore to quit my village. It was here that I was born, and here lie
the bones of many friends and relations. For this spot I felt a sacred reverence,
and never could consent to leave it without being forced therefrom.* Likewise:
the Blackfoot Indians, who lived on the land around the upper Mis-
souri River and who were pushed to the brink of starvation when the
white man killed off the buffalo, etc. *The blackness of the black box
recorder,* the remains of which would perhaps have carried some trace
of the vanished ghost of my mother's brother, who died in a crash in
the mid-sixties, or the remains of my college acquaintance who died
in the crash over Lockerbie; *the blackness of black Americans,* imported
here from sub-Saharan Africa, first into the West Indies by the Spanish and later by the British monarchy, the black Americans who later
Africanized Christianity and Africanized the English tongue, and
who diluted (bringing us much good) the culture of those black-
hearted villains who believed their *white* culture impervious to or
somehow better than the blackness of Crispus Attacks, the blackness
of Nat Turner, the blackness of Martin Luther King Jr., the blackness
of Malcolm X, the blackness of Ralph Ellison, the blackness of Louis
Armstrong and John Coltrane and Miles Davis, etc.; *the blackness of
the Black Panther Party for Self Defense,* as articulated by Huey Newton, Bobby Seale, Eldridge Cleaver, et al., *WE BELIEVE that this
racist government has robbed us and now we are demanding the overdue debt
of forty acres and two mules. Forty acres and two mules was promised* 100
years ago as restitution for slave labor and mass murder of black people.

Black magic, the putative means by which the witches of Salem attempted to bring down the Mathers and others of a Puritan persuasion, its most potent rituals including the Black Mass, which follows the Roman mass but with everything upside down and backward, with crucifixes upended and unclothed women serving as altars; and then there is the *blackness of black lung disease,* by which many a miner was brought low; *blackness of the black market* and its scalped tickets and bootlegged smokes, and black light, and black belts, and Black Sabbath and their stateside hit "Iron Man," and the blackness of *black comedy,* defined in my encyclopedia as *dark humor that provokes laughter and makes the audience ill at ease. Motion pictures that feature black comedy show irreverence toward death, sex, and established moral values, inciting laughter where it might otherwise be inappropriate.* Black Mountain Poets, such as Creeley, Levertov, Olson, their revolution in the poetic tongue. And two last things, two last things to remember, one being that most American of institutions, *the blacklist,* wherein people are deprived of livelihood because of political belief, wherein all is fear and delusion about the motives of others and no conversation is without its dark stratagems and even those closest are suspect, and, finally, the *black rain* of Hiroshima and Nagasaki, that precipitation which falls over a city after the three-part devastation of blast, heat, and radiation, that precipitation which falls upon the incinerated bodies, the irradiated bodies, that precipitation which falls on civilians, that precipitation which falls on rubble and devastation. *Red, white, and blue is just marketing rhetoric,* therefore, the sloganeering to which we aspire in order not to terrify foreign nationals; *the real American color is black,* primordial, eternal, heartless, infinite, full of sorrow, *For though consciences are unlike as foreheads, every intelligence has one,* upon every forehead the burdensome ornament of the black conscience, and a recognition that the civilization we founded, the civilization of the strip mall and the subdivision and the online cosmetic surgeon, *all built upon the color black;* when I wore the lonely, annihilating veil I felt the blackness of it, as above, but *mostly insinuated,* a howling inside me about history and remorse and loneliness and madness and the need to capture these somehow, and I feel it still; my roots, which are *your roots,* go back to the first syllable of language, my roots are in cave painting, my roots precede the first guilty confessor who attempted to be shriven by a guilty priest, my roots precede the light upon the world, dwelling equally in its darkness; it's a history of honesty, dignity, and courage on the one hand, and *brutality, bloodthirstiness, and murder* on the other. To be an American, to be a citizen of the West, is to be a murderer. Don't kid yourself. Cover your face.

THE MINISTER'S BLACK VEIL

BY NATHANIEL HAWTHORNE

A PARABLE*

The sexton stood in the porch of Milford meeting-house, pulling lustily at the bell-rope. The old people of the village came stooping along the street. Children, with bright faces, tript merrily beside their parents, or mimicked a graver gait, in the conscious dignity of their Sunday clothes. Spruce bachelors looked sidelong at the pretty maidens, and fancied that the Sabbath sunshine made them prettier than on week-days. When the throng had mostly streamed into the porch, the sexton began to toll the bell, keeping his eye on the Reverend Mr. Hooper's door. The first glimpse of the clergyman's figure was the signal for the bell to cease its summons.

"But what has good Parson Hooper got upon his face?" cried the sexton in astonishment.

All within hearing immediately turned about, and beheld the semblance of Mr. Hooper, pacing slowly his meditative way towards the meeting-house. With one accord they started, expressing more wonder than if some strange minister were coming to dust the cushions of Mr. Hooper's pulpit.

"Are you sure it is our parson?" inquired Goodman Gray of the sexton.

---

*Another clergyman in New England, Mr. Joseph Moody, of York, Maine, who died about eighty years since, made himself remarkable by the same eccentricity that is here related of the Reverend Mr. Hooper. In his case, however, the symbol had a different import. In early life he had accidentally killed a beloved friend; and from that day till the hour of his own death, he hid his face from men.

"Of a certainty it is good Mr. Hooper," replied the sexton. "He was to have exchanged pulpits with Parson Shute of Westbury; but Parson Shute sent to excuse himself yesterday, being to preach a funeral sermon."

The cause of so much amazement may appear sufficiently slight. Mr. Hooper, a gentlemanly person of about thirty, though still a bachelor, was dressed with due clerical neatness, as if a careful wife had starched his band, and brushed the weekly dust from his Sunday's garb. There was but one thing remarkable in his appearance. Swathed about his forehead, and hanging down over his face, so low as to be shaken by his breath, Mr. Hooper had on a black veil. On a nearer view, it seemed to consist of two folds of crape, which entirely concealed his features, except the mouth and chin, but probably did not intercept his sight, farther than to give a darkened aspect to all living and inanimate things. With this gloomy shade before him, good Mr. Hooper walked onward, at a slow and quiet pace, stooping somewhat and looking on the ground, as is customary with abstracted men, yet nodding kindly to those of his parishioners who still waited on the meeting-house steps. But so wonder-struck were they, that his greeting hardly met with a return.

"I can't really feel as if good Mr. Hooper's face was behind that piece of crape," said the sexton.

"I don't like it," muttered an old woman, as she hobbled into the meeting-house. "He has changed himself into something awful, only by hiding his face."

"Our parson has gone mad!" cried Goodman Gray, following him across the threshold.

A rumor of some unaccountable phenomenon had preceded Mr. Hooper into the meeting-house, and set all the congregation astir. Few could refrain from twisting their heads towards the door; many stood upright, and turned directly about; while several little boys clambered upon the seats, and came down again with a terrible racket. There was a general bustle, a rustling of the women's gowns and shuffling of the men's feet, greatly at variance with that hushed repose which should attend the entrance of the minister. But Mr. Hooper appeared not to notice the perturbation of his people. He entered with an almost noiseless step, bent his head mildly to the pews on each side, and bowed as he passed his oldest parishioner, a white-haired great-grandsire, who occupied an arm-chair in the centre of the aisle. It was strange to observe, how slowly this venerable man became conscious of something singular in the appearance of his pastor. He seemed not fully to partake of the prevailing wonder, till Mr. Hooper had ascended the stairs, and showed himself in the pulpit, face to face with his congregation, except for the black veil. That mysterious emblem was never once withdrawn. It shook with his measured breath as he gave out the psalm; it threw its obscurity between him and the holy page, as he read the Scriptures; and while he prayed, the veil lay heavily on his uplifted countenance. Did he seek to hide it from the dread Being whom he was addressing?

Such was the effect of this simple piece of crape, that more than one woman of delicate nerves was forced to leave the meeting-house. Yet perhaps the pale-faced congregation was almost as fearful a sight to the minister, as his black veil to them.

Mr. Hooper had the reputation of a good preacher, but not an energetic one: he strove to win his people heavenward, by mild persuasive influences, rather than to drive them thither, by the thunders of the Word. The sermon which he now delivered, was marked by the same characteristics of style and manner, as the general series of his pulpit oratory. But there was something, either in the sentiment of the discourse itself, or in the imagination of the auditors, which made it greatly the most powerful effort that they had ever heard from their pastor's lips. It was tinged, rather more darkly than usual, with the gentle gloom of Mr. Hooper's temperament. The subject had reference to secret sin, and those sad mysteries which we hide from our nearest and dearest, and would fain conceal from our own consciousness, even forgetting that the Omniscient can detect them. A subtle power was breathed into his words. Each member of the congregation, the most innocent girl, and the man of hardened breast, felt as if the preacher had crept upon them, behind his awful veil, and discovered their hoarded iniquity of deed or thought. Many spread their clasped hands on their bosoms. There was nothing terrible in what Mr. Hooper said; at least, no violence; and yet, with every tremor of his melancholy voice, the hearers quaked. An unsought pathos came hand in hand with awe. So sensible were the audience of some unwonted attribute in their minister, that they longed for a breath of wind to blow aside the veil, almost believing that a stranger's visage would be discovered, though the form, gesture, and voice were those of Mr. Hooper.

At the close of the services, the people hurried out with indecorous confusion, eager to communicate their pent-up amazement, and conscious of lighter spirits, the moment they lost sight of the black veil. Some gathered in little circles, huddled closely together, with their mouths all whispering in the centre; some went homeward alone, wrapt in silent meditation; some talked loudly, and profaned the Sabbath-day with ostentatious laughter. A few shook their sagacious heads, intimating that they could penetrate the mystery; while one or two affirmed that there was no mystery at all, but only that Mr. Hooper's eyes were so weakened by the midnight lamp, as to require a shade. After a brief interval, forth came good Mr. Hooper also, in the rear of his flock. Turning his veiled face from one group to another, he paid due reverence to the hoary heads, saluted the middle-aged with kind dignity, as their friend and spiritual guide, greeted the young with mingled authority and love, and laid his hands on the little children's heads to bless them. Such was always his custom on the Sabbath-day. Strange and bewildered looks repaid him for his courtesy. None, as on former occasions, aspired to the honor of walking by their pastor's side. Old Squire Saunders, doubtless by an accidental lapse of memory, neglected to invite Mr. Hooper to his table, where the good clergyman had been wont to bless the food, almost every Sunday since his settlement. He returned, therefore, to the parsonage, and, at the moment of closing the door, was observed to look back upon the people, all of whom had their eyes fixed upon the minister. A sad smile gleamed faintly from beneath the black veil, and flickered about his mouth, glimmering as he disappeared.

"How strange," said a lady, "that a simple black veil, such as any woman might wear on her bonnet, should become such a terrible thing on Mr. Hooper's face!"

"Something must surely be amiss with Mr. Hooper's intellects," observed her husband, the physician of the village. "But the strangest part of the affair is the effect of this vagary, even on a sober-minded man like myself. The black veil, though it covers only our pastor's face, throws its influence over his whole person, and makes him ghost-like from head to foot. Do you not feel it so?"

"Truly do I," replied the lady; "and I would not be alone with him for the world. I wonder he is not afraid to be alone with himself!"

"Men sometimes are so," said her husband.

The afternoon service was attended with similar circumstances. At its conclusion, the bell tolled for the funeral of a young lady. The relatives and friends were assembled in the house, and the more distant acquaintances stood about the door, speaking of the good qualities of the deceased, when their talk was interrupted by the appearance of Mr. Hooper, still covered with his black veil. It was now an appropriate emblem. The clergyman stepped into the room where the corpse was laid, and bent over the coffin, to take a last farewell of his deceased parishioner. As he stooped, the veil hung straight down from his forehead, so that, if her eye-lids had not been closed for ever, the dead maiden might have seen his face. Could Mr. Hooper be fearful of her glance, that he so hastily caught back the black veil? A person who watched the interview between the dead and the living, scrupled not to affirm, that, at the instant when the clergyman's features were disclosed, the corpse had slightly shuddered, rustling the shroud and muslin cap, though the countenance retained the composure of death. A superstitious old woman was the only witness of this prodigy. From the coffin, Mr. Hooper passed into the chamber of the mourners, and thence to the head of the staircase, to make the funeral prayer. It was a tender and heart-dissolving prayer, full of sorrow, yet so imbued with celestial hopes, that the music of a heavenly harp, swept by the fingers of the dead, seemed faintly to be heard among the saddest accents of the minister. The people trembled, though they but darkly understood him, when he prayed that they, and himself, and all of mortal race, might be ready, as he trusted this young maiden had been, for the dreadful hour that should snatch the veil from their faces. The bearers went heavily forth, and the mourners followed, saddening all the street, with the dead before them, and Mr. Hooper in his black veil behind.

"Why do you look back?" said one in the procession to his partner.

"I had a fancy," replied she, "that the minister and the maiden's spirit were walking hand in hand."

"And so had I, at the same moment," said the other.

That night, the handsomest couple in Milford village were to be joined in wedlock. Though reckoned a melancholy man, Mr. Hooper had a placid cheerfulness for such occasions, which often excited a sympathetic smile, where livelier merriment would have been thrown away. There was no quality of his disposition which made him more beloved than this. The company at the wedding awaited his arrival with impatience trusting that the strange awe, which had gathered over him throughout the day, would now be dispelled. But such was not the result. When Mr. Hooper came, the first thing that their eyes rested on was the same horrible black veil, which had added deeper gloom to the funeral, and could portend nothing but evil to the wedding. Such was its immediate effect on the guests that a cloud seemed to have rolled duskily from beneath the black crape, and dimmed the light of the candles. The bridal pair stood up before the minister. But the bride's cold fingers quivered in the tremulous hand of the bridegroom, and her death-like paleness caused a whisper, that the maiden who had been buried a few hours before, was come from her grave to be married. If ever another wedding were so dismal, it was that famous one, where they tolled the wedding-knell. After performing the ceremony, Mr. Hooper raised a glass of wine to his lips, wishing happiness to the new-married couple, in a strain of mild pleasantry that ought to have brightened the features of the guests, like a cheerful gleam from the hearth. At that instant, catching a glimpse of his figure in the looking-glass, the black veil involved his own spirit in the horror with which it overwhelmed all others. His frame shuddered — his lips grew white — he spilt the untasted wine upon the carpet — and rushed forth into the darkness. For the Earth, too, had on her Black Veil.

The next day, the whole village of Milford talked of little else than Parson Hooper's black veil. That, and the mystery concealed behind it, supplied a topic for discussion between acquaintances meeting in the street, and good women gossiping at their open windows. It was the first item of news that the tavern-keeper told to his guests. The children babbled of it on their way to school. One imitative little imp covered his face with an old black handkerchief, thereby so affrighting his playmates, that the panic seized himself, and he well nigh lost his wits by his own waggery.

It was remarkable, that, of all the busy-bodies and impertinent people in the parish, not one ventured to put the plain question to Mr. Hooper, wherefore he did this thing. Hitherto, whenever there appeared the slightest call for such interference, he had never lacked advisers, nor shown himself averse to be guided by their judgment. If he erred at all, it was by so painful a degree of self-distrust, that even the mildest censure would lead him to consider an indifferent action as a crime. Yet, though so well acquainted with this amiable weakness, no individual among his parishioners chose to make the black veil a subject of friendly remonstrance. There was a feeling of dread, neither plainly confessed nor carefully concealed, which caused each to shift the responsibility upon another, till at length it was found expedient to send a deputation of the church, in order to deal with Mr. Hooper about the mystery, before it should grow into a scandal. Never did an embassy so ill discharge its duties. The minister received them with friendly courtesy, but became silent, after they were seated, leaving to his visitors the whole burthen of introducing their important business. The topic, it might be supposed, was obvious enough. There was the black veil, swathed round Mr. Hooper's forehead, and concealing every feature above his placid mouth, on which, at times, they could perceive the glimmering of a melancholy smile. But that piece of crape, to their imagination, seemed to hang down before his heart, the symbol of a fearful secret between him and them. Were the veil but cast aside, they might speak freely of it, but not till then. Thus they sat a considerable time, speechless, confused, and shrinking uneasily from Mr. Hooper's eye, which they felt to be fixed upon them with an invisible glance. Finally, the deputies returned abashed to their constituents, pronouncing the matter too weighty to be handled, except by a council of the churches, if, indeed, it might not require a general synod.

But there was one person in the village, unappalled by the awe with which the black veil had impressed all beside herself. When the deputies returned without an explanation, or even venturing to demand one, she, with the calm energy of her character, determined to chase away the strange cloud that appeared to be settling round Mr. Hooper, every moment more darkly than before. As his plighted wife, it should be her privilege to know what the black veil concealed. At the minister's first visit, therefore, she entered upon the subject, with a direct simplicity, which made the task easier both for him and her. After he had seated himself, she fixed her eyes steadfastly upon the veil, but could discern nothing of the dreadful gloom that had so overawed the multitude: it was but a double fold of crape, hanging down from his forehead to his mouth, and slightly stirring with his breath.

"No," said she aloud, and smiling, "there is nothing terrible in this piece of crape, except that it hides a face which I am always glad to look upon. Come, good sir, let the sun shine from behind the cloud. First lay aside your black veil: then tell me why you put it on."

Mr. Hooper's smile glimmered faintly.

"There is an hour to come," said he, "when all of us shall cast aside our veils. Take it not amiss, beloved friend, if I wear this piece of crape till then."

"Your words are a mystery too," returned the young lady. "Take away the veil from them, at least."

"Elizabeth, I will," said he, "so far as my vow may suffer me. Know, then, this veil is a type and a symbol, and I am bound to wear it ever, both in light and darkness, in solitude and before the gaze of multitudes, and as with strangers, so with my familiar friends. No mortal eye will see it withdrawn. This dismal shade must separate me from the world: even you, Elizabeth, can never come behind it!"

"What grievous affliction hath befallen you," she earnestly inquired, "that you should thus darken your eyes for ever?"

"If it be a sign of mourning," replied Mr. Hooper, "I, perhaps, like most other mortals, have sorrows dark enough to be typified by a black veil."

"But what if the world will not believe that it is the type of an innocent sorrow?" urged Elizabeth. "Beloved and respected as you are, there may be whispers, that you hide your face under the consciousness of secret sin. For the sake of your holy office, do away this scandal!"

The color rose into her cheeks, as she intimated the nature of the rumors that were already abroad in the village. But Mr. Hooper's mildness did not forsake him. He even smiled again — that same sad smile, which always appeared like a faint glimmering of light, proceeding from the obscurity beneath the veil.

"If I hide my face for sorrow, there is cause enough," he merely replied; "and if I cover it for secret sin, what mortal might not do the same?"

And with this gentle, but unconquerable obstinacy, did he resist all her entreaties. At length Elizabeth sat silent. For a few moments she appeared lost in thought, considering, probably, what new methods might be tried, to withdraw her lover from so dark a fantasy, which, if it had no other meaning, was perhaps a symptom of mental disease. Though of a firmer character than his own, the tears rolled down her cheeks. But, in an instant, as it were, a new feeling took the place of sorrow: her eyes were fixed insensibly on the black veil, when, like a sudden twilight in the air, its terrors fell around her. She arose, and stood trembling before him.

"And do you feel it then at last?" said he mournfully.

She made no reply, but covered her eyes with her hand, and turned to leave the room. He rushed forward and caught her arm.

"Have patience with me, Elizabeth!" cried he passionately. "Do not desert me, though this veil must be between us here on earth. Be mine, and hereafter there shall be no veil over my face, no darkness between our souls! It is but a mortal veil — it is not for eternity! Oh! you know not how lonely I am, and how frightened, to be alone behind my black veil. Do not leave me in this miserable obscurity for ever!"

"Lift the veil but once, and look me in the face," said she.

"Never! It cannot be!" replied Mr. Hooper.

"Then, farewell!" said Elizabeth.

She withdrew her arm from his grasp, and slowly departed, pausing at the door, to give one long, shuddering gaze, that seemed almost to penetrate the mystery of the black veil. But, even amid his grief, Mr. Hooper smiled to think that only a material emblem had separated him from happiness, though the horrors which it shadowed forth, must be drawn darkly between the fondest of lovers.

From that time no attempts were made to remove Mr. Hooper's black veil, or, by a direct appeal, to discover the secret which it was supposed to hide. By persons who claimed a superiority to popular prejudice, it was reckoned merely an eccentric whim, such as often mingles with the sober actions of men otherwise rational, and tinges them all with its own semblance of insanity. But with the multitude, good Mr. Hooper was irreparably a bugbear. He could not walk the street with any peace of mind, so conscious was he that the gentle and timid would turn aside to avoid him, and that others would make it a point of hardihood to throw themselves in his way. The impertinence of the latter class compelled him to give up his customary walk, at sunset, to the burial ground; for when he leaned pensively over the gate, there would always be faces behind the grave-stones, peeping at his black veil. A fable went the rounds, that the stare of the dead people drove him thence. It grieved him, to the very depth of his kind heart, to observe how the children fled from his approach, breaking up their merriest sports, while his melancholy figure was yet afar off. Their instinctive dread caused him to feel, more strongly than aught else, that a preternatural horror was interwoven with the threads of the black crape. In truth, his own antipathy to the veil was known to be so great, that he never willingly passed before a mirror, nor stooped to drink at a still fountain, lest, in its peaceful bosom, he should be affrighted by himself. This was what gave plausibility to the whispers, that Mr. Hooper's conscience tortured him for some great crime, too horrible to be entirely concealed, or otherwise than so obscurely intimated. Thus, from beneath the black veil, there rolled a cloud into the sunshine, an ambiguity of sin or sorrow, which enveloped the poor minister, so that love or sympathy could never reach him. It was said, that ghost and fiend consorted with him there. With self-shudderings and outward terrors, he walked continually in its shadow, groping darkly within his own soul, or gazing through a medium that saddened the whole world. Even the lawless wind, it was believed, respected his dreadful secret, and never blew aside the veil. But still good Mr. Hooper sadly smiled, at the pale visages of the worldly throng as he passed by.

Among all its bad influences, the black veil had the one desirable effect, of making its wearer a very efficient clergyman. By the aid of his mysterious emblem — for there was no other apparent cause — he became a man of awful power, over souls that were in agony for sin. His converts always regarded him with a dread peculiar to themselves, affirming, though but figuratively, that, before he brought them to celestial light, they had been with him behind the black veil. Its gloom, indeed, enabled him to sympathize with all dark affections. Dying sinners cried aloud for Mr. Hooper, and would not yield their breath till he appeared; though ever, as he stooped to whisper consolation, they shuddered at the veiled face so near their own. Such were the terrors of the black veil, even when death had bared his visage! Strangers came long distances to attend service at his church, with the mere idle purpose of gazing at his figure, because it was forbidden them to behold his face. But many were made to quake ere they departed! Once, during Governor Belcher's administration, Mr. Hooper was appointed to preach the election sermon. Covered with his black veil, he stood before the chief magistrate, the council, and the representatives, and wrought so deep an impression, that the legislative measures of that year, were characterized by all the gloom and piety of our earliest ancestral sway.

In this manner Mr. Hooper spent a long life, irreproachable in outward act, yet shrouded in dismal suspicions; kind and loving, though unloved, and dimly feared; a man apart from men, shunned in their health and joy, but ever summoned to their aid in mortal anguish. As years wore on, shedding their snows above his sable veil, he acquired a name throughout the New England churches, and they called him Father Hooper. Nearly all his parishioners, who were of mature age when he was settled, had been borne away by many a funeral: he had one congregation in the church, and a more crowded one in the church-yard; and having wrought so late into the evening, and done his work so well, it was now good Father Hooper's turn to rest.

Several persons were visible by the shaded candlelight, in the death-chamber of the old clergyman. Natural connexions he had none. But there was the decorously grave, though unmoved physician, seeking only to mitigate the last pangs of the patient whom he could not save. There were the deacons, and other eminently pious members of his church. There, also, was the Reverend Mr. Clark, of Westbury, a young and zealous divine, who had ridden in haste to pray by the bed-side of the expiring minister. There was the nurse, no hired handmaiden of death, but one whose calm affection had endured thus long in secrecy, in solitude, amid the chill of age, and would not perish, even at the dying hour. Who, but Elizabeth! And there lay the hoary head of good Father Hooper upon the death-pillow, with the black veil still swathed about his brow, and reaching down over his face, so that each more difficult gasp of his faint breath caused it to stir. All through life that piece of crape had hung between him and the world: it had separated him from cheerful brotherhood and woman's love, and kept him in that saddest of all prisons, his own heart; and still it lay upon his face, as if to deepen the gloom of his darksome chamber, and shade him from the sunshine of eternity.

For some time previous, his mind had been confused, wavering doubtfully between the past and the present, and hovering forward, as it were, at intervals, into the indistinctness of the world to come. There had been feverish turns, which tossed him from side to side, and wore away what little strength he had. But in his most convulsive struggles, and in the wildest vagaries of his intellect, when no other thought retained its sober influence, he still showed an awful solicitude lest the black veil should slip aside. Even if his bewildered soul could have forgotten, there was a faithful woman at his pillow, who, with averted eyes, would have covered that aged face, which she had last beheld in the comeliness of manhood. At length the death-stricken old man lay quietly in the torpor of mental and bodily exhaustion, with an imperceptible pulse, and breath that grew fainter and fainter, except when a long, deep, and irregular inspiration seemed to prelude the flight of his spirit.

The minister of Westbury approached the bedside.

"Venerable Father Hooper," said he, "the moment of your release is at hand. Are you ready for the lifting of the veil, that shuts in time from eternity?"

Father Hooper at first replied merely by a feeble motion of his head; then, apprehensive, perhaps, that his meaning might be doubtful, he exerted himself to speak.

"Yea," said he, in faint accents, "my soul hath a patient weariness until that veil be lifted."

"And is it fitting," resumed the Reverend Mr. Clark, "that a man so given to prayer, of such a blameless example, holy in deed and thought, so far as mortal judgment may pronounce; is it fitting that a father in the church should leave a shadow on his memory, that may seem to blacken a life so pure? I pray you, my venerable brother, let not this thing be! Suffer us to be gladdened by your triumphant aspect, as you go to your reward. Before the veil of eternity be lifted, let me cast aside this black veil from your face!"

And thus speaking, the Reverend Mr. Clark bent forward to reveal the mystery of so many years. But, exerting a sudden energy, that made all the beholders stand aghast, Father Hooper snatched both his hands from beneath the bed-clothes, and pressed them strongly on the black veil, resolute to struggle, if the minister of Westbury would contend with a dying man.

"Never!" cried the veiled clergyman. "On earth, never!"

"Dark old man!" exclaimed the affrighted minister, "with what horrible crime upon your soul are you now passing to the judgment?"

Father Hooper's breath heaved; it rattled in his throat; but, with a mighty effort, grasping forward with his hands, he caught hold of life, and held it back till he should speak. He even raised himself in bed; and there he sat, shivering with the arms of death around him, while the black veil hung down, awful, at that last moment, in the gathered terrors of a lifetime. And yet the faint, sad smile, so often there, now seemed to glimmer from its obscurity, and linger on Father Hooper's lips.

"Why do you tremble at me alone?" cried he, turning his veiled face round the circle of pale spectators. "Tremble also at each other! Have men avoided me, and women shown no pity, and children screamed and fled, only for my black veil? What, but the mystery which it obscurely typifies, has made this piece of crape so awful? When the friend shows his inmost heart to his friend; the lover to his best-beloved; when man does not vainly shrink from the eye of his Creator, loathsomely treasuring up the secret of his sin; then deem me a monster, for the symbol beneath which I have lived, and die! I look around me, and, lo! on every visage a Black Veil!"

While his auditors shrank from one another, in mutual affright, Father Hooper fell back upon his pillow, a veiled corpse, with a faint smile lingering on the lips. Still veiled, they laid him in his coffin, and a veiled corpse they bore him to the grave. The grass of many years has sprung up and withered on that grave, the burial-stone is moss-grown, and good Mr. Hooper's face is dust; but awful is still the thought, that it mouldered beneath the Black Veil!

SELECTED BIBLIOGRAPHY

My style of quotation in this book sometimes asks the reader to suspend the question of who exactly is doing the speaking. A dangerous undertaking, to be sure, and one that I seek to redress here. The aspiration concealed in this strategy is one in which, hopefully, the literature present will properly appear to be quilted together from the texts of the past, sometimes consciously, sometimes less so. For the sake of completeness, however, please note the following: the vast majority of uncited quotations in these pages, as well as all the chapter titles, come from the work of Nathaniel Hawthorne. There are also some phantom observations from Herman Melville, as well as Cotton Mather (chapter six), Roland Barthes (chapter seven), Robert Held (on firearms, in chapter nine), Robert Burton (chapter ten), Alice Earle and Charles Banks (on colonial life, chapter eleven, and also in chapter fifteen), Philip Woodwell and Steven Watson and Gail M. Potter (chapter fifteen), C. P. Moody (chapter sixteen), George Francis (on South Station), the National Lime Association (on lime), Lyle Dorsett (on D. L. Moody), and D. L. Moody (chapter seventeen). A more complete list of my sources is below.

Alschuler, Glen C. *American Transcendental Quarterly,* 24, Suppl. 2 (1974).

Anderson, Joseph Crook, II, and Lois Ware Thurston, C. G., Eds. *Maine Families in 1790,* vol. 4. Camden, ME: Picton Press, 1994.

Arvin, Newton. *Hawthorne.* New York, NY: Russell & Russell, 1961.

Barthes, Roland. Translated by Richard Howard. *A Lover's Discourse: Fragments.* New York, NY: Hill and Wang, 1978.

————. Translated by Annette Lavers. *Mythologies.* New York, NY: Hill and Wang, 1972.

Bell, Charles H. *History of the Town of Exeter, New Hampshire.* Exeter, NH: Higginson Book Company, 1888.

Bell, Michael Davitt. *Hawthorne and the Historical Romance of New England.* Princeton, NJ: Princeton University Press, 1971.

Bellis, Peter J. "Mauling Governor Pyncheon." *Studies in the Novel,* 26:3 (Fall, 1994).

Benoit, Raymond. "Hawthorne's Psychology of Death: 'The Minister's Black Veil.'" *Studies in Short Fiction,* 8:4 (Fall, 1971).

Bockris, Victor. *With William Burroughs: A Report from the Bunker.* New York, NY: St. Martin's Press, 1996.

Burroughs, William S. *Junky.* New York, NY: Penguin Books, 1977.

————. Ed. Oliver Harris. *The Letters of William S. Burroughs: 1945–1959.* New York, NY: Penguin Books, 1994.

————. *Queer.* New York, NY: Penguin Books, 1987.

Burton, Robert. *The Anatomy of Melancholy: What It Is, With All the Kinds, Causes, Symptomes, Prognostickes & Several Cures of It.* Ed., with an introduction by Holbrook Jackson. New York, NY: Vintage, 1977.

Chapin, Alice Moody. *The Family Tree, by Alice Moody Chapin: Seven Hundred Years of Moody Ancestors,* 1988, manuscript, courtesy of Old York Historical Society Library, York, ME.

Clark, James Freeman. "The Funeral of Mr. Hawthorne." *Nathaniel Hawthorne Journal,* 1972.

Cochran, Robert W. "Hawthorne's Choice: The Veil or the Jaundiced Eye." *College English,* 23:5 (Feb., 1962).

The Concise Columbia Encyclopedia, second edition. New York, NY: Columbia University Press, 1989.

Crews, Frederick. *The Sins of the Father: Hawthorne's Psychological Themes.* Berkeley, CA: University of California Press, 1989.

Derrida, Jacques. *Limited Inc.* Evanston, IL: Northwestern University Press, 1988.

————. Ed. Elisabeth Weber. Translated by Peggy Kamuf and others. *Points . . . : Interviews 1974–1994.* Stanford, CA: Stanford University Press, 1995.

Dorsett, Lyle W. *A Passion for Souls: The Life of D. L. Moody.* Chicago, IL: Moody Press, 1997.

Earle, Alice Morse. *Child Life in Colonial Days.* Williamstown, MA: Corner House Publishers, 1975.

Fogle, Richard Harter. "An Ambiguity of Sin or Sorrow." *New England Quarterly,* 21:3 (Sept., 1948).

Foucault, Michel, ed. *I, Pierre Rivière, Having Slaughtered My Mother, My Sister, and My Brother . . . : A Case of Parricide in the Nineteenth Century.* Translated by Frank Jellinek. Lincoln, NE: Bison Books, 1982.

Francis, George B. *The South Terminal Station.* Boston, MA: John C. Gray, 1899.

Freedman, William. "The Artist's Symbol and Hawthorne's Veil: 'The Minister's Black Veil' Restartus." *Studies in Short Fiction,* 29:3 (Summer, 1992).

Fuller, John G. *Incident at Exeter / The Interrupted Journey: Two Landmark Investigations of UFO Encounters in One Volume.* New York, NY: MJF Books, 1965.

Garber, Marjorie. *Vested Interests: Cross-Dressing and Cultural Anxiety.* New York, NY: Routledge, 1992.

Gartner, Matthew. "Hawthorne and the Fictions of Family History." *Nathaniel Hawthorne Review,* 22:2 (Fall, 1996).

Genthner, Nancy Moody. *What's Cooking at Moody's Diner: 60 Years of Recipes and Reminiscences.* West Rockport, ME: Dancing Bear Books, 1989.

German, Norman. "The Veil of Words in 'The Minister's Black Veil.'" *Studies in Short Fiction,* 25:1 (Winter, 1988).

Hawthorne, Nathaniel. *Collected Novels: Fanshawe, The Scarlet Letter, The House of the Seven Gables, The Blithedale Romance, The Marble Faun.* New York, NY: The Library of America, 1983.

———. *The Scarlet Letter.* New York, NY: Bantam Books, 1965.

———. *Tales and Sketches.* New York, NY: The Library of America, 1982.

———. *Twice-Told Tales.* Boston, MA: American Stationers Co., 1837.

———. Ed. and with an introduction by Newton Arvin. *Hawthorne's Short Stories.* New York, NY: Alfred A. Knopf, 1946.

———. Ed. Edward H. Davidson, Claude M. Simpson, and L. Neal Smith. *The Elixir of Life Manuscripts* (Volume XIII of *The Centenary Edition of the Works of Nathaniel Hawthorne*). Columbus, OH: Ohio State University Press, 1962–1988.

———. Ed. James McIntosh. *Nathaniel Hawthorne's Tales.* New York, NY: W. W. Norton & Co., 1987.

———. Ed. Claude M. Simpson. *The American Notebooks* (Volume VIII of *The Centenary Edition of the Works of Nathaniel Hawthorne*). Columbus, OH: Ohio State University Press, 1962–1988.

Hickerson, J. M., ed. *How I Made the Sale That Did the Most for Me: Sixty Great Sales Stories Told by Sixty Great Salesmen.* New York, NY: Prentice-Hall, 1951.

Kences, James E. "'Overtaken by Death': Dying, Death, and Burial in Early York." York, ME: Old York Historical Society, 1995.

Knight, Brenda, ed. *Women of the Beat Generation: The Writers, Artists & Muses at the Heart of the Revolution.* Berkeley, CA: Conors Press, 1996.

Laighton, Oscar. *Ninety Years at the Isles of Shoals.* Boston, MA: Beacon Press, 1930.

Lepore, Jill. *The Name of War: King Philip's War and the Origins of American Identity.* New York, NY: Alfred A. Knopf, Inc., 1998.

Longfellow, Henry Wadsworth. *Poems and Other Writings.* New York, NY: The Library of America, 2000.

Mather, Cotton. *Diary of Cotton Mather: Volume I, 1681–1709.* New York, NY: Frederick Ungar Publishing, 1964.

———. Ed. Kenneth B. Murdock. *Selections from Cotton Mather.* New York, NY: Hafner Publishing, 1926.

McAleer, John. *Ralph Waldo Emerson: Days of Encounter.* Boston, MA: Little, Brown and Company, 1984.

McCarthy, Judy. "'The Minister's Black Veil': Concealing Moses and the Holy of Holies." *Studies in Short Fiction,* 24:2 (Spring, 1987).

McFarland, Ronald E. "Community and Interpretive Communities in Stories by Hawthorne, Kafka, and García Márquez." *Studies in Short Fiction,* 29:4 (Fall, 1992).

Miller, Edwin Haviland. *Salem Is My Dwelling Place: A Life of Nathaniel Hawthorne.* Iowa City, IA: University of Iowa Press, 1991.

Miller, J. Hillis. *Hawthorne and History.* Cambridge, MA: Basil Blackwell, 1991.

Monteiro, George. "The Full Particulars of the Minister's Behavior — According to Hale." *Nathaniel Hawthorne Journal,* 1972.

Moodey, Joshua. "Souldiery Spiritualized."

Moody, Charles C. P. *Biographical Sketches of the Moody Family: Embracing Notices of Ten Ministers and Several Laymen, From 1633 to 1842.* Boston: Samuel G. Drake, 1847.

Moody, D. L. *Echoes from the Pulpit and Platform.* Hartford, CT: A. D. Worthington & Co., 1900.

———. *Heaven; Where It is; Its Inhabitants, and How to Get There.* Chicago, IL: F. H. Revell, 1880.

———. *Sowing and Reaping.* Chicago, IL: The Bible Institute Colportage Association, 1896.

Moody, Herbert A. *Historical Notes Concerning the Moody Family.* Milford, NH: The Cabinet Press, 1947.

Moody, William R. *The Life of Dwight L. Moody.* Chicago, IL: Fleming H. Revell Company, 1900.

Moore, Thomas. "Lalah Rookh," in *The Poetical Works of Thomas Moore, Vol. III.* Boston, MA: Houghton, Mifflin and Company, 1856.

Morgan, Ted. *Literary Outlaw: The Life and Times of William S. Burroughs.* New York: Avon Books, 1990.

Morse, F. L. S. *Thomaston Scrapbook.* Thomaston, ME: Thomaston Historical Society, 1977.

Morseburger, Robert E. "The Minister's Black Veil: Shrouded in a Blackness, Ten Times Black." *New England Quarterly,* 46:3 (Sept., 1973).

Newberry, Frederick. "The Biblical Veil: Sources and Typology in Hawthorne's 'The Minister's Black Veil.'" *Texas Studies in Literature and Language,* 31:2 (Summer, 1989).

Newman, Lea Bertani Vozar. "One Hundred-and-Fifty Years of Looking At, Into, Through, Behind, and Around 'The Minister's Black Veil.'" *Nathaniel Hawthorne Review,* 13:1 (Spring, 1987).

Noyes, Sybil. *Genealogical Dictionary of Maine and New Hampshire.* Baltimore, MD: Genealogical Publishing Company, 1983.

Odier, Daniel. *The Job: Interviews with William S. Burroughs.* New York: Penguin Books, 1989.

Potter, Gail M. "The Legend of Handkerchief Moody," in *Mysterious New England.* Ed. and compiled by the editors of *Yankee.* Dublin, NH: Yankee, Inc., 1971.

Rabinow, Paul, ed. *The Foucault Reader.* New York, NY: Pantheon Books, 1984.

Reece, James B. "Mr. Hooper's Vow." *ESQ,* v. 21, 2nd quarter, 1975.

Roberts, Kenneth. *The Kenneth Roberts Readers.* Garden City, NY: Doubleday, Doran and Co., 1945.

————. *Northwest Passage.* Garden City, NY: Doubleday, Doran and Co., 1937.

Turner, Frederick W., III. "Hawthorne's Black Veil." *Studies in Short Fiction,* 5:2 (Winter, 1968).

Voigt, Gilbert. "The Meaning of 'The Minister's Black Veil.'" *College English,* 13, #6 (March, 1952).

Warner, Michael, ed. *American Sermons: The Pilgrims to Martin Luther King.* New York, NY: Library of America, 1999.

Warren Historical Society. *Old Warren, Maine.* Warren, ME: Warren Historical Society, 1997.

Watterson, William C., and Wihhey, John P. "The Haunting of the Hawthornes." *Bowdoin,* v. 69, #2.

Westcott, Brooke Foss, and Fenton John Anthony Hortt, eds. *Revised Greek-English New Testament.* New York, NY: Harper & Brothers, 1882.

Williams, Daniel E., ed. *Pillars of Salt: An Anthology of Early American Criminal Narratives.* Madison, WI: Madison House, 1993.

Woodwell, Philip McIntire, ed. *Handkerchief Moody: The Diary & the Man.* Portland, ME: Colonial Offset Printing Co., 1981.

Acknowledgments

The John Simon Guggenheim Memorial Foundation (for the honor of a fellowship), the Board and Corporation of Yaddo, the New York Public Library, the New England Genealogical Historical Society, the Old York Historical Society, the Whitefield Historical Society, Town of Whitefield, ME, the Warren Historical Society, the Old Manse of Concord, the Trustees of Reservations, Columbia University, the Newberry Library, the Boston Athenaeum, Helen Aylon, Bill Henderson, Barry Werth, Lucinda Ebersole, Laura Iglehart, Mona Jimenez, Alec Michod, the Rev'd Thomas T. Parke, the Bishop Frank Griswold, Randy Polumbo, Elizabeth Robbins, Stacey Richter, Nancy Withington, Virginia S. Spiller, Michael Sundell, Thomas B. Johnson, Gary Hackett, Robert Nedelkoff, Laura Miller, Steven Watson, Ryan Harbage, the indispensable Cathleen Bell, Russell Banks, David Shields, Frank Bidart, Mary Robison, Allan Gurganus, Julia Slavin, the totally essential Mary-Beth Hughes, Walter Donahue, Michael Pietsch, Melanie Jackson (as always), Amy Osborn, and my family, especially my father.

The Black Veil

by Rick Moody

A READING GROUP GUIDE

An entry from Rick Moody's Slate diary

Thursday, May 2, 2002, at 10:01 A.M. PT

Some days, in order to avoid writing, all you have to do is stare at the wreckage.

Last Friday, when I was holed up in Idaho, a friend IM'd me while I was checking e-mail in my motel, to say that she was having a bad time lately. Well, it became clear fast that this was an understatement. She mentioned having failed in love; she said that she was having a hard time finding lovers who could *see the inner beauty,* but that was the least of her problems. There was something unsettling about the density of typos and bad grammar in her remarks, especially since she's a literary critic. I had a feeling there was something else going on. So I asked. I said, *Are you using?* And she admitted, yes, that she had just bought fifteen bags of dope and had already done four of them. Fifteen seemed, uh, like a lot. I said, *Would you consider throwing out the rest?* She said she wouldn't and that, furthermore, she was going to do all of them. I pointed out that there wasn't any guarantee she would survive, and she said she didn't really want to live that much anyhow.

This had already happened once this year, and I'd been counseling her occasionally on ways to stay clean. In fact, that she contacted me at all was a pretty good sign. Most people in my circle of acquaintances know that I had a problem with drinking and drugs when I was young and that I no longer do. I am a pretty sturdy and good person to talk to if you are trying to give up destroying yourself, and my friend (let's say she's called Nina) contacted *me*. Admittedly, she had gone to see the dealer first, but still.

She said she was having difficulties with the *small keys* on her keyboard and would I call her instead? I said I'd call, sure, but I agreed only because it would give me a minute or so to get in touch with some people in New York who might be able to reach Nina's apartment before she managed to shoot the other eleven bags of heroin. I made these calls fast, and then I called Nina. All this from Idaho, of course, from my drab, grim motel room.

The thing about junkies is that they all sound the same. The same with drunks. Nina is my friend, and she is a sprite, a pixie, full of life and a kind of furious cynicism that I associate with having seen a lot of life, with knowing the truth, with having endured. But in the cold storage of junk ecstasy, she was just another complainer and self-satisfied in some ways, remarking that some people were too smart for the twelve steps, that she couldn't be bothered to go to rehab again. There's a shiver that always travels down my spine when I'm in close proximity to genuine mental illness, a recognition of the potential for trouble. And though I loved Nina, I found myself experiencing this shiver of recognition. In fact, I only stayed on the line because I figured I could get her to part with the telephone number of her therapist.

I guess it worked out all right. My friends from the city descended on Nina's apartment, managed to take her out for sushi (!) so that she'd have some food in her, likewise to spirit away the rest of the heroin. (They consigned it to the NYC sewer system, somewhere on the Upper East Side.) On the other hand, Nina is not in rehab or the psych ward where she belongs, at least the way I see it. *And I've been thinking about this all week.* It's been like a shadow over the week. All the things that I've been talking about instead — my house, my inability to write, my travels — have been undergirded by this anxiety, by this sense of watching somebody I really love do really awesome amounts of damage to herself. During lunch, Nina's madness, during dinner out, Nina's madness, out in the sunshine, Nina's madness, everywhere and always the potential for real trouble.

Then, yesterday, some more wreckage. I was back in the city, avoiding the fact that there was *no heat in my house* when Amy, my fiancée, called to say that she had just been laid off from her computer programmer job. They didn't give her time to back up her files, they locked her out of the system, she was on her way home, et cetera. She sounded giddy about it at first, but I knew that sensation, having once been fired myself, and I knew that giddiness would come to an end. Later in the day, she was numb. Weeping. For perspective, I called a friend who has been struggling to find a job in the media business for some months now, since his office, too, got downsized. He said, *Don't let anyone tell you about this recovery we're supposedly having; that's just business writers, and they're about as effective as movie reviewers are.*

Sometimes when you look at all this stuff, all this suffering, all this heartache, all this struggle, it's hard to figure out how to say anything at all about it. I mean, for example, the only thing that could illustrate what Wednesday was like for me was the view out Amy's window. She lives in Prospect Heights, and so on a clear day with lots of sun, you can see all the way to Lower Manhattan, where there used to be two towers.

Reprinted with permission. Each of the five diary entries that Rick Moody contributed to *Slate* the week of April 29 to May 3, 2002, can be found at slate.msn.com.

Reading Group Questions and Topics for Discussion

1. The secrets encoded in lineage are essential to Rick Moody's examination of himself in *The Black Veil*. How does the author's desire for connection with his father and grandfather relate to his desire for a genealogical link to Handkerchief Moody?

2. The veil is one of the book's most salient symbols. What does it stand for? Identify various veils that we use today and describe our purposes in using them; for example, to conceal our shame, or to keep ourselves apart from others.

3. *The Black Veil* details a history of suffering — not just Rick Moody's own depression and alcoholism, but the difficulties of his ancestors, family members, friends, and lovers. Why do you think that suffering, a condition familiar to all people, so frequently breeds loneliness and alienation?

4. How is *The Black Veil* different from other memoirs you've read? Discuss the author's intent in embracing both style and subject matter that are unusual by the genre's standards.

5. What do you make of the author's incorporation of Nathaniel Hawthorne, one of the first truly American canonical writers, into the book? Is Rick Moody recognizing his debt to Hawthorne? Positioning himself as one of Hawthorne's literary heirs? Neither? Both?

6. What do the book's structure and narrative style say about Rick Moody's identity, and the way in which we all forge

our identities? Do we discover ourselves in fits and starts, by accident?

7. What do you suspect was behind Rick Moody's decision to write a memoir after writing many works of fiction? Do you think that writing an autobiographical work can lead to a deeper knowledge of yourself? Do you think it's a catharsis?

8. Rick Moody's distinctive style sets him apart from most other contemporary writers. In fact, many people have said his writing more closely resembles poetry or music than conventional prose. What do you think? Are there any artists, musicians, poets, or other writers whose work you would compare to Rick Moody's?

9. Melancholy and alcoholism are two of the oldest literary associations — from the dark clouds following Shakespearean characters to the notoriety of Hemingway and Fitzgerald. In what ways does Moody's account of his experiences with depression and addiction comment on the vast heritage that he is becoming a part of? Does he come to any conclusions?

10. Rick Moody has suggested that, rather than "a memoir," *The Black Veil* is: "A book. A think. An encyclopedia. A catalogue. A brushfire. A building collapse. A think tank. A prose poem. A deed of sale. A crie de coeur. A lost cause. A dampened enthusiasm. A night of the living dead. A soldiering on. An all-hopes-lost. A listing to one side. A breath of fresh air. A crown of thorns. A land of enchantments. An American notebook." What justifies describing the book in this fashion? How is *The Black Veil* a work that evades categorization?